# DEBATE AND CRITICAL ANALYSIS:
## The Harmony of Conflict

# COMMUNICATION
# TEXTBOOK SERIES
Jennings Bryant – Editor

---

# Rhetoric and Public
# Address
Donovan Ochs – Advisor

---

BRANHAM • Debate and Critical
Analysis: The Harmony
of Conflict

# DEBATE AND CRITICAL ANALYSIS:
## The Harmony of Conflict

## Robert James Branham
### Bates College

Routledge
Taylor & Francis Group

NEW YORK AND LONDON

Permissions

Excerpts from "Against a One-Term, Six-Year Presidency," by Arthur Schlesinger, Jr., Copyright © 1986 by The New York Times Company. Reprinted by permission.

Excerpts from "Shouting 'Fire?' "reprinted by permission of Alan Dershowitz, Professor of Law, from *The Atlantic Monthly*.

Amnesty International Publication, *When the State Kills* (AI Index: ACT 51/07/89). Reprinted with permission.

*Who Decides? A Reproductive Rights Issues Manual*, 1990, The NARAL Foundation, Washington, DC. Reprinted by permission.

Excerpts from "Why Blacks Need Affirmative Action," by Jesse Jackson, reprinted with the permission of the American Enterprise Institute for Public Policy Research, Washington, DC.

First Published by
Lawrence Erlbaum Associates, Inc., Publishers
365 Broadway
Hillsdale, New Jersey 07642

Routledge
711 Third Avenue, New York, NY 10017, USA
2 Park Square, Milton Park, Abingdon, Oxon, OX14 4RN

Routledge is an imprint of the Taylor & Francis Group, an informa business

First issued in paperback 2011

**Library of Congress Cataloging-in-Publication Data**

Branham, Robert J.
   Debate and critical analysis : the harmony of conflict / Robert
James Branham.
      p.  cm.
   Includes bibliographical references and index.
   ISBN 0-8058-0724-1
   1. Debates and debating.  I. Title.
PN4181.B694   1991
808.53 – dc20                                                    90-23429
                                                                 CIP

**Publisher's Note**
The publisher has gone to great lengths to ensure the quality of this reprint
but points out that some imperfections in the original may be apparent.


ISBN 978-0-805-80724-0 (hbk)
ISBN 978-0-415-51557-3 (pbk)

*To Celeste*

# Contents

# PREFACE

Some years ago, in sorting through the old books left in my faculty office by its previous occupant, I stumbled upon a copy of William Trufant Foster's 1908 text, *Argumentation and Debating*. It was everything I had despaired of finding in a debate text. Foster systematically explored the processes and strategies of analysis and argumentation in ways that rang true to my own experiences as a debater and teacher of debate. He approached debate not as an isolated activity for specialized competition, but rather as the stuff of our political, moral, and everyday lives. To illustrate techniques of argument, Foster drew upon historical and current controversies and added his own wry Yankee comments. Although Foster's book had been out of print for decades and was dated and incomplete in many ways, it provided an extraordinary model of what a text for classes in debate, argumentation and critical analysis *could be*. In countless ways, it has been the inspiration and daunting model for this book.

There have been other, more contemporary inspirations: people who have contributed greatly to the development of the ideas in this book. I gratefully acknowledge the work of my teachers, particularly Herb James and Bob Shrum; Matt Mason and Tom Foley, who were my partners not only in competition but in learning debate; John Meany, whose dedication to the intellectual and ethical integrity of debate change all who have the joy to work with him; and the many students of my own who have helped develop, sharpen, and challenge my understandings of debate theory and strategy. W. Barnett Pearce talked me into this project and has supported it throughout; his integration of debate and scholarship in his own professional career has left its imprint here. My colleagues Paul Rosenthal and Steve Dolley, and my Erlbaum editor, Robin Marks Weisberg, offered helpful suggestions in their readings of earlier drafts. Finally, my thanks to Celeste Branham, whose editorial suggestions, patience, willingness to shoulder additional burdens, and encouragement have played more of a role in this production than any such list could possibly suggest.

# THE NATURE AND HISTORY OF DEBATE

Human beings are opinionated creatures. We hold strong beliefs about such diverse matters as who should be elected President of the United States, what is the best restaurant in town, or whether women should have access to abortion on demand. Whatever our opinions may be on any given matter and no matter how strongly we may hold them, we should recognize that these opinions are, in fact, argumentative claims, subject to dispute.

Debate is the process by which opinions are advanced, supported, disputed, and defended. Debates are not always formal or even adjudicated. We engage in debate when we argue with friends about the meaning or merit of a movie we have seen, or with an employer about some matter of company policy. Debates need not be oral exchanges. Brilliant debates have been conducted through the exchange of letters and through the publication of scientific papers, for example, in which different scientists may refute the experimental findings of others or challenge theoretical claims advanced in prior research.

These varied exchanges share certain characteristics that identify them as debates. In debate, an opinion must be clearly stated, supported by reasoning and evidence, and defended against conflicting views. "If argumentation is the art of convincing others of the truth or falsity of a disputed matter," wrote Raymond Alden in 1900, "debate may be said to be the art of doing this under conditions such that both sides of the case can be heard and that the advocates of each side can reply directly to those of the other"(Alden, 1900, p. 1). Debate is thus a matter not only of declamation, in which conflicting opinions are aired, but of *resolution*, in which these conflicting opinions are compared and tested against each other in the process of decision making.

The process of debate raises certain fundamental questions about our opinions: How did we arrive at them? Why do we hold them? What alternative opinions exist and how do they compare with our own? The ability to pose and answer these questions has long been considered the hallmark of a truly educated person. In his essay *On Liberty*, political philosopher John Stuart Mill (1859/1947) identified the ability and willingness to subject opinions to debate as a prerequisite for the attainment of wisdom and, ultimately, of liberty itself.

> In the case of any person whose judgment is really deserving of confidence, how has it become so? Because he has kept his mind open to criticism of his opinions and conduct. Because it has been his practice to listen to all that could be said against him; to profit by as much of it as was just, and expound to himself, and upon occasion to others, the fallacy of what was fallacious. Because he has felt, that the only way in which a human being can make some approach to knowing the whole of a subject, is by hearing what can be said about it by persons of every variety of opinion, and studying all modes in which it can be looked at by every character of mind. No wise man ever acquired his wisdom in any mode but this; nor is it in the nature of human intellect to become wise in any other manner. (p. 20)

Mill distinguished between "received opinion," uncritically accepted by an audience from some figure of authority, and an opinion formed through controversy and critical deliberation. It is only through the latter process, Mill argued, that the individual should be able to hold and express an opinion with genuine conviction. An untested opinion, he insisted, even if it happens to be *true*, "is but one superstition the more accidentally clinging to the words that enunciate a truth" (p. 35).

> There is the greatest difference between presuming an opinion to be true, because, with every opportunity for contesting it, it has not been refuted, and assuming its truth for the purpose of not permitting its refutation. Complete liberty of contradicting and disproving our opinion, is the very condition which justifies us in assuming its truth for purposes of action; and on no other terms can a being with human faculties have any rational assurance of being right. (p. 19)

For Mill, debate is a process by which firm convictions on important issues are formed. These convictions may not be the opinions that one took into the dispute, for these may be proven partly or completely wrong through the process of debate. Yet one may expect to emerge from the process of debate with a far more detailed and accurate understanding of the issues involved and with far greater confidence in the conclusions one has drawn from the dispute. "The steady habit of correcting and completing his own opinion by collating it with those of others," Mill insisted, "so far from causing doubt and hesitation in carrying it into practice, is the only stable foundation for a just reliance on it" (p. 20).

Mill was himself a person of strong opinions tested through disputation. He debated many of the great issues of his day and some of the timeless issues of the human condition, such as the responsibilities of representative government, the nature of human freedom, and the dynamics of power and oppression in the subjugation of women. But Mill did not view the proper scope of debate as limited to political or legal questions or its proper forum as limited to the formal deliberations of organized bodies. He instead conceived of debate as a "habit of mind" that should be cultivated by individuals for application to all affairs, whether personal, religious, political, scientific, or those drawn from what he termed "the business of life." "On every subject on which difference of opinion is possible," Mill insisted, "the truth depends on a balance to be struck between two sets of conflicting reasons" (p. 36). We should withhold our confident endorsement of opinions until they have withstood the test of reasoned disputation. We should, he advised, issue "a standing invitation to the whole world to prove them unfounded" (p. 21) and not be satisfied until that invitation has been accepted.

Willingness to subject one's opinions to disputation is a necessary but not sufficient condition for the achievement of true debate. For an opinion to be truly tested, it must first be given the strongest possible expression. The best available arguments for the opinion must be advanced, and supported by the most powerful evidence and reasoning that can be mustered. It is not enough to hold an opinion that turns out to be true; one must have come to that opinion for the best reasons. Furthermore, for an opinion to be truly tested, it must be confronted with the strongest possible counterarguments, also supported by the most persuasive evidence and reasoning that can be found.

The clash of varying opinions is best achieved through genuine debate, in which the conflicting positions are advocated by different parties who are committed to them. The presentation of different views by a single speaker is no substitute for real debate. Although it is possible for a single speaker to both support a given position and describe and refute contrary views, such a presentation is likely to produce a lesser challenge to the position being advocated than would an actual debate. In an ideal debate, Mill wrote, the opposing sides would be defended by knowledgeable persons who earnestly believe the positions they advocate in the dispute.

Mill recognized, however, that such disputants are often not available to discuss matters of immediate importance. In order to provide the best possible disputation of ideas in this common circumstance, Mill endorsed a form of academic debate familiar to modern students: a debate in which the participants skillfully defend positions that do not necessarily represent their own personal beliefs. "So essential is this discipline to a real understanding of moral and human subjects," he insisted, "that if opponents of all important truths do not exist, it is indispensable to imagine them, and supply them with the strongest arguments which the most skilful devil's advocate can conjure up" (p. 37).

The abilities to identify the strongest positions and counterpositions on a given issue and to support and defend them in the best ways possible are precisely the skills of debate that this text aims to enhance. It is designed to familiarize students with the range of argumentative resources and strategies that are available to the skillful disputant and to describe the processes of reasoning and critical analysis through which these strategies may best be employed. This text is conceived as a practical guide to the persuasive and sound expression of one's own opinions and to the powerful refutation of the positions one may oppose.

Most of the skills, strategies, and purposes that guide today's debaters are ancient in origin. The importance Mill placed on the intellectual activity of debate was hardly novel. Indeed, it reflected a centuries-old understanding of debate in many cultures as a hallmark of civilization, social order, and knowledge. The remainder of this chapter will explore the development of formal debate in a variety of cultures and ages. Among the questions to be pursued are these: Why have most of the world's cultures placed such a high value on debate?; How have conceptions of debate differed among cultures?; and, How have ancient and global traditions of debate influenced the modern practice of disputation? At the end of this chapter we return to the question raised but not fully answered by Mill's essay *On Liberty:* What are the characteristics of true debate?

## A BRIEF HISTORY OF DEBATE

Debate has been an important part of most cultures and ages. Indeed, in lands ranging from ancient Athens to India and modern America to Eastern Europe and Africa, debate has been central to the culture's social operation, intellectual discourse, political life, and self-image.

Although it has been argued that debate is only possible in a democracy and that it is the distinctive flower of Western civilization, neither claim holds up under scrutiny. Democratic societies, it is true, may place a particular premium on public debate as the basic means by which citizens participate in the formulation of policy. But debate has played important roles in even the most feudal, doctrinaire, and totalitarian societies, if only among the privileged elites. Comparatively closed societies may place restrictions on who may debate, the topics that may be debated, and what may be said about the topics, but debate nevertheless persists even in such societies.

In a broader sense, debate may be viewed as the process of decision making in which alternative choices are expressed and compared. The decisions-to-be-made range from the highest questions of state (Should we go to war? How should we administer a system of criminal justice?) to matters of scientific inquiry (Does the sun circle the Earth? What causes AIDS?) to personal decision making and choices of the most mundane and rudimentary sorts (Where is the best hunting to be found? How should we invest our money?).

Most cultures have developed systems of organized debate. Debate may be organized in the sense that it occurs on scheduled occasions, is available to designated participants, considers particular subjects, and is conducted according to a specified format. Debates may be organized according to very different principles, as is apparent when one examines the history of debating around the world.

Understanding what subjects have been set aside for organized debate, with what constraints, and who has been permitted to participate in them provides invaluable insight to the character of societies and their ages. It also tells us a great deal about the assumptions and practice of modern debate.

## Greek and Roman Debate

Debate has long been regarded as a form of verbal warfare, a fight to the finish between combatants armed with reason and evidence. In fact, the Latin root for the terms *debate* and *battle* is the same: *battuere*, "to beat."

The *Iliad*, perhaps the oldest surviving work of Greek literature, is a record of great battles and tragic losses, peopled with heroes who bridge the worlds of gods and mortals. It is also, however, a record of the debates on diplomacy and military strategy that led to and guided these battles. Homer contrasted the resolution of disputes by weapons and by words throughout the *Iliad*, attributing the greatest follies to those occasions when debate and reasoned discourse have been swept aside by primitive impulses.

Homer paired each of the most important military leaders with a great debater: Hector with Poulydamas and, to a lesser extent, Achilles with Nestor. Poulydamas was "Hector's comrade, and born in the same night,/ he was better with words, Hector with weapons" (Homer, Book 18, lines

251–252). Similarly, Achilles debates with "soft-spoken" Nestor, "the clearest orator in Pylos,/ from whose tongue speech could run sweeter than honey" (Book 1, lines 247–249). At critical moments of decision making, the warriors debate the orators and hold sway. Despite their superior arguments, these skilled debaters lose the battle for the minds of their audiences when confronted with the warriors' appeals to base instincts.

> So Hector spoke; the Trojans roared. Poor fools,
> For Pallas took their wits away from them,
> They gave applause to Hector's evil counsel;
> Poulydamas, who'd made good sense, got none. (Book 18, lines 310–313)

Homer vindicated the "losing" debaters, proving their counsel wise and their reasoning correct. Those who fail to abide by the "good sense" of the superior arguments in the *Iliad*'s debates do so at their peril.

At least in the realm of intranational disputes, the *Iliad* emphasizes the virtue of debate in preference to impulsive decisions or actual violence. "Come, stop this squabble!", wise Athena counsels Achilles; "Do not draw your sword./ Attack each other, if you will, with words" (Book 1, lines 210–211). The ability to resolve disputes through reasoned discourse is presented in the *Iliad* as the mark of a truly advanced culture.

The contrast of cultures dependent on warfare to settle disputes and those willing and able to do battle with words is clearly drawn in Homer's description of the great shield of Achilles, the extraordinary central image of the *Iliad*. The shield is etched with depictions of the vast range of human activity set amidst a vision of the cosmos. At the center of the shield are images of two cities, one peaceful and joyous, the other fraught with warfare and treachery. In the city of peace and order, Homer described a scene of legal disputation:

> The people thronged the forum, where arose
> The strife of tongues, and two contending stood:
> The one asserting that he had paid the mulct,
> The price of blood for having slain a man;
> The other claiming still the fine as due.
> Both eager to the judges made appeal.
> The crowds, by heralds scarce kept back, with shouts
> And cheers applauded loudly each in turn.
> On smooth and polished stones, a sacred ring,
> The elders sat, and in their hands, their staves
> Of office held, to hear and judge the cause;
> While in the midst two golden talents lay,
> The prize of him who should most justly plead. (Book 18, lines 497–508)

Despite the bitter issue that has motivated the dispute, the principals (serving as their own advocates, as was the custom of the time) were able to entrust their disagreement to an orderly process of resolution, to substitute the "strife of tongues" for the clash of swords. Thus Homer implied, according to critic Kenneth John Atchity (1978), that "even intranational strife can be beneficial, as long as it is expressed within a *customary*, social framework; it may even be a progressive factor, since peaceful settlement automatically becomes a precedent, an example for others to follow" (p. 185). The proper social framework for the resolution of disputes is verbal, not martial. In the *Iliad*, the development of social institutions capable of providing such customary recourse is a hallmark of cultural advancement. "The unstated sources of the orator's prize," as Atchity observed, is "the ideal, orderly society itself" (pp. 185–186).

Oratory and debate were common features of early Greek literature and historical writing. As classicist George Kennedy (1980) noted, the historical treatises of Herodotus and Thucydides employ debates to enliven their discussion of various topics, such as the consideration of possible constitutions for the Persian Empire. The debates are probably fictional, in the sense of not representing actual encounters between two historical disputants, but may be true to the broad-based discussion of these issues in their periods. By staging them as debates, the historians strive not only to create a livelier presentation, but one that clearly identifies competing currents of thought and the issues perceived to be at stake.

Organized debate seems to have found its place at the center of public life in Greece during the 6th century B.C., with the reforms of Solon. During the reign of Pericles (461–445 B.C.), the popular assembly (ecclesia) in Athens offered regular opportunities for public declamation and debate on a wide range of subjects. When the assembly was convened every 8 to 10 days, any adult male citizen might speak on any side of any matter, public or private.

It was in the popular assembly, for example, that the great orator Demosthenes warned of the coming tyranny of Philip of Macedon and sought through his "phillipics" to arouse the Athenian resistance. As debate historian and teacher Alan Nichols (1941) has written:

> In the Assembly, questions of war and peace, national defense, taxation, and the most important policies of state were decided after argument in which any citizen might take part. The ecclesia thus developed into a great forensic forum, where discussion and debate enjoyed a rigidly practical exercise. (p. 444)

The Athenian courts also organized debate as a basis for decision making. With no attorneys, the litigants were generally expected to present and argue their own cases before large juries (usually featuring more than 500 citizens). A majority vote of the jury determined the outcome.

> Thus before large audiences in the courts of Athens, as an everyday routine, there were debates on which hinged questions of life and death, banishment, imprisonment, and property rights. In such forensic contests Socrates was condemned to drink the hemlock; (and) Demosthenes to go into exile. (Nichols, 1941, p. 446)

In contrast to the more broadly based public participation in the political and legal debates of ancient Greece, debate as a matter of governance in the Roman empire was largely restricted to designated representatives. Of particular importance as a forum for debate was the Roman Senate. The 300 appointed members of the Senate debated and decided most major questions of foreign and domestic policy and fixed procedures governing the conduct of their discussions.

The Roman court system, unlike that of the Greeks, generally relied on trained judges rather than citizen juries. Moreover, cases were ordinarily argued by skilled advocates rather than the actual parties to the dispute. As a result, Roman court forensics were often quite specialized, employing technical concepts and sophisticated strategies of argument.

The Roman Forum provided a venue for public oratory and debate. The open-air Forum, with its elevated speaking platform (*rostrum*), bordered the marketplace and featured discourse ranging from funeral eulogies to disputes over national policy.

The debates of ancient Greece and Rome continue to influence debating today. Despite their many differences, both societies prized and refined debate as an activity essential to proper governance. In both societies, the practice of debate was systematized: Formats were defined, strategies were forged, and critical concepts were identified. Many of these systematic elements, from the design of formal debating chambers to the actual argumentative strategies employed, survive today. The basic assumption of Greek and Roman debate is widely held today--that wise decisions (whether in governance or the administration of justice) can only be reached through the clash of conflicting points of view.

But the debating practices of the Greeks and Romans are not the only progenitors of contemporary debate. Other cultural traditions, both Western and non-Western, have made important and sometimes very different contributions to contemporary practices and understandings of debate.

## Debate in India

Debating in India originated as a part of religious ceremony, and later evolved into an important medium for the conduct of theological inquiries and disputes. The ancestor of Indian debating was the *brahmodya*, a set of riddles and charades performed by actors in ceremonies accompanying animal sacrifices.

The *brahmodya* riddles were scripted in the form of questions and answers and were designed to offer an entertaining demonstration of intellectual prowess. Originally, the dialogues were memorized and recited. Later, however, the performances were extemporaneous and each rival sought to outshine the other. These debates became popular entertainment. No longer a minor diversion during sacrifices, debates were featured in public assemblies. Indian kings sponsored debating contests in the royal courts and offered great prizes for the victors who proved themselves the wisest brahmins.

Those who devoted themselves most avidly to the contests were called "the brahmins addicted to debate" (Jayatilleke, 1963, p. 45). In order to prepare themselves and others for debating contests, such brahmins developed systematic instruction in logic, reasoning, and debate strategy. As in the West, debate thereby played a vital role in the development of Indian philosophical, scientific, and political thought. "The first awareness of the validity and invalidity of reasoning," as K.N. Jayatilleke (1963) has observed, "seems to have arisen out of the debate in India as much as in Greece" (p. 43).

After the rise of Buddhism, debating became the primary forum through which rival philosophical schools conducted their doctrinal disputes. Debates were generally public events, governed by established procedures, and chaired by an umpire. Topics were generally drawn from the theological rifts that divided the competing sects represented by the disputants.

> One of the earliest lists of topics said to be vigorously debated by "many and various heretical teachers, recluses, brahmins and paribbajakas" contains the ten theses on which the Buddha refused to express an opinion, namely the *avyakatas*. Each of these theses is said to be held by a school of recluses and brahmins who were at loggerheads with each other in maintaining the truth of its own thesis. (Jayatilleke, 1963, p. 242)

The 10 theses "on which the Buddha refused to express an opinion" represent the different possible answers to four metaphysical questions: Is the world eternal?; Is the world finite?; Is the soul identical with the body?' and Do saints exist after death? The possible answers to these questions were then framed affirmatively as propositions to be defended and refuted in debate:

The world is eternal.

The world is not eternal.

The world is finite.

The world is infinite.

The soul is identical with the body.

The soul is different from the body.

The saint exists after death.

The saint does not exist after death.

The possible permutations were sometimes expanded in framing topics to reflect the beliefs of splinter groups. Thus, "The saint does and does not exist after death; or The saint neither does nor does not exist after death" (Jayatilleke, 1963, p. 243).

The systematic instruction in Buddhist debating paid particular attention to matters of evidence. Spiritual theses were to be supported and refuted by reference to sensory data, acquired experience, examples, analogies, and authoritative testimony. Elaborate tests for each type of evidence were prescribed and fallacies in reasoning from evidence to theses were identified.

Around the 2nd century, A.D., a manual that described the methods of debating was produced by one of the competing schools. It offers a defense of debate against its critics, proclaiming it to be "necessary to protect the truth" (Warder, 1970, pp. 416–417). Although Buddhist debaters were anxious to emerge victorious from the debates, the contests were viewed by most participants as ways of seeking spiritual truth and proving the correctness of their deeply held beliefs.

## Debate in East Asia

As in India, debate in China played an important role in religious training, theological disputation, and the development of logic and philosophical reasoning. The collapse of the Han Dynasty in 220 C.E., however, led to great tumult in Chinese society and significant changes in the forms and purposes of Chinese debate.

The Han Dynasty's collapse produced doubts, especially among the literati, about the classic texts and doctrines of Confucianism which had been, as Mary Garrett (1989) has written, its "ideological engine" (p. 3). Metaphysical questions (such as the relationship between being and nothingness) were raised with new vigor, and the competing texts and teachings of Taoism and Buddhism gained influence. Unlike the strict social order prescribed in Confucianism, Taoist texts (such as the *Chuang-tzu* and *Lao-tzu*) seemed to promote non-conformity and "rejection of societal standards of judgment" (Garrett, 1989, p. 3). The conflict between these competing world views fueled renewed interest in debate.

One of the most interesting forms of discussion and debate to emerge from this period of uncertainty and upheaval was the practice of "pure talk." Pure talk, as Garrett has described it, was conducted by circles of educated people, often taking the form of competitive debates conducted before audiences that would last an entire day and night. The report of one such contest records that, after the topic was announced,

> [T]here rang out a chorus of great debate. They threaded their way through yin and yang, with literary embellishments sprouting in every direction. Rather than quote from the sages and ancient records, they concentrated on bringing to light the natural order of things. Tzu-ch'un and all the assembled scholars joined the attack. The points and retorts thrusted back and forth like spears. But Lu answered each and every assault with a reply that was more than adequate. They continued the entire day, until dusk fell, without even pausing for food and drink. (Kuan Ch'en, quoted in Garrett, 1989, p. 7)

Topics for pure talk debates varied from metaphysical theses to questions of how a particular literary text should be interpreted or judged, such as: "The Symbols of *The Book of Changes* are More Subtle than the Visible Shapes of Nature" (Garrett, 1989, p. 8).

Normally, one person (designated as the "host") would defend the thesis for debate and another (the "guest") would refute it. Members of the audience would sometimes join in the fray in order to clarify the arguments of one side for the other, but the debate remained focused on the encounter between the two main participants. The debaters were expected to support their arguments with strong evidence (drawn from historical records, examples, or statements of textual authorities) and were held to standards of logical rigor and consistency.

Skillful and elegant argument by the practitioners of pure talk was much admired. Good performances could lead to career advancement and patronage. Yet the ostensible purpose of these debates was not primarily entertainment nor advancement, but the discovery of *truth*. The debates were highly competitive, and structured as a game, but "the goal of the game itself," noted Garrett (1989), "was to reach the truth about a thesis that was important to everyone involved, to determine whether the thesis was sustainable or not, to 'honor the heart of truth' " (p. 13).

Having eventually reached a point in the debate at which all significant objections to the opponent's position had been successfully refuted, the loser in a pure talk debate was expected to concede and adopt the position that had proven to be superior. If, even after one debater had been silenced by the other, members of the audience still had reservations about the winning position, the host of the gathering might then call upon someone more capable of refuting it. The point of Chinese pure talk debates was to arrive at some consensus regarding the truth or falsity of the proposition.

Debates on literary and historical texts were also an important part of scholarly life in feudal Japan. Although literary, religious, and political debating societies were not organized until the 1860s, informal debate was common among students who strove to test wits with their fellows.

The autobiography of Yukichi Fukuzawa (1834–1901) offers a glimpse of the informal debating practices of young scholars in mid-19th century Japan (Fukuzawa, 1966). Eager to test himself against his fellow students, Fukuzawa would often initiate extracurricular debates on scholarly matters, such as the meaning of a classical Chinese poem or the interpretation of a controversial event in Japanese history.

The perennial favorite among historical topics for debate in Japan was the story of the Forty-Seven Ronin. Around the year 1700, a feudal lord wounded an official of the Shogun who had insulted him. The lord was forced to commit suicide and his properties were confiscated. Forty-seven of the lord's retainers pledged themselves to avenge their master by killing the official. They eventually succeeded in this plan, and then surrendered themselves to justice, expecting to die. A great debate arose concerning their fate. Some, including the Shogun himself, believed that the act of the ronin should be approved as in accord with Confucian principles of loyalty. Other scholars insisted that Confucian principles must be observed in accordance with the law, not freely interpreted by individuals. The latter opinion eventually held sway, after more than a year of deliberation, and the ronin were ordered to commit suicide. They became folk heroes, and their fate has been vigorously debated ever since.

More than a century after the fact, the debate was joined by Fukuzawa and his schoolmates.

> If the theme of the Forty-Seven Ronin came up, I would challenge my comrades, "I will take whichever side you are against. If you say the Forty-Seven Ronin were loyal, I will prove they were disloyal. Or if you want to prove the contrary, I will take the opposite side, for I can make them loyal men or disloyal men with the twist of my tongue. Now, come, all of you together."
>
> Such were our innocent debates; sometimes I won, sometimes I was beaten; and our voices often were loud, but that made it all the livelier. Never did our debates grow so serious that the debaters had to decide the absolute right or wrong of the problem. (Fukuzawa, 1966, p. 78)

The controversy over the actions of the Forty-Seven Ronin has proven to be an unresolvable dispute, enduring over centuries. Although Fukuzawa's debates resumed the task of the original judicial deliberation, it is clear that for him the topic bore the additional interest of providing a challenging dispute over issues at the center of Japanese culture.

After Japan opened contact with the West in the 1850s, Fukuzawa was among the first Japanese to visit the United States and Europe. During his travels, he observed political speeches and debates in Parliament, the U.S. Congress, and elsewhere. Upon his return to Japan, he created the first public speech and debate hall in Japan, and organized a campaign to broaden participation in speech and debate as vehicles through which he believed the Japanese could develop and propagate genuine *independence* of thought.

Fukuzawa challenged the Confucian dictates that one must accept the way things are and accept one's assigned place within an established social and political order. He encouraged doubt, critical scrutiny of ideas, and independence of thought and expression. Speech and debate, he believed, best encouraged these vital habits of mind.

Fukuzawa's belief that political speech and debate represented the most effective challenge to the established order was apparently shared by the Japanese government, which banned all political speech and debate activities in 1878.

## Debate in the Medieval Universities

Modern institutions of higher education are, in most fundamental respects, the descendants of the universities that arose in Paris, Bologna, and elsewhere in medieval Europe. Emerging in the renaissance of the 12th century, these universities organized societies of masters and scholars in a system of lectures, individual studies, and examinations devoted to the liberal arts of learning.

It is scarcely an exaggeration to say that debate was the central feature of the medieval university curriculum. "To analyse, to subdivide, to know the *pros* and *cons* of every argument, to be alert in disputation, in posing questions and in suggesting replies–these were the arts that appealed to teacher and scholar alike," wrote Oxford historian C.E. Mallet (1924, p. 186).

Progressive training in debate provided the very structure of the educational experience. At medieval Oxford, modeling the system of the continental schools, the first 2 years of a student's education were devoted to the acquisition of knowledge in a variety of fields, including the formal study of argument technique. After achieving the rank of "General Sophister," the student then spent at least 1 year in formal disputation, advancing and opposing propositions with fellow students. One topic debated at medieval Oxford was "Whether more than one angel can occupy one place at the same time." Disputations were often technical and abstract, as indicated in the following excerpt of an exchange from the 13th century:

> **Opponent:** What think you of this question, whether universal ideas are formed by abstraction?
> **Respondent:** I affirm it.
> **Opponent:** Universal ideas are not formed by abstraction, therefore you are deceived.
> **Respondent:** I deny the antecedent.
> **Opponent:** I prove the antecedent. Whatever is formed by sensation alone, is not formed by abstraction. But universal ideas are formed by sensation alone: therefore universal ideas are <not> formed by abstraction. (*The Oxford Book of Oxford*, p. 7)

In the fourth year, the students engaged in disputations on grammar and logic with the masters themselves. If certified as upright and capable, the scholars then took part in an exercise called the Determinations, where they sought to make their professional reputations in debate as their arguments were scrutinized for fallacies and irrelevancies. At last, after an additional 3 years of study, the scholars took part in a final ceremony in which they offered a lecture to the community of masters they proposed to join and engaged in a final, extraordinary disputation. In the grueling Inception, the scholars were matched against "a succession of opponents who relieved each other at intervals from six in the morning till six in the evening" (Rashdall, 1936, pp. 479–480).

Those who triumphed at the public examination and Inception were duly celebrated. A letter sent home by a student at Bologna who had just passed through the final trial exclaimed:

> "Sing unto the Lord a new song, praise him with stringed instruments and organs, rejoice upon the high-sounding cymbals," for your son has held a glorious disputation, which was attended by a great multitude of teachers and scholars. He answered all the questions without a mistake, and no one could prevail against his arguments. (Haskins, 1957, pp. 48–49)

Why did the medieval university place such a premium on training in disputation and debate? Debate seems to have been valued both as a means by which to gauge the student's command of certain bodies of knowledge and as a "habit of mind," valuable in its own right.

As a form of examination, debate was used to test the depth of a student's knowledge in a given subject area. Moreover, frequent disputation was believed to cultivate certain skills in the use of knowledge, such as in the ability to apply a body of learning to a particular question or task.

But debate was much more than a useful tool or yardstick for evaluation; it reflected an analytical approach that was at the heart of the intellectual life for medieval scholars. "Syllogism, disputation," and "the orderly marshalling of arguments for and against specific theses," wrote historian Charles Homer Haskins (1957), "became the intellectual habit of the age in law and medicine as well as in philosophy and theology" (p. 30).

## Debate in the Constitutional Democracies

In the West, the "first great modern forum of public discussion," as Alan Nichols (1941, p. 454) has observed, was the English Parliament. The House of Commons was founded in 1265 and the importance of freedom to debate first acknowledged during the reign of Edward III (1327-1377). Over succeeding centuries, Parliament became more influential in governance and the importance of the debates through which it conducted its deliberations grew correspondingly.

In the last half of the 18th century, parliamentary debating flourished amidst the controversies generated by England's colonial expansion and the American and French revolutions. The great parliamentary debaters of this period, including Edmund Burke, William Pitt, Richard Brinsley Sheridan, and Charles James Fox, achieved international celebrity and enormous political influence.

The concept of parliamentary debate took root in England's American colonies. Each of the colonies had an elective assembly that governed most local affairs. After the American Revolution, the growth in power of the federal government was accompanied by the increased importance and influence of debate in the setting of national policy. The rules of the First and Second Continental Congresses and later the bicameral Congress of the United States were designed to maximize the opportunities for virtually unlimited debate. The Congress became the principal forum in which the great issues of the new nation – states' rights, slavery, territorial expansion, and, eventually, secession – were aired.

In a sense, members of the U.S. House of Representatives and Senate were often elected as debating gladiators for their constituents. They were expected to be able to articulate their constituents' concerns and defend their positions and interests against other competitors. Floor speeches and debates were widely reported. Understandably, the political campaigns of aspirants to these offices were dominated by stump speeches and, occasionally, by formal debating encounters between rival candidates. Perhaps the most famous of these candidate debates in the 19th century were those conducted in 1858 between Abraham Lincoln and Stephen Douglas as they campaigned for the office of U.S. senator from Illinois. Their debates over the question of whether slavery should be permitted in new American territories elevated Lincoln to national prominence (despite his loss in the 1858 Senate race, he was elected president of the United States in 1860) and framed a national discussion over the issue that fueled the Civil War.

Although political campaigns throughout much of the world are now dominated by television advertising, candidate debates remain an important part of national elections in many countries (including not only the United States and Britain, but such nations as Japan, Peru, and the Soviet Union).

Debating activity in Britain and the United was by no means limited to members of the national governments. As early as 1631, the citizens of Dorchester, Massachusetts organized a system of town meetings at which problems facing the community could be discussed by its residents and support for solutions could be forged. For centuries thereafter, the New England town meeting provided the basic system of municipal governance for citizens of that region.

Nor was debate restricted to the affairs and forums of government. Debating clubs and societies were widespread in England by the mid-18th century. These societies were especially popular among aspiring members of the middle and lower classes and were seen as a means of social improvement and advancement (Browne, 1989, pp. 5–6). Members gathered to discuss major political and moral questions of the day and to hone valuable skills in oratory and advocacy. Beyond their material advantages in facilitating career advancement, the clubs reflected the values of the Enlightenment. By encouraging the expression of diverse opinions and creating some sense of empowerment among members of social classes historically excluded from power, the clubs embodied an "openness to ideas, rationality, tolerance, commitment to human rights and liberty, dedication to progressive ideals, (and) faith in the possibility of social and political improvement" (Fawcett, 1980, p. 229).

In the United States, debating societies emerged from the lyceum movement. The first lyceum was formed in Millbury, Massachusetts in 1826 as an evening study group. Debates and speeches were frequently held and followed by an open forum for discussion. Within 8 years, more than 3,000 town lyceums had been formed across the country, the best-known of which was that directed by famed orator Daniel Webster in Boston. Major political, literary, and judicial figures appeared at the lyceum gatherings to express and defend their views on various subjects.

The topic most widely and vigorously debated in the United States during much of the 19th century was slavery. Abolitionist societies provided regular gatherings at which the evils of slavery could be described and potential strategies to abolish it could be debated. Should slavery be abolished altogether and at once? Excluded from the new territories?

Would abolition bring economic loss and, if so, should that be a deciding consideration?

Abolitionist societies provided opportunities for speech and debate to people who had been systematically denied any sort of public voice: African-Americans and women. Freed slaves, such as Frederick Douglass, were especially popular speakers at Abolitionist meetings because, as historian Philip Foner (1975) has noted, "Who else could refute so effectively the testimony of those who upheld slavery and argued that slaves actually benefitted from their bondage and were happy to be human property?" (p. 5). The powerful, insightful, and eloquent speeches of Douglass and other African-Americans also "helped to demolish the myth of the natural inferiority of black people," and thus supported by tangible demonstration the claims of African-Americans to full human rights (Foner, 1975, p. 2).

Prohibitions against African-American speakers were very strong. When the Abolitionists engaged in debates or lectures before the general public, their speakers—particularly if they were black—were frequently jeered or even stoned. Such segregation has persisted in American and British politics. Until 1935, prospective members of the most prestigious American debate honor society (Delta Sigma Rho) were required to swear at their initiation that they were "not a Negro."

The great skill and success demonstrated by African-American speakers and debaters challenged negative stereotypes. Frederick Douglass, one of the greatest orators in American history, was advised to speak less eloquently in order not to cast doubt on his status as a former slave. Douglass refused to stifle or diminish his voice, as have countless other African-American men and women who have found in speech and debate not only a platform for expression but a powerful source of self-definition and validation. Benjamin Elijah Mays, later President of Morehouse College, civil rights leader, and mentor of Martin Luther King, Jr., among others, wrote in his autobiography of what his experiences as an intercollegiate debater for Bates College from 1917–1920 meant to him:

> Through my competitive experience, I had finally dismissed from my mind for all time the myth of the inherent inferiority of all Negroes and the inherent superiority of all whites—articles of faith to so many in my previous environment. I had done better in academic performances, in public speaking, and in argumentation and debate than the vast majority of my classmates. . . . Bates College did not emancipate me; it did the far greater service of allowing me to emancipate myself, to accept with dignity my own worth as a free man. (Mays, 1971, p. 60)

The Abolitionist movement also provided American women with their first significant public speaking opportunities. As in many cultures, women in the United States were expected to follow the dictum of St. Paul: "Let a woman learn in silence with all submissiveness. . . . I permit no woman to teach or have authority over men; she is to keep silent." Scientific "experts" from Aristotle to Darwin maintained that women were biologically unsuited to speaking (Jamieson, 1988, pp. 68–70). If women engaged in active thought or speech, Aristotle warned, they would become infertile.

Women were consigned to the domestic sphere and denied access to public affairs. They were excluded for centuries from the professions of the ministry, politics, and the law, which provided most important occasions for public address. The abolitionist movement (and later the temperance and suffrage movements) provided alternative occasions and forums for speaking that proved more accessible to women. Indeed, women were among the greatest Abolitionist leaders, speakers, and debaters.

Maria W. Stewart was an outspoken abolitionist and generally believed to be the first recorded native-born American woman to engage in public speaking. An African-American, she spoke from and about the double burdens of her gender and race, each of which was held by much of the public to delegitimize her as a speaker. Undaunted by hostile reactions, she maintained, "It was contempt for my moral and religious opinions in private that drove me thus before a public" (Foner, 1975, p. 67). She viewed her public speeches as opportunities in which to address and challenge the preconceptions of her audience, confident that "Brilliant wit will shine, come from whence it will; and genius and talent will not hide the brightness of its lustre" (p. 66).

But even where women were able to secure the right to speak their views, they were excluded from the right to *debate* them with others. Debate was widely held to be contrary to the gentle and submissive nature appropriate to womanhood. Angelina Grimke, as Kathleen Jamieson and David Birdsell have described, was among the first American women to challenge the restrictions on women's participation in public debate, pronouncing them to be:

> *a violation of human rights, a rank usurpation of power,* a violent seizure and confiscation of what is sacredly and inalienably hers–thus inflicting upon woman outrageous wrongs, working mischief incalculable in the social circle, and in its influence on the world producing only evil and that continually. (Jamieson & Birdsell, 1988, p. 78)

Grimke accepted the invitation of two young men to debate in Amesbury, Massachusetts on the subject of slavery. The outraged editor of the Amesbury *Morning Courier* refused to publish the results of the debate.

In the United States, Great Britain, and other nations, debate is a crucial element of power, decision making, and national self-definition. Debate as a means of decision making signals an openness to diverse opinions and a commitment to participatory democracy, rather than autocratic power. This self-image has often been more imaginary than real, however, as access to public speech, debate, and decision making has been restricted. Groups and individuals excluded from traditional opportunities for speech and debate have created their own, offering eloquent rebuttal to the claims of a dominant society.

## Debate Then and Now

This brief survey of the development of organized debating in various cultures is by no means a comprehensive one. It should, however, provide some sense of both the different approaches to debate in disparate cultures and of commonalities in their understandings of debate as an important intellectual and civic activity.

Debate has been viewed in many cultures and ages as an essential element of individual intellectual development and as a hallmark of civilized society. It is through the contest of competing ideas that opinions and convictions may best be formed. In matters of religious belief, scientific inquiry, literary interpretation, or matters of law and governance, debate provides not only a "marketplace of ideas," but a means through which "comparison shopping" may be conducted among competing ideas in that marketplace. As the self-styled "public philosopher" Walter Lippmann (1982) has written:

> In the absence of debate, unrestricted utterance leads to the degradation of opinion. By a kind of Gresham's law the more rational is overcome by the less rational, and the opinions that will prevail will be those which are held most ardently by those with the most passionate will. For that reason the freedom to speak can never be maintained merely by objecting to interference with the liberty of the press, of printing, of broadcasting, of the screen. It can be maintained only by promoting debate. (p. 196)

The freedom to conduct public debate is a basic and highly prized right. It signals not only a societal tolerance for diversity of opinion, but some level of public participation and responsibility in matters of policy. During the remarkable last months of 1989, when Eastern European nations declared and established their independence, public debate flourished. Streetcorners in East Germany, Czechoslovakia, and elsewhere were filled for the first time in half a century with groups of people vigorously debating current events and future plans.

But virtuosity in debating, as has been recognized by many cultures over thousands of years, requires systematic instruction and dedicated practice. For this and other reasons, debate has long flourished in academia.

The individual skills required for success in debate are precisely those skills most valued in scholarship. As Raymond Alden (1900) wrote in *The Art of Debate:*

> The mental habits which go to make a good debater are of the highest type, and are usually developed only by considerable training. They involve: the ability to find out as well as to defend the truth, the ability to analyze keenly and sift the essential from the trivial, the willingness to consider questions apart from the prejudices with which one is tempted to view them, and finally, the power of expression. . . . These are not every-day qualities. . . . (p. 3)

Because of the correspondence between the skills necessary for competitive success in debate and those qualities most prized in scholarship, debate has been a central feature of the educational systems of many cultures from ancient times to the present. The rhetorical training of students in ancient Greece, the disputations of medieval European university students, the rigorous debate training of Buddhist monks, and the interscholastic and classroom debates of contemporary students have all been designed to provide students with methods of critical analysis, research, organization, and communication that have been deemed essential to their more general academic and personal development. "It is one of the highest aims of education," Alden (1900) insisted, "to bring about conditions under which opinions will be held because they have been legitimately earned, not lazily inherited or borrowed" (p. 4).

Despite its long history, debate is a subversive, even revolutionary, force in education. Debate may be conceived as a struggle against received opinion, in which knowledge is not "lazily inherited" from one's instructors or textbooks, but *earned* by viewing the opinions so received as *argumentative claims*, to be tested against other possible opinions. "Over-indulgence in being lectured-to," wrote Arthur Quiller-Couch, "is a primrose path to intellectual sloth, the more fatally deceitful because it appears vituous." (1928, p. 34) Participation in debate removes students from their accustomed roles as note-takers and "exam-crammers" and accords them a more ambitious, independent, and active status.

Debate is an *attitude* as well as an activity. Debate abides no limits: for a debater, everything is debatable (including this statement). For a trained debater, there are indeed two (or more) sides to every issue, and these alternative perspectives must be examined and compared before a reasoned decision can be reached. For a debater, claims must be *proven,* supported by evidence that will withstand the most arduous scrutiny (which the debater is willing and able to provide). This attitude toward true debate is the hallmark of scholarship, citizenship, and, as Fukuzawa, observed, personal growth and independence.

## THE CHARACTERISTICS OF TRUE DEBATE

To the popular mind, the term *debate* evokes certain images of a particular form of contest: Two or more speakers who appear on the same stage and speak within set time limits on opposing sides of a common question. In fact, however, such exchanges are often not true debates and many genuine debates, as noted earlier, are neither formally nor orally transacted.

Even in organized oral exchanges, debate is not synonymous with format. The best designed format may fail to produce genuine debate, as when, for example, the participants fail to seize the opportunity to engage each other's arguments and remain "two ships passing in the night." In such a case, no true debate has occurred. On the other hand, formats that seem unconducive to debate may be overcome by adversaries who are dedicated and skilled enough to do so.

The format adopted for the "debates" between American presidential candidates, for example, has often been criticized (and properly so) as unconducive to genuine debate. In the presidential debate format, the candidates respond to questions from journalists, rather than raising issues themselves. Moreover, they are denied sufficient opportunity to support their own positions (because of the brief times allotted for response to each question). Candidate statements such as "I oppose the death penalty because it doesn't work," remain undeveloped (What "work" is it supposed to do? What evidence is there to support the claim that it has failed to meet this objective?) and unchallenged by the opponent. Little opportunity is provided in the Presidential "debate" format for candidates to respond to the arguments of their adversaries.

Unsurprisingly, this format produces little true debate in the sense that we have defined it. Indeed, several major news organizations refused to refer to the 1988 candidate encounters as debates. CBS News, for instance, substituted the term *joint appearance* in their reports of the contests.

Nevertheless, some genuine debate did occur in this format, however unlikely that outcome may have been. The 1988 debate between vice-presidential candidates Lloyd Bentsen and Dan Quayle defied the odds. Most arguments of both candidates were clearly developed and supported with examples and other evidence. They frequently clashed with each other's statements. They identified what they believed to be the most important issues in the contest (and the election) and related their individual arguments to these larger issues.

Thus, true debate is to be found not in the *format*, but in particular characteristics of the arguments that occur within the format. Although various formats for the interchange of ideas may be more or less likely to produce real debate, it is in the qualities of the arguments themselves that true debate may be found.

If debate is "the process by which opinions are advanced, supported, disputed, and defended," the fulfillment of these actions in turn requires that the arguments of the disputants possess certain attributes. Thus, true debate depends on the presence of four characteristics of argument:

1. **Development,** through which arguments are advanced and supported;
2. **Clash,** through which arguments are properly disputed;
3. **Extension,** through which arguments are defended against refutation; and
4. **Perspective,** through which individual arguments are related to the larger question at hand.

These four characteristics form the basic outline of this book. In the succeeding chapters, each is explained in detail, along with the methods and strategies that debaters may use to achieve these qualities in their own performances. Here, each of these central concepts is briefly defined and illustrated.

## Development

In a true debate, the positions of the contending sides must be clearly articulated, adequately explained, and supported by reasoning and evidence. These qualities are prerequisites for informed controversy and decision making; without them, debate is impossible. To say that "the death penalty does not work" is to utter an opinion, but not to make an argument sufficient to engage or sustain debate. In order to engage in profitable debate, the advocate must explain what the death penalty is *supposed* to do (e.g., deter criminals, incapacitate them, or provide some sense of retribution) and demonstrate with convincing evidence that it has failed to do so. Amnesty International (1989), an organization committed to the worldwide abolition of the death penalty, develops its argument that the death penalty fails to work in the following section of its 1989 report:

## Deterrence

The argument most frequently used for the death penalty is deterrence: it is necessary to kill an offender to dissuade other people from committing the same kind of crime.

At first glance, this appears to be a plausible argument. What could more effectively stop those willing to kill or commit other serious crimes than the threat of the most terrible of punishments, death? What more forceful way could be found to respond to the strong desire of ordinary people to be protected against crime?

Empirical evidence, however, does not support the argument. Moreover, its common sense logic rests on questionable assumptions.

It is incorrect to assume that all or most of those who commit such serious crimes as murder do so after rationally calculating the consequences. Murders are most often committed in moments of passion, when extreme emotion overcomes reason. They may also be committed under the influence of alcohol or drugs, or in moments of panic, for example when the perpetrator is caught in the act of stealing. Some people who commit violent crime are highly unstable or mentally ill. In none of these cases can fear of the death penalty be expected to deter.

A Japanese prison psychiatrist studied 145 convicted murderers between 1955 and 1957. He could find none who remembered thinking they might be sentenced to death before committing the crime. "Despite their knowledge of the existence of the death penalty" the prisoners had been "incapable because of their impulsiveness and their inability to live except in the present, of being inhibited by the thought of capital punishment."

After 35 years in the Prison Medical Service, a British doctor found that "Deterrence is by no means the simple affair that some people think . . . A high proportion of murderers are so tensed up at the time of their crime as to be impervious to the consequences to themselves; others manage to persuade themselves that they can get away with it."

This last point underlines another weakness in the deterrence argument. Those offenders who plan serious crimes in a calculated manner may decide to proceed despite the risks in the belief that they will not be caught. The key to deterrence in such cases is to increase the likelihood of detection, arrest and conviction. The death penalty may even be counter-productive in that it diverts official and public attention from efforts needed to bring about real improvements in combating crime.

The deterrence argument is not borne out by the facts. If the death penalty did deter potential offenders more effectively than other punishments, one would expect to find that in analyses of comparable jurisdictions, those which have the death penalty for a particular crime would have a lower rate of that crime than those which do not. Similarly, a rise in the rate of crimes hitherto punishable by death would be expected in states which abolish the penalty and a decline in crime rates would be expected among states which introduce it for those crimes. Yet study after study has failed to establish any such link between the death penalty and crime rates.

The first major report on capital punishment prepared for the UN and published in 1962 considered the possible effects of removing various offences from the list of capital crimes. The report concluded that "All the information available appears to confirm that such a removal has, in fact, never been followed by a notable rise in the incidence of the crime no longer punishable with death.

The United Kingdom Royal Commission on Capital Punishment (1949-1953) examined the available statistics on jurisdictions which had abolished or ceased using the death penalty for murder. From its survey of seven European countries, New Zealand and individual states within Australia and the USA, the Commission concluded that "there is no clear evidence in any of the figures we have examined that the abolition of capital punishment has led to an increase in the homicide rate, or that its reintroduction has led to a fall.

Recent crime figures from abolitionist countries similarly fail to show that abolition has harmful effects. Although there were more murder and manslaughter convictions in South Australia in the five years after abolition than in the five years before, a longer-term study showed "that abolition of the death penalty had no effect on homicide trends in that state". The death penalty was abolished there in 1976. In Jamaica, there was little change in the homicide rate during a moratorium on executions between 1976 and 1980, despite a rash of political shootings during the 1980 general election. In Canada, the homicide rate per 100,000 population fell from a peak of 3.09 in 1975, the year before the abolition of the death penalty for murder, to 2.74 in 1983, and in 1986 it reached its lowest level in 15 years. In the United Kingdom, the number of homicides has risen since the abolition of the death penalty for murder, but the increase has been far smaller than for other serious violent offences.

Reviewing the evidence on the relation between changes in the use of the death penalty and crime, the report on the death penalty prepared for the UN Committee on Crime Prevention and Control in 1988 stated that, although no definite conclusions could be drawn about the impact of changes in the death penalty alone (as these could have been associated with other social and penal changes affecting crime), nevertheless "the fact that all the evidence continues to point in the same direction is persuasive a priori evidence that countries need not fear sudden and serious changes in the curve of crime if they reduce their reliance upon the death penalty."

As Mill (1859/1947) insisted, "If the cultivation of the understanding consists in one thing more than in another, it is surely in learning the *grounds* of one's own opinions" (p. 35). In debate, the grounds of an opinion must be developed by (a) identifying, explaining, and organizing one's arguments on behalf of the opinion and (b) supporting these arguments with sound reasoning and evidence. Through such development, the worth of the opinion itself may best be tested.

## Clash

Clash is the characteristic most readily associated with debate. More than the "venting of opinion," it is, as Lippmann (1982) observed, the "confrontation of opinion" (p. 232). Clash is not simply a matter of disagreement, as in the childish refrains of "Yes it is!"/"No it isn't!" Clash is the product of demonstrated conflict between two competing argumentative positions. Arguments compete in the sense that one must choose between them—both cannot be true. Clash may occur at the level of argument initiated in the first claim ("Murder rates have dropped in states that have instituted the death penalty" vs. "Murder rates have risen in states that have instituted the death penalty") or at another level of abstraction ("Murder rates have dropped in states that have instituted the death penalty" vs. "Murder rates have dropped at a slower rate in states that have instituted the death penalty than in those that have eliminated it").

The conflict between competing arguments must be *demonstrated* in the sense that the arguer must *explain* how his or her argument refutes or accounts for that of the opponent.

Debate affords the opportunity for competing advocates to explain how their positions differ and why, in the opinion of each advocate, one of these positions is better than the other. When debaters take advantage of this opportunity, their positions clash.

## Extension

Extensions are "responses to responses" in a debate. A distinguishing feature of true debate is the ability and willingness of the debaters representing two opposing sides not simply to state their two positions, but to continue or *extend* this clash through multiple speeches. The argument presented earlier by Amnesty International refutes the best known argument offered on behalf of the death penalty. In a debate, however, not only would we have heard the proponents of capital punishment offer their own best case for the deterrent effect of the death penalty, we would also have the opportunity to hear them *respond* to the arguments and evidence of Amnesty International, and to hear the representatives of Amnesty International respond in turn to these responses.

In June 1988, the "MacNeil-Lehrer Newshour" broadcasted a debate between Jack Watson, former White House Chief of Staff for U.S. President Carter, and Arthur Schlesinger, Jr., historian and advisor to President Kennedy. The debate format employed by the "Newshour" usually features two speakers and a moderator. In order to encourage on-point clash and extension of arguments, at the end of each speech the moderator (in this case Robert MacNeil) briefly reiterates the most important point made by the previous speaker and asks the next speaker to address it. As a result, lines of argument developed in the speakers' original comments are clearly extended through multiple speeches, thus providing a richer, more detailed view of the competing positions.

Watson and Schlesinger debated the question: "Should the office of the vice-president be retained or abolished?" Watson began by explaining the value of the vice-presidency.

> **Watson:** The main reason for having a Vice-President to begin with is that we want to have somebody ready, willing, able, and prepared to assume the Presidency in the event that it becomes necessary to do so. In recent years, the preparation of the Vice-President for that role in the event that role is thrust upon him has been much better . . .

Schlesinger, who supported the abolition of the vice-presidency, was then asked to respond to Watson's claim that the vice-presidency provides useful preparation for being president.

> **Schlesinger:** The Vice-President has nothing to do except to wait around for the President to die. Every effort to give some meaning to the office has failed. Far from it being an experience which prepares people for the Presidency, it may well be in many cases that the frustrations inseparable from the Office make people *less* well-prepared for the Presidency than when they undertook the Office.
>
> The Vice-President is a man deprived of identity; he is condemned to being an echo of the President. He cannot admit any independence of thought or independence of judgment. That's a grueling experience for people, and I'm not sure it's the best preparation for the kind of leadership the Presidency demands.

Watson was then asked to address Schlesinger's claim that, instead of preparing him or her to assume the presidency, serving as vice-president actually maims those who then succeed to the higher office.

> **Watson:** Look at history. There are four Vice-Presidents who succeeded to the Presidency in this century that later gained the Presidency by their own election. Theodore Roosevelt was one, Harry Truman was one, Lyndon Johnson was one, Richard Nixon was another. In the case of the first three men in particular that I mentioned, Theodore Roosevelt and Harry Truman and Lyndon Johnson . . . it's absolutely true, as Dr. Schlesinger said, that while they were Vice-President they were clearly in a subordinated role to the President. That must be the way it is; the executive power of the country is indivisibly invested in the President of the United States under the Constitution, which is as it should be. But when these three men became

President, succeeded to the Presidency upon the death of their predecessor, they were in the opinion of many historians, either near-great Presidents (in the case of Teddy Roosevelt and Harry Truman) or above-average Presidents (in the case of Lyndon Johnson). So, I don't think that the experience of being Vice-President, though it's clearly and should be a subordinated role to the President's role, is a "maiming" experience. I think it's a preparatory experience.

Finally, Schlesinger responded to the examples raised by Watson and offered new ones to support and extend his own arguments.

**Schlesinger:** What Jack Watson said should be remembered in the context. That is, Teddy Roosevelt and Harry Truman were Vice-Presidents for a very short time. Teddy Roosevelt, having served as both Vice-President and President himself, was in favor of the abolition of the Vice-Presidency. Lyndon Johnson was a man of a very powerful personality and served with a President who was relatively considerate toward him, as Presidents go.

One of the real problems is that with the increasing visibility of the Vice-Presidency and with the decline of the political parties, the Vice-President has an unfair advantage over his competitors in the contest for the Presidency, for the *nomination*. But then, once he gets the nomination, he finds himself trapped in that he is identified with the policies of the President whom he has served and when he tries to distance himself from that President he is likely to invite charges of disloyalty to him. We can see how that hurt Hubert Humphrey in 1968, how it hurt Fritz Mondale in 1984, and how it's hurting George Bush today – three admirable men.

The process of clash and extension in this exchange can best be visualized through the use of a *flowsheet,* a system of notation specially designed to provide an organized record of the arguments in a debate. The process of flowsheet notation is described in detail in chapter 8. Each of the four speeches you have just read is outlined in one of the vertical columns in Fig. 1.1, moving left to right from the first speech to the last. Arguments made about a given issue are flowed next to each other, so that you can follow the extensions of that issue through the entire debate by following a horizontal line directly across the flowsheet.

The exchange between Watson and Schlesinger improved as it was extended. Evidence and arguments became more refined and, in this case, less clear-cut for either side. As we leave this debate, the "last words" for each side were yet to be heard. Each debater could presumably have continued to extend these arguments through several more successive exchanges.

It is the dynamic of extension, the ability to "respond to responses," that distinguishes debates from other sorts of argumentative clashes. By the

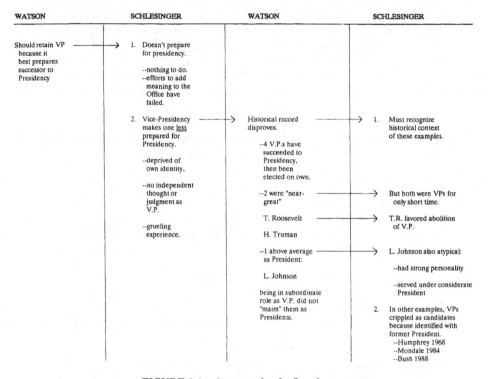

| WATSON | SCHLESINGER | WATSON | SCHLESINGER |
|---|---|---|---|
| Should retain VP because it best prepares successor to Presidency → | 1. Doesn't prepare for presidency.<br><br>--nothing to do.<br>--efforts to add meaning to the Office have failed. | | |
| | 2. Vice-Presidency makes one <u>less</u> prepared for Presidency. →<br><br>--deprived of own identity.<br><br>--no independent thought or judgment as V.P.<br><br>--grueling experience. | Historical record disproves. →<br><br>--4 V.P.s have succeeded to Presidency, then been elected on own.<br><br>--2 were "near-great" →<br><br>T. Roosevelt →<br><br>H. Truman<br><br>--1 above average as President: →<br><br>L. Johnson<br><br>being in subordinate role as V.P. did not "maim" them as Presidents. | 1. Must recognize historical context of these examples.<br><br>But both were VPs for only short time.<br><br>T.R. favored abolition of V.P.<br><br>L. Johnson also atypical:<br><br>--had strong personality<br><br>--served under considerate President<br><br>2. In other examples, VPs crippled as candidates because identified with former President.<br>--Humphrey 1968<br>--Mondale 1984<br>--Bush 1988 |

**FIGURE 1.1.**   An example of a flowsheet.

end of the process of clash and extension, the debaters and their audience should be in a better position to resolve not only these issues, but the larger question on which they bear.

## Perspective

True debate involves more than an extended clash of well-developed arguments. True debate centers on a specific proposition to be affirmed or denied (e.g., "Resolved: that the United States should continue its economic sanctions against South Africa"). The many individual arguments and issues in the debate are ultimately only important in relation to that proposition. The arguments over the deterrent effect of the death penalty as presented by Amnesty International are important only insofar as they contribute to the proposition "Resolved: that the death penalty should be abolished."

Thus, a true debate always occurs on at least two levels: the level of individual issues and the level of the proposition. At the level of the proposition, the debate is over how one should *judge* the debate itself. It is a "meta-debate," a debate about the debate, in which the debaters argue about:

Which issues are the most important?

How should the debate be decided?

What burdens of proof does each side possess?

Who should win?

In the presidential debates, each candidate might reasonably be expected to sort through the many issues raised and identify those most important in the election. But beyond the topical issues, the candidates are called to reflect on the ultimate topic of the debate, which is not for most voters a matter of a single issue or set of issues, but rather the questions of "Who should be president?," "What makes a good president?," and "Why would I make a better president than my opponent?"

True debate requires that the participants establish some perspective with which to view the contest itself, and through which the importance of individual issues and arguments may be judged.

## CONCLUSION

True debate, as practiced in many cultures through the centuries, is distinguished by the clash and extension of well-developed argumentative positions, through which some perspective is gained on a governing question or proposition.

In the following chapters, the reader embarks on the systematic study of those debate structures, strategies, and techniques that enable one to engage in true debate.

# THE STRUCTURES OF ADVOCACY AND OPPOSITION

The characteristics of true debate can only emerge from a discussion that is clearly structured and focused on the pivotal issues of the dispute. This in turn requires a common understanding of what is being disputed. There must be agreement among the participants as to the topic and division of sides in the dispute. It is only when these basic arrangements have been agreed on that meaningful *dis*agreement can take place.

In order for proper *development, clash,* and *extension* to occur, the disputants must know what issues should be developed, which should be the focus of clash, and how that clash should be organized and extended. In order to provide perspective by relating individual arguments to the larger question under dispute, the disputants must first have a clear sense of what that question *is* and be able to distinguish the individual arguments that pertain to it.

Thus, it is the responsibility of both sides in a debate to promote a clear understanding of the issues at stake and to provide sufficient structure in the dispute to enable cogent discussion.

The structure of a debate is determined partly by the format in which it occurs, designating the order and length of speeches (a subject explored in chapter 8). But the content of debates is primarily structured by the ways in which the issue under dispute is framed, and by the ways in which the cases and arguments for each side are organized.

In order to properly frame a dispute for the purposes of debate:

1. An appropriate proposition for debate must be agreed on; and
2. Key terms in the dispute must be defined.

To be properly organized for debate, the cases and arguments of the disputants must adhere to:

1. The argumentative responsibilities of propositional advocacy; and
2. The appropriate structures for propositional advocacy and opposition.

Each of these four elements of debate structure is examined in turn.

## THE DEBATE PROPOSITION

The proposition in a formal debate provides the governing question of the dispute. All other issues raised are subordinate to it, important only in so far as they are brought to bear upon it. In the deliberations of legislative bodies, the proposition is usually provided in the form of a motion, resolution, or bill. Members of the house are ultimately asked to reach a decision regarding it, and their deliberation is facilitated by parliamentary debate.

Legal proceedings are similarly framed by definite propositions, in the form of criminal charges (e.g., "$X$ has violated law $y$") or civil claims ("$A$ has incurred $q$ damages because of $B$"). The precise statement of charges and claims is essential to the justice system. Only with such a clear and prior understanding of the proposition under dispute can the parties adequately prepare and present their cases.

Without a clear proposition (whether agreed on before the dispute or arrived at during the discussion), true debate cannot occur. Framing a proper resolution for debate, however, is no simple matter. As William Trufant Foster (1908/1932) observed:

> It is not easy to phrase the proposition so that it shall mean precisely what we wish to argue; so that it shall include the whole matter at issue, nothing more and nothing less; so that there shall be no possible ambiguity. Yet, unless the proposition is so phrased, a debate may degenerate into a lifeless quibble concerning the meaning of terms, under which the living heart of the question is buried. (p. 2)

In order to facilitate true debate, the proposition should conform to certain guidelines:

*The Proposition Should Present an Argumentative Claim.*   True debate requires more than a *topic* (or subject matter for discussion); it requires a *proposition,* through which those who defend it make some argumentative claim subject to dispute. Thus, "The relationship between the United States and Puerto Rico" may be a fine topic for discussion, but it is insufficient as a topic for *debate.* Panelists preparing to discuss such an issue may feel no obligation to commit themselves to a particular course of action regarding Puerto Rico. Moreover, the topic does not ensure clear disagreement or that competing ideas emerge from among the panelists. On the other hand, the following propositions would serve these functions:

> "Be it resolved: that Puerto Rico should be an independent and sovereign nation;"
> "Be it resolved: that the American colonization of Puerto Rico is deplorable;" or
> "This House believes that Puerto Rico should become the fifty-first state of the Union."

A proper topic for debate should enforce controversy by stating a claim, rather than merely identifying a subject, and by clearly dividing the sides and positions of the participants.

*The Proposition Should Be Debatable.*   The basic function of a proposition is to facilitate cogent disagreement regarding a controversial subject. A proposition is not debatable "(a) if it is obviously true or obviously false; or (b) if it cannot be proved at least approximately true or false" (Foster, 1908/1932, p. 3).

Not all argumentative claims make suitable topics for debate. An obviously true or obviously false proposition, such as "Resolved: that child pornography is reprehensible" renders debate pointless. The best propositions for debate are those that provide the disputants on both sides with potentially strong positions. As a general rule, the more even the sides in a debate, the more interesting and valuable it will be.

At the same time, it should be recognized that the purpose of debates, as the standard wording of its propositions suggests, is to *resolve* the dispute at hand. The proposition and format of the debate should facilitate decision making, a choice between the positions of competing advocates. Propositions that cannot be proven at least approximately true or false are unsuitable for debate. As Foster (1908/1932) observed:

> One of the early presidents of Harvard College wrote a dissertation on the question, "Whether angels speak any language; if so, whether it is Hebrew." Much futile discussion on such questions has at various times brought

debating into ill repute. A question should offer something more than an ingenious exercise: it should offer the chance of arriving at some conclusion regarded by the particular audience or disputants as of some practical importance. It should be discarded if, like the proposition, "The pen is mightier than the sword," it offers no possibility of arriving at reasonably sound conclusions through the process of argument. (pp. 4–5)

Debate propositions should frame matters of genuine controversy in language that divides the sides as evenly as possible and that makes possible an informed resolution of the dispute.

*The Proposition Should Be Phrased Clearly and Simply.*    Propositions should be phrased so as to focus discussion on the major issues of concern. Ambiguous words or phrases should be avoided, for they tend to generate controversy regarding the *meaning* of the proposition rather than on the fundamental issues of the topic. Debates about semantics or definitions are almost invariably less interesting than debates regarding the substantive issues of the topic.

At the turn of the last century, a leading textbook suggested the following "standard question for young debaters: "Are the works of nature more beautiful than those of art?" Yet this topic almost ensures a fruitless and frustrating debate on the meanings of its key terms: *nature, art,* and *beauty.* The topic invites its proponents to define *beauty* in such a way as to advantage *nature* and its opponents to offer a competing standard of *beauty* that privileges *art.* Thus, the debate seems destined to focus (with little prospect for resolution) on the "proper" definition of *beauty.*

Unfortunately, such mistakes in the wording of debate resolutions remain common today. Both participants and spectators are better served by propositional wording that is clear and that focuses attention on the genuine issues of the topic.

*The Proposition Should Be Limited in Scope.*    The appropriate breadth for the debate proposition depends on the number of times it will be debated and the forum(s) in which debate will occur. If the same topic is to be used for an entire semester or year of interscholastic competition, it should be broad enough to permit diverse approaches and avoid tedious repetition of arguments. The full discussion of the topic would unfold over the course of the competitive season, rather than in any single debate.

For most debates, however, the proposition should be clear and very limited. In most classroom and political debates, the proposition will be debated only once (or, at most, a few times). Thus, the proposition must be sufficiently limited to permit satisfactory treatment of it in the time allotted. The proposition "Resolved: that the United States should expand its exploration of outer space" cannot be satisfactorily examined in a single debate; there are too many potential and dissimilar ways in which such exploration might take place. The proposition "Resolved: that the United States should send astronauts to Mars by the year 2000," although still a major issue, is far more amenable to discussion in a single debate.

Narrow topics are also preferable because they facilitate clash between the disputants, enabling each side to have a better idea of what the other will argue and to prepare accordingly. Such focused preparation will almost always produce better debates and more informed decisions by the audience.

*The Proposition Should Be Interesting.* The proposition for debate should be of immediate concern and interest both for the disputants and the audience. Good topics for academic debate generally reflect current issues – matters that have generated considerable attention and controversy at the time they are debated. British university debating societies, for example, often hold what they term "emergency debates" regarding controversial actions just taken or about to be taken, such as: "This House condemns the American intervention in Panama" or "Be it resolved: that this House has no confidence in Prime Minister Thatcher."

"Emergency" debates are held at the peak of public interest in a topic and provide a forum for the members of a community to make their varied opinions heard, see them developed, and hear how they fare when controverted by advocates of competing opinions. What is sacrificed in preparation time is generally compensated for by enthusiasm and relevance.

Issues should be debated not simply to reward argumentation skills or "for the sake of argument," but because the participants genuinely care about the issue being discussed.

## Types of Propositions

Traditionally, topics for debate have been classified as belonging to one of three categories: propositions of *fact*, *value*, or *policy*. For reasons we soon explore, these categories are not actually discrete; each one necessarily overlaps with the others. These categories do, however, describe real differences among the various ways that propositions are worded. Furthermore, each of the three types of proposition poses somewhat different demands for advocates and opponents, altering the structures and burdens of argument.

Propositions of fact make claims about what is, was, or will be true. Although propositions of fact are not only issued by scientists (indeed, *I* am stating a proposition of fact in this very sentence), scientific inquiry provides clear models of their various forms.

Scientists make claims about what *is* through the statement of hypotheses that may be confirmed or disproven through investigation. Examples of such propositions include the claims that:

"Children who are exposed to violence on television are more likely to commit violent acts;"
   "The 'Loch Ness monster' truly exists;" or
   "The experiments of scientists at the University of Utah have in fact produced 'cold nuclear fusion.' "

Each of these claims about what *is* has been subjected to dispute. Empirical observations have been conducted in the effort to support or deny the hypotheses. Competing scientists have scrutinized each other's data, sometimes arriving at different interpretations of the same observations. In other instances, competing scientists have generated different data, perhaps using different experimental designs.

Propositions of fact regarding what *is* are generally either claims of *causality* (*x* results in *y*, as in the aforementioned television violence example) or *definition* (*a* belongs to classification *q*, as in the aforementioned "cold fusion" hypothesis).

Propositions of fact regarding what *was* are hypotheses regarding events or conditions of the past. Such hypotheses may involve historical claims (e.g., "Vikings landed on North America before Columbus" or "Harriet Taylor was an influential collaborator on works credited to John Stuart Mill") or *pre*historical claims, such as: "The mass extinction of dinosaurs was caused by the impact of a huge asteroid on the surface of the Earth" or "The 'big bang' theory best explains the origins of the universe."

Propositions of fact regarding what *will be* are, of course, predictions. Predictive claims generally draw on an understanding of the past and present to extrapolate future events. In order to predict what the responses of China might be to increased economic sanctions, for example, one might examine Chinese (or other nations') responses to past sanctions. In order to predict the weather in a given area for next Thursday, meteorologists must know the current status of relevant fronts and the past directional patterns of wind and fronts.

Propositions of fact are, in fact, highly debatable. People's understandings of what is, was, or will be are often quite diverse. Even "common knowledge" changes, and usually through the process of scientific debate on propositions of fact.

Propositions of value represent claims of *evaluation*, stipulating something as good or ill, ugly or beautiful, important or inconsequential, great or mediocre, for example. Propositions of value are commonly associated with disputes on matters of ethics, religion, philosophy, or aesthetics, but are also a regular part of our own conversational arguments. When we dispute the merits of a movie we have just seen or a restaurant we have just visited, we are debating propositions of value. When we hope to "do the right thing" but are uncertain about what the right thing *is* in a given situation, we will probably dispute propositions of value with others or ourselves (in a struggle of conscience) in an effort to determine the proper course.

Propositions of value normally include an *evaluative term* and identify an *object of evaluation.* In the proposition, "Resolved: that investment in South Africa is immoral," "investment in South Africa" is the object of evaluation and "immoral" is the evaluative term. In the proposition "Resolved: that efficiency is a deplorable fetish of modern life," "efficiency" is the object of evaluation and "deplorable fetish" the evaluative term.

The proposition of value may represent an absolute judgment (e.g., "This House believes that the atomic bombing of Hiroshima was immoral") or a comparative evaluation ("This House believes that the bombing of Pearl Harbor was a greater crime than the bombing of Hiroshima" or "Resolved: that freedom speech is of greater importance than the right to privacy").

The proposition of policy is a claim that a particular course of action should be or should have been taken. Most policy propositions support some action that should be taken in the future (e.g., "Resolved: that the United States should recognize Lithuania as an independent nation"). Some policy propositions address historical controversies by supporting some action that was or might have been taken in the past (e.g., "This House believes that the South should have been allowed to secede").

The policies disputed may refer to potential governmental action at the national level (e.g., "Resolved: that the United States should permit the use of human fetal tissue for scientific research"), the international level (e.g., "Resolved: that all nations should cease the killing of whales"), the state or provincial level (e.g., "Resolved: that Quebec should secede" or "Resolved: that Maine should establish a state-run lottery"), or the local level (e.g., "Resolved: that the city of Lewiston should adopt mandatory recycling procedures").

Propositions of policies need not, however, be restricted to the actions of governments. Policy propositions may focus on matters of personal decision and action, as in the resolution that "This house supports $X$ for president of the United States." Members of academic debating societies or courses may also find it valuable to debate matters of school policy, such as "Resolved: that this university should establish a system of pass/fail grading," "This house believes that knowledge of at least one foreign language should be required for graduation from this university" or

"Resolved: that the university should prohibit racist speech on campus." Debates on matters of school policy draw on issues and circumstances that are usually familiar to the disputants and audience. Moreover, such debates can sometimes play an important role in the actual decision-making process regarding the matter discussed, whether by raising campus awareness of the issues or by organizing diffuse campus opinions on controversial matters.

Policy propositions may be serious or humorous or, in British fashion, both. The proposition "Resolved: that presidential candidates should be required to appear on 'Jeopardy!' [a television game show]," provides a humorous vehicle for the discussion of real issues (e.g., "What *should* the president know about the Constitution?," and "How have gaps in presidential knowledge of basic geography, history, and diplomacy impeded proper governance?").

Having delineated the three basic types of propositions, it should be made clear that these categories are not entirely discrete. Debating about propositions of fact or value often requires the evaluation of policies; debating policy propositions *always* requires that the disputants debate subordinate propositions of fact and value.

Propositions of value are often prescriptive–accepting or rejecting them may entail certain courses of action. If we uphold the proposition of value that "investment in South Africa is immoral," we are presumably obligated to discontinue such investment. Accepting the proposition of value entails acceptance of a proposition of policy. On the other hand, it might be argued that if more horrible consequences could be predicted to follow divestment, then continued investment may be moral. In either case, the proposition of value can only be fully assessed with reference to the courses of action it entails.

All propositions of policy necessarily subsume propositions of fact and value. Policies are endorsed because of their anticipated net benefits. The claim that a given action will produce certain benefits requires the advocate to make predictive claims (propositions of fact) about what results will ensue from the contemplated action and evaluative claims (propositions of value) about how these results should be appraised. In order to debate the policy proposition "Resolved: that the United States should impose more severe sanctions against China," the proponent would presumably make both factual claims about human rights abuses in China and the predicted effects of economic sanctions and value claims regarding the importance of human rights and the moral obligation of the United States to attempt to encourage their observance.

Propositions of fact, value, and policy make different sorts of claims and, as we shall soon discuss, present somewhat different argumentative burdens for their advocates and opponents. They are nevertheless inter-related, and those engaged in any form of debate must acquire an understanding of all three.

## DEFINITIONS

Debates without clear and accepted definitions are usually futile exercises. Unless there is agreement as to what the debate is *about*, there is not likely to be much substantive clash. In a "Firing Line" debate nationally televised in 1990, with host William F. Buckley joined by leading members of Congress and other political figures, the topic was "Resolved: that drugs should be legalized." Neither side, however, clearly defined either *drugs* or *legalized*. Does the term *drugs* include not only marijuana but heroin, cocaine, LSD, and PCP? Does legalize mean that *anyone* (including minors and psychotics, for example) may purchase drugs in *any quantities* they desire? Because of these and other points of confusion, no true debate occurred. It was only at the conclusion of the program, when the operative definitions of the proponents had at last been clarified to some extent, that the two sides were prepared to debate.

As Foster (1908/1928) warned,

> Unless disputants understand the meaning attached by each other to the terms of a controversy, they may worry along indefinitely without making an inch of progress. The contending parties may think they agree on the proposition, when, as a matter of fact, their apparent agreement is due to ambiguity in the use of terms. On the other hand, the contending parties may work themselves into a quarrel over imaginary disagreements concerning ideas, when in fact they are merely confused as to the meaning of words. Disputes which seem interminable are sometimes ended abruptly and happily upon the accidental discovery that the parties in dispute agreed all the time as to the real questions at issue, while neither side understood what the other side meant. (p. 24)

Clear definitions of all potentially ambiguous terms are thus essential for the conduct of meaningful debate. In order for clash to occur, the terms that dictate the clash must be understood by both parties. *Definitions of all key terms should be provided at the outset of the debate.* The first speaker in defense of the proposition should make clear what the proposition *means* to its advocates. The opposition may then choose to accept this interpretation of the topic as legitimate and proceed to dispute the case advanced by the proponents in defense of it, or to *dispute* the definitions of terms offered by the affirmative, suggest other more reasonable definitions, and then dispute the case offered on behalf of the proposition according to *both* sets of definitions.

The standards by which definitions for the purposes of disputation are judged vary according to the nature of the dispute. In legal argument, statutory definitions are essential to the determination of *jurisdiction*, which "alone gives the court power to hear, determine, and pronounce judgment on the issues before it" (*Ex Parte Cavitt*, 118 P. 2d 846, 37 CA 2d 698). Similar standards may be imposed in the deliberations of task forces or committee hearings in which the ability to keep the discussion "on-track," devoted to issues that are germane to a prescribed mission, may be essential to their productivity and success.

In most classroom or public debates, definitions serve a similar purpose in one sense, providing assurance that the proposition proved by the affirmative *is* the given one that the audience has gathered to hear disputed, and not "another which (the affirmative) has substituted for it by means of arbitrary definitions" (Foster, 1908/1928, p. 27). In another sense, however, definitions in classroom or public debate serve a more complex purpose. If, as discussed earlier, true debate requires a proposition about which strong and reasoned disagreement may exist, proper definitions should *enable* such disagreement, rather than rendering the proposition less debatable by virtue of being too one-sided.

In debating the topic "Resolved: that the atomic bombing of Hiroshima was justified," the key term to be defined (because it is both important to the topic and ambiguous) is *justified*. The *Random House Dictionary of the English Language* (2nd ed.) lists two different meanings of the transitive verb *justify:* "to *be* just or right;" and "to *defend* as warranted or well-grounded." The first definition, when used to interpret the preceding debate resolution, provides for substantial disagreement – whether it was right to bomb Hiroshima remains an open and heatedly disputed question after half a century. On the other hand, to use the second definition of *justify*, which would amount to the proposition that "the atomic bombing of Hiroshima was defended by some people as warranted," would render the proposition indisputable. It is undeniable that many of those involved with the bombing did (rightly or wrongly) defend it as warranted. Although the second definition would present obvious strategic advantages for the proponents, it would be unreasonable because it renders the debate one-sided (hence, no longer a true "debate").

Definitions of terms in the resolution should meet certain basic criteria in order to be reasonable:

1. **The definition should not be *tautological*.** A tautology is a proposition that is necessarily true by definition or logical structure, as in the claim that the animal burrowing in your backyard is either a woodchuck or

not a woodchuck. If in defense of the proposition, "Resolved: that the practice of lecturing is over-emphasized in undergraduate instruction," *lecturing* were to be defined as "an instructor's undue reliance on his or her own words," the definition is tautological. If it is an "undue reliance," then it is by definition "overemphasized."

2. **The proposition should not be defined as a *truism*.** The proposition should be defined in such a way that makes it *debatable*. A truistic definition is one that no reasonable person could oppose. If in defense of the proposition "Resolved: that euthanasia is immoral," the term *euthanasia* were to be defined as "the forcible killing of healthy adults," exemplified by the Holocaust of World War II, the topic would have been rendered truistic.

3. **The definition should *limit* the scope of the debate.** Definitions should make it easier for participants to understand what *is* at issue in the debate at least partly by explaining what is *not:* "To define is to express with precision the constituent ingredients of the essence of that which is to be defined: incongruous, accidental, and extraneous features being left out in such a manner that the definition will not apply to any other object than that defined" (*McDougall v. Monlezon* 38 La.Ann. Reports, *Words and Phrases*, 1971, p. 377).

4. **The definition should be true to the context of the dispute.** Disputes rage before formal debates begin. Every proposition for debate, as we discuss in chapter 4, emerges from a particular history and context in which concern over certain issues has been generated. For most debates, this context provides a backdrop of audience expectations concerning what issues the debate will cover. Debaters who violate such expectations do so at their peril.

In order to be true to the context of the dispute, it should be recognized that definitions of phrases or topics as a whole are more useful than definitions of individual words and that such definitions may be drawn from many sources other than, and arguably better than, dictionaries. Of particular value are those definitions generated from within the field of inquiry or activity most directly related to the topic.

Having discussed the appropriate standards for reasonable definitions, let us remember that for most audiences, debates about definitions are less than entertaining. If the goal of the participants (debaters and audience alike) is to hear disputation on some set of issues, definitional disputes should be resolved if possible prior to the debate and through greater precision in the wording of the topic.

Definitional disputes are more common and more influential in technical debates before specialized audiences (such as legal argument, scientific disputes, and competitive tournament debate). In a technical debate on a proposition of policy, definitions are used to forge a relationship between the more general terms of the topic (e.g., "Resolved: that the United States should substantially increase its exploration of outer space") and the specific policy advocated by the affirmative team (e.g., a program to send astronauts to Mars by the year 2010). There are many ways in which the U.S. might increase its exploration of outer space. The affirmative will presumably not wish to defend *all* possible forms of space exploration, but rather one or more of the most beneficial forms. The advocate *affirms* the statement of the proposition by the defense of a policy that exemplifies the resolution. Because it would be beneficial to send astronauts to Mars by the year 2000, the advocate maintains, we can affirm the proposition that the U.S. should substantially increase its exploration of outer space (at least in this one instance).

It is through definitions that the link between general proposition and specific policy is forged. Because "sending astronauts" may be judged a form of "increased exploration" and "Mars" may be defined as in "outer space," the defense of the specific policy in this instance may be judged as a defense of the more general proposition. The relationship between policy and proposition is called *topicality*.

The opposition may dispute the topicality of the proposal, arguing that it does not meet or enact the terms of the proposition. If the affirmative team were to propose a policy of increased funding for the Strategic Defense Initiative ("Star Wars"), the opposition might well argue that this does not constitute *exploration* of outer space. Hence, even if increased funding of S.D.I. were to prove desirable, this would not constitute a reason to affirm the *proposition* agreed on for the debate. The opposition might claim the debate to be forfeit on the grounds that the advocates have failed to provide a case on behalf of the proposition.

## ARGUMENTATIVE RESPONSIBILITIES FOR ADVOCACY

No matter what type of proposition is debated or how its terms are defined, the advocate who upholds the proposition must always address a basic question from the audience: "Why should I accept the proposition as true?" In order to answer this question, the advocate must provide a case that supports the proposition, good reasons, and evidence that would lead the listener to affirm it.

### Organization

In order to establish a case in defense of the proposition, the first speaker in a debate must present an *organized* discussion of the issues that are pertinent to it. The case is organized by offering clear and discrete reasons that one should accept the proposition, arranged according to some rational principle. These reasons may be offered in the form of *contentions* (a list of basic claims) or, in the case of a policy advocacy, *advantages* that will be gained by adopting the policy.

The first speech in a debate is usually prepared to some extent (and often entirely scripted) in advance. In a debate that is orally and spontaneously conducted, the first speech is the only one in the debate that can be fully prepared or even completely outlined in advance. All others are obliged to respond or adapt to arguments that have been made in previous speeches. Advance preparation of the opening speech, which enables the affirmative speaker to refine reasoning and wording, carefully select evidence, and organize his or her strongest arguments, is among the principal strategic advantages of the affirmative side in any debate.

Clear organization of arguments is beneficial to the advocate in several ways.

*Organization Strategically Frames the Discussion of Issues.* By offering a clear organization, the advocate directs the focus of the debate to those issues most relevant and beneficial to his or her side. The opening speech offers the advocate an opportunity to base the case on certain reasons, while disavowing (at least implicitly) other potential arguments on behalf of the proposition. By providing a clear case for the proposition, the advocate compels the opposition to address the issues as framed or to justify abandonment of that structure in favor of another. As a result, the organization of the opening speech normally provides the structure for the discussion of all significant issues pertaining to the case for the remainder of the debate.

*Organization Stresses the Independence of Multiple Reasons.* A skilled advocate normally offers more than one reason to accept his or her position. In defense of continued economic sanctions against South Africa, an advocate might claim: (a) The economic pressure from sanctions will hasten the abolition of apartheid; and (b) Sanctions are morally required in order to avoid lending economic *support* to apartheid.

Even if sufficient doubt is cast upon Reason A in the course of debate to render it unlikely (sanctions may not prompt reform), it could be argued that Reason B is independently compelling. Regardless of whether sanctions work to reduce apartheid, it may be said that we have a moral obligation not to contribute materially to the apartheid regime.

Ideally, the multiple reasons offered in support of a proposition should be independent of one another, so that if one or more is defeated, another may yet prevail. If an advocate identifies three benefits to a potential change in the nation's immigration policy, and two are substantially diminished through the course of the debate, there remains one significant and independent advantage to be gained by adoption of the proposal. If a college admissions officer tells you of four particular strengths of his or her college and you discover that two of these strengths are present in equal measure at other schools to which you have been admitted, you are still left with two unique strengths of the first school.

In 1900, Alden offered the following organization of a case in support of the proposition that "Women should have the right of suffrage in the United States," stressing the different and independent reasons why one might support the proposition.

**Introductory.**
The problem of suffrage is of grave importance in America.
Originally, the right to take part in government was based on physical force.
In the U.S., however, it is supposed to be based on principle, not tradition.

**I. To deny women this right is unreasonable according to the principles of go;ernment in America.**
A. Here suffrage is called "universal."
(It is no denial to say that suffrage is denied to certain classes by law, for
   This denial is largely based on assumed incapacity, as in the case of idiots, criminals, and minors.)
(Neither is it sufficient to say that women are excepted because of incapacity for military service, for
   Men are not disfranchised when incapacitated by age or infirmity.)
B. Here the principle is accepted that taxation implies representation; and women are taxed.

**II. To deny it is unjust.**
A. Suffrage is a natural right of citizens, for
It is the means by which they are to protect and exercise the freedom and equality guaranteed them by the Declaration of Independence.
B. Women need the suffrage to protect their interests.
1. Many of them have business interests.
2. Many are interested in the education of children.
3. Many still suffer from laws unfavorable to their personal rights (as in the case of holding property, guardianship of children, etc.)
(It cannot be said that they are represented in these matters by men, for
   In the nature of the case a man cannot represent the interests of a woman; and
   Unmarried women are not even professedly represented.)

**III. To deny it is contrary to the interests of the nation.**
The influence of women in politics would be beneficial.

Women are, broadly speaking, more moral than men.

Women are more interested in reforms.

(It cannot be urged that the interests of the home would be injured, for
This is contrary to the nature of women; and Experience in Colorado,
Wyoming, and elsewhere, proves the contrary.)

**Conclusion.**

This movement has grown beyond all expectation, and has been successful
in many localities.

The present is an opportune plan for trying it in the United States.

(Alden, 1900, pp. 55–57)

Alden's outline of the case for women's suffrage organizes some of the
major arguments in a national debate that raged for half a century. Alden's
organization stresses the independence of the three reasons presented.
The audience may decide that women should be granted the vote if they
accept *any one* of the three contentions: that to deny women the vote is
hypocritical (a consistency standard); that suffrage is an inalienable right
to which women are entitled; *or* that women's suffrage will bring practical
benefits to the nation.

Historically, the women's suffrage movement gained support from
diverse quarters among groups and individuals who had very different
reasons for lending their support. Reasons that motivated some supporters were unappealing to others, who lent their support for different
reasons entirely. The ultimate political success of the movement to amend
the United States Constitution depended on a coalition of diverse interests
forged by the ability of advocates to present different and *independent*
reasons to support it.

Proper organization of the advocate's case, clearly dividing different
possible reasons to embrace the proposition, can stress the independent
sufficiency of these reasons, thus providing a greater probability of success.

*Organization Facilitates Memory, Extension, and Rebuttal.* A properly designed case should frame the issues of the debate in such a
memorable way that the organizational structure and wording is still
referred to by the debaters in their closing remarks and implanted in the
audience's minds during the process of decision making. My decision to
demarcate the "four purposes of organization" in this section, for example,
is partly to make different ideas clear, but also to increase the likelihood
that they will be retained.

*Proper Organization Makes Clear the Logical Development and Com-
pleteness of Your Position.* A proper organization should follow the form
of an outline. Major points should be clearly identified as such, and

supported by subordinate ones. Clear transitions should be provided when moving from one major point to the next.

The sequence in which the major points should be arranged varies according to topic and purpose. It is sometimes necessary to begin by providing certain background information on the events or issues under discussion. If powerful preconceptions exist on the topic, the advocate may wish to address these before proceeding. Generally, the sequence of contentions follows a *topical* arrangement (in which the case is organized by dividing independent reasons to support the proposition), a *problem-solution* organization (in which a problem is identified, current approaches to it are discounted, and a new solution proposed), or a *syllogistic* format (in which a sequence of premises are listed which, if true, lead to a necessary conclusion).

Ida B. Wells was a crusading African-American journalist and an outstanding speaker of the late 19th and early 20th centuries. She was a leading campaigner against the crime of lynching and, despite numerous threats to her life, wrote a series of revelatory newspaper articles and the first book, (Wells, 1892/1969), documenting its magnitude and horror. In 1909, she addressed the newly founded National Negro Conference on the topic of "Lynching, Our National Crime." Wells began her address by delineating the three major points of her organization:

> The lynching record for a quarter of a century merits the thoughtful study of the American people. It presents three salient facts:
>
> First: Lynching is color-line murder.
>
> Second: Crimes against women is the excuse, not the cause.
>
> Third: It is a national crime and requires a national remedy. (Foner, 1975, p. 71)

Wells' appeal for national anti-lynching legislation (contained in her third point) was preceded by two factual contentions, designed to demonstrate the significance of the problem and to dismiss false preconceptions and defenses of it. Both of her first two contentions were prerequisites for the third. In the first contention, Wells established the crime as racially specific and abhorrent:

> During the last ten years from 1899 to 1908 inclusive the number lynched was 959. Of this number 102 were white, while the colored victims numbered 857. No other nation, civilized or savage, burns its criminals; only under the Stars and Stripes is the human holocaust possible. Twenty-eight human beings burned at the stake, one of them a woman and two of them children, is the awful indictment against American civilization–the gruesome tribute which the nation pays to the color line. (Foner, 1975, p. 72)

In her second contention, Wells dismissed the prevailing myth used to rationalize lynching, "the shameless falsehood that 'Negroes are lynched to protect womanhood.'" She refuted this claim by statistically demonstrating that in the vast majority of lynching cases, not even the perpetrators claim such motives. Instead, she argued, lynching is motivated by the desire to prevent African-Americans from voting or from competing with whites for jobs.

Having demonstrated the significance of the problem and dismissed its primary rationalization, Wells then explained why national legislation was needed to address the problem and to offer specific details as to how such legislation would work.

Wells clearly identified and divided her three main arguments. Each is an important claim in its own right; the statistical backing she provided to support the first two contentions was the newsworthy product of her original research. Moreover, her organization reflected a logical progression, directing the audience toward a specific conclusion as she sought their support for specific legislation.

The organization of a case should arrange the principal arguments in such a way as to be clear, memorable, and strategically located for further reference. It should also make plain that the case is logically complete, fulfilling the burdens of proof implicit in defense of the proposition.

In defense of a proposition, the following two basic organizational patterns are most commonly used:

Need-Plan/Problem-Solution Outline
1. A significant problem exists.
2. The present system is incapable of dealing with this problem.
3. Our proposal will better address the problem.

Comparative Advantage Outline
Our proposal will gain the following advantages over the present system:
1. Statement of first advantage.
  A. The advantage is of significant value.
  B. The present system is unable to gain the advantage.
  C. Our proposal will gain the advantage.
2. Statement of second advantage, third, etc. Repeat aforementioned development steps.

Although one organizational pattern may prove more useful than another in expressing the case on behalf of a given proposal, the burdens of proof represented by these two structures are, as we see here, identical.

## Burdens of Proof in Advocacy

The arguments offered by an advocate must be more than well-organized; they must be logically complete and sufficient to support the proposition for debate. The advocate, in short, must assume a *burden of proof* in the establishment of a case. The burden of proof in debate has been defined by Raymond Alden (1900) as "the obligation resting upon one or other of the parties to a controversy to establish by proofs a given proposition, before being entitled to receive an answer from the other side" (p. 61).

Argumentative burdens of proof are well-established in legal advocacy. In a criminal trial the prosecutor seeks to affirm a charge or complaint against a defendant. In order to do so, the prosecutor must counter a *presumption* (that which is assumed to be true unless disproven) of the defendant's innocence. The defendant must be proved guilty if he or she is to be convicted.

In a civil trial, the plaintiff alleges that he or she has suffered some sort of damage or loss at the hand of another. The plaintiff must shoulder the burden of proof for such a charge at the outset of the proceeding. As Lord Justice Bowen wrote:

> In every lawsuit somebody must go on with it; the plaintiff is the first to begin, and if he does nothing he fails. If he makes a *prima facie* case, and nothing else is done by the other side to answer it, the defendant fails. The test, therefore as to the burden of proof is simply to consider which party would be more successful if no evidence at all was given, or if no more evidence was given than is given at this particular point of the case. (*Abrath v. No.E. Ry. Co.*, Alden, 1900, p. 62)

A *prima facie* case is one that is complete and sound "on its first making" and that fulfills the burdens of proof implicit in the proposition. The requirement of a *prima facie* case is normally imposed on the opening speech in a debate, the speech in which a case must be established to support the proposition. Just as the plaintiff in a civil case or the prosecutor in a criminal one is expected to begin the trial with sufficient proof of the charge against the defendant (otherwise, the case may be dismissed), so too must the advocate who supports the proposition in a debate.

Debate topics, when properly worded, require the audience to endorse some change in beliefs or action. The proposition may promote some new policy, requiring the indictment of what now exists and the creation of some measure of confidence in what *might* exist. The proposition may issue a firm moral judgment or endorse some controversial claim of fact. A proposition that will be accepted by its audience as presumptively true before any case is presented is generally unsuitable for debate. Therefore, debate propositions are framed as statements requiring support for affirmation, with the expectation that "s/he who affirms must prove."

The opening affirmative speaker in a debate must provide a case for the proposition that is *prima facie*, sufficient in that single speech to compel belief unless challenged. Otherwise, there is no logical necessity for the other side to respond. A general test for the logical completeness, or *prima facie* status, of the case is this: If, at the end of the opening speech in support of the proposition, the debate were to suddenly end due to a fire or other calamity, would the affirmative win?

In other words, if there were for some reason to be no refutation from the opposition, would the affirmative's case have been sufficiently established to induce support for the proposition? If this question may be answered affirmatively at the end of the opening speech, then the burden of proof has substantially shifted to the opposition, who must now endeavor to *disprove* the affirmative's claim that the proposition should be upheld. In a criminal trial, if the prosecutor has substantiated the charges against the defendant, the burden then shifts to the counsel for the defendant who must create some reasonable doubt regarding the adequacy of the prosecution's case. In one sense, then, the job of the opening affirmative speaker is to shift the burden of proof to those who would oppose the proposition.

But what exactly *are* the argumentative burdens borne by an advocate? What must be proven in order to establish a *prima facie* case and shift the burden of proof to the members opposite? Logical burdens of proof vary according to the type of proposition being debated, but are most clearly defined for the defense of policy propositions.

Propositions of policy, as we have previously discussed, are confronted in matters of individual as well as governmental decision making. In order to identify the burdens of proof implicit in defense of any proposition of policy, you need only examine in detail the process by which you arrived at some recent personal decision. What questions did you ask before deciding? What proof was required to convince you? Imagine that, for example, when visiting a car dealer's showroom, a salesperson asks that you buy a Model $X$ car. What details and assurances would you need before you could assent to such a proposal?

First, you would need to know the details of the proposal: Which model is being offered? With what features? At what price? With what sort of trade-in allowance for your current automobile? Until such details are provided, you cannot fully evaluate the proposal.

Second, you must be given some reason to buy the new car, in the form of advantages or benefits that you will gain by purchasing it. The salesperson would be expected to identify the "selling points" of the Model $X$ car (e.g., good fuel economy, abundant cargo space, or low rates of repair), demonstrating (perhaps through specification charts or independent consumer reports) that these benefits are in fact attributable to this model car; that you would have a high probability of *achieving* these benefits if you purchased a Model *X*.

Third, you must assess the significance or value of these benefits. Exactly how good *is* the gas mileage? How much money would this save you in fuel expenditures for an average driving year? What *is* the cargo capacity and how often and for what purposes would such space be important to you? By asking these questions, you would be attempting to establish both the quantitative significance (how much of the benefit would be gained?) and qualitative significance (how valuable are these benefits?) of the advantages claimed.

Fourth, before buying a new car, you would probably compare the benefits claimed for the new Model *X* car and those available from your current car or from other available new and used cars. When you compare the available benefits from different competing options, you are attempting to establish the uniqueness of the benefits claimed on behalf of Model *X*. Must you buy Model *X* to gain 40 square feet of cargo space? How much cargo space does your current vehicle contain? How much is available from other available vehicles? One beneficial feature of the Model *X* car may be that it has four doors. But if your current car also has four doors, there is no unique advantage in this feature to be gained by buying Model *X*.

Finally, before you could make a reasonable decision to purchase a Model *X* car, you must be convinced that the unique advantages of buying one will outweigh the disadvantages of doing so. No matter how wonderful the features of the Model *X* car, you would probably decide not to purchase it if doing so were to seriously jeopardize your financial well-being. Similarly, no matter how spacious its cargo area, you would probably decide not to purchase Model *X* if, according to safety reports, it were shown to be abnormally susceptible to life-threatening mechanical failures.

These basic requirements of the case to buy a car are the same touchstones or "stock issues" of all policy debate and decision making. In any policy debate, he or she who upholds the proposition must:

1. Describe the proposed course of action in sufficient detail to permit meaningful debate;
2. Identify benefits or advantages that will be gained by adopting the proposed course of action;
3. Demonstrate that these benefits are significant;
4. Demonstrate that these benefits are unique to the proposal; and, ultimately,

5. Show that the benefits associated with adopting the proposal outweigh the costs.

These basic responsibilities of the advocate deserve individual attention.

*The Advocate Must Present a Policy in Sufficient Detail To Be Debated.* In order to determine the effectiveness, benefits, and liabilities of a policy, one must first have a clear understanding of what that policy *is.* The amount of detail required will depend on the policy under discussion, the forum, and the purpose of the debate.

For a public debate held before a general audience, fewer details of a proposal will normally be required than for Congressional deliberations over a matter of legislation. The entertainment and interest value of listing the mechanics of program administration is obviously limited.

But no matter what forum in which the debate occurs, sufficient detail of a proposal must be provided to permit meaningful assessment of the policy, in order to predict what sorts of problems it might face or to evaluate what benefits it may reasonably be expected to produce. Ben Wattenberg and Karl Zinsmeister, among others, have proposed that the United States admit more skilled immigrants from other nations. They criticize existing immigration policy both for admitting too few immigrants and for valuing reunification of families above the admission of skilled workers. In making "The Case for More Immigration," Wattenberg and Zinsmeister (1990) proposed increased numbers of immigrants and specific modifications in current immigration procedures, which they detailed:

> As under current policy, we propose that refugee visas be allotted independently, and adult citizens of the U.S. be able to bring in any bona-fide spouses, minor children, or parents without limit (but not more distant relatives, who would be judged under meritocratic criteria). These two categories together – refugees and immediate family – would make up a little more than half of the yearly total of immigrants to the U.S. All other entrants would be selected through a skill-based system, with points awarded for years of school completed, apprenticeship or vocational training, knowledge of English, high professional status or special educational achievements, and some carefully drawn blueprint of occupational demand in the U.S.. . . . At the end of each year's scoring process, the available entrance slots would be filled simply by accepting, in order, the top scorers on the list. This is similar to the way Canada, Australia, and New Zealand already select most of their immigrants, and with a great deal of success. (p. 24)

Although Wattenberg's and Zinsmeister's description of their proposal lacks the detail that would be necessary for legislation or administration, it provides sufficient description to permit debate and is well-suited to the proposal's appearance in a general-interest magazine.

In a more technical policy debate, in which the dispute is aimed not at a general audience but rather at decision makers who must assess the prospective operation of the proposed policy in detail, the statement of the proposal should include at least the following information:

1. **Mandates.** What is it, exactly, that you propose to do? In the case of Wattenberg's and Zinsmeister's proposal, the mandates would consist of the specific changes they propose in immigration policy;

2. **Implementation.** *When* will the proposal take effect? What *agent* will enact the proposal (e.g., the Federal government or the shareholders of corporation *O*)?;

3. **Administration.** Who will carry out the policy once adopted? With what sorts of resources (staff, facilities, jurisdictional authority, powers)?;

4. **Funding and finance.** How much will the proposal cost? From where will these funds come?

5. **Enforcement.** If the proposal is one for which compliance is an issue (e.g., a proposal that all students at *X* university should be required to take course *Y*), the proponents should specify how such compliance is to be gained. These specifications may be of *incentives* to comply (e.g., those who take course *Y* will receive two course credits instead of one) or *penalties* for those who do not comply (those who do not take course *Y* will not graduate).

6. **Checks and review.** In order to ensure the proper administration of the proposal, it may be desirable to provide some process for oversight and review of its operations, whether on an on-going basis or after some specified interval of time.

7. **Spikes.** A well-designed policy proposal will include provisions designed to obviate potential objections. Although argument "spikes" in general will be discussed in Chapter 4, it is the "plan spike" that commands our immediate attention.

In designing a policy proposal for presentation, an effort should be made to anticipate and preempt the objections of one's opponents. The *plan spike* is one means by which to do this. Later in this section, we discuss the various forms of arguments opponents are likely to present against a proposal. Policy advocates should not wait until these objections have been made in a debate to begin their defense against them. Careful design of the proposal itself can usually weaken or render irrelevant certain potential objections. A proposal designed to head off strong potential objections is a better policy, more beneficial because it will produce fewer negative side effects.

There are three types of plan spikes that are commonly used not only in competitive debate but in actual policy decision making:

1. **Exemptions** limit the scope of the plan, making its provisions inapplicable to certain groups, regions, actions, and so on. A proposal to ration fuel supplies in the event of future shortages might well include exemptions for certain categories of consumers (e.g., such as emergency vehicles). A proposal for the federal government to mandate national high school graduation requirements might reasonably exempt schools administered on Indian reservations, thereby honoring tribal sovereignty over their educational systems. Failure to provide such exemptions would entail significant disadvantages.

2. **Compensation** offers some sort of relief (whether money or services) to groups or individuals disadvantaged by the proposal. A proposal to curb U.S. sales of tobacco products might include some sort of transitional assistance for those currently employed in tobacco farming, for example. This assistance would be designed to limit the extent to which the proposal would entail a disadvantage of increased unemployment.

3. **Limits on interpretation** are efforts to control the ways in which the proposal will be used to establish precedents or to prevent potential misunderstandings of its mandates. In 1990, the U.S. Senate sought to pass a new Civil Rights Act, which would restore legal protections for minorities (particularly in combatting employment discrimination) invalidated in a series of recent Supreme Court decisions. According to the bill, the charge of hiring discrimination could be supported against an employer whose workforce included substantially lower proportions of minorities than were available in the labor pool, unless such underrepresentation were the result of demonstrated business necessities. In order to defuse the Bush Administration's objection that such a policy would result in "racial quotas," as employers sought to protect themselves from potential suits, the bill's sponsors added an interpretation spike to its wording: "Nothing in this legislation may be construed to require racial quotas."

A well-crafted plan enables clear understanding by both sides in the debate of the proposal at its center. It also reflects the strategic advantages of thoughtful anticipation of an opponent's potential arguments.

*The Advocate Must Identify Benefits or Advantages That Will Be Gained by the Adoption of the Policy.* Implicit in the demand that advocates identify the "selling points" of their proposal is the burden to prove the extent to which these benefits would actually be *achieved* as a result of the proposed policy.

Traditionally, cases offered in support of policy propositions have been conceived in terms of problems and solutions: A significant problem is identified, shown to be beyond the capacity of current efforts to remedy it, but remediable through the new course of action proposed. This structure, however, is more a reflection of rhetorical style than of logical necessity.

Ultimately, the obligation of the advocate is to demonstrate that the proposed course of action will produce advantageous *benefits*, which may come in the form of reductions in some existing problem. Advocates of a proposal to send food shipments to famine-stricken country $X$ must demonstrate what benefits such shipments will produce (e.g., how much starvation will be prevented and for how long; how much malnutrition-related illness will be prevented, etc.). The benefits or advantages of the food-shipment proposal come in the form of reductions in the problems that plague country $X$. Specifying problems is only important insofar as it assists decision makers in determining the extent of the benefits to be gained through adoption of the proposal.

Demonstrating the general scope of a problem (beyond the specific reductions of it that may be attributable to the proposal) is ultimately irrelevant to the evaluation of a policy. To show how many people in total are starving in country $X$ is of dubious relevance; what *is* relevant is the number of people who might be prevented from starving by adoption of the proposal.

Wattenberg and Zinsmeister (1990)–who, among others, have proposed that the United States should accept more immigrants from other nations–identified three main advantages of their proposal to increase the number of immigrants admitted into the United States:

1. Increased immigration will diminish looming labor shortages in the United States, because "immigrants flow not to areas of labor surplus but to the regions and the occupations where demand is the greatest" (p. 22);

2. Increased immigration "can keep America from aging precipitously and fill in the demographic holes that may harm our pension and health-care systems" (p. 23), because immigrants tend to be at the beginning of their careers, whereas an increasing proportion of native-born Americans are elderly.

3. Increased immigration will "bring us significant numbers of bold creators and skilled workers," because immigrants tend to significantly out-perform native-born Americans in educational performance and a higher proportion are professionals (p. 23).

For each of the three benefits of increased immigration that they cited, Wattenberg and Zinsmeister offered reasons to expect that the proposal would actually produce these benefits.

*The Advocate Must Demonstrate the Significance of These Advantages.*
The proposal to adopt a given policy is compelling only when the predicted
outcomes of that policy are regarded as *valuable.* We are motivated to
perform actions by the prospect of achieving significantly greater benefits
than would otherwise be available. Just *how* significant the prospective
benefits must be varies according to the costs and difficulties that must be
borne to achieve them. The greater the effort and cost required to achieve
prospective benefits, the more valuable those benefits must be. In order to
persuade you that we should drive for an hour in order to dine at a
particular restaurant this evening, I would have to convince you that the
prospective meal would be quite extraordinary (or that other significant
benefits, such as a beautifully scenic drive, would be gained). On the other
hand, if our dining choice were between two restaurants–one next door
and one two blocks away–my burden would be substantially less in
convincing you to dine at the slightly more distant one. A modest advantage attributable to the more distant restaurant might suffice.

In their case for more immigration, Wattenberg and Zinsmeister
claimed that increased immigration will beneficially alter the demographics of the current U.S. population. In order to demonstrate the
significance of this advantage, they sketched the dimensions of the current
problem and the degree to which the presence of more immigrants could
reduce it:

> Immigrants typically bring something else to the country, and that is their
> youth. The U.S. is in the midst of becoming a significantly grayer nation.
> Census Bureau projections show median age rising from 33 to 42 over the
> next 40 years. Just from 1990 to 2000, the number of young adults aged 25 to
> 34 is expected to drop from 44 million to 37 million. The ratio of working age
> taxpayers to elderly people will shrink from the 5:1 of today to 2.5:1 in 2030.
> (Wattenberg & Zinsmeister, 1990, p. 22)

Because fewer working-age people will be available to support a larger
elderly population's social services and benefits (particularly medical
care), Wattenberg and Zinsmeister argued that the prospect is one of
substantially higher taxes, lowered benefits, or both. These, in turn, may
produce a marked deterioration in the quality of life for most Americans.

Increased immigration, they argued, will produce the benefit of
averting such problems: "Restoring some demographic equilibrium to the
system by more nearly balancing the number of workers and retirees
would lessen the need for tax increases or benefit reductions for many
decades" (Wattenberg & Zinsmeister, 1990, p. 23). "Immigration," they
claimed, "can begin to ameliorate these imbalances fairly quickly" because
"each payroll-taxpaying immigrant adds thousands of dollars per year to
the Social Security trust funds" (p. 23).

Thus, Wattenberg and Zinsmeister attempted to establish the significance of the demographic advantage attributable to increased immigration by demonstrating (at least in a general way) the extent to which the plan will alter the balance, what the effects of that change in the balance will be, and why these effects should be perceived as valuable.

There are two basic dimensions to significance: a quantitative dimension and a qualitative one. In order to prove that a problem is significant, one must ascertain both how widespread and numerous is its incidence (quantitative significance) and how dire are its effects when it occurs (qualitative significance).

Asia Watch, a human rights advocacy organization, has been at the forefront of efforts to encourage the United States and other nations to impose more severe economic sanctions against China as a result of its crackdown against political dissidents in June 1989, and after. Asia Watch supported its position by offering detailed reports of human rights abuses in China, thus demonstrating the significance of the problem. In its February, 1990, report, *Punishment Season: Human Rights in China After Martial Law* (Asia Watch Committee, 1990), Asia Watch claimed that as many as 1,000 pro-democracy demonstrators were killed on the streets of Beijing by Chinese troops on the nights of June 3 and 4 alone (p. 7).

But the deaths at Tiananmen Square and elsewhere play a relatively small part in Asia Watch's case for sanctions nearly a year later. The benefits available from increased sanctions do not include the resurrection of those already killed. Although sanctions might bring some sense of retribution with respect to the killings, or conceivably deter similar incidents in the future, Asia Watch based its case for sanctions on more tangible benefits achievable in the shorter-run. The bulk of its report is devoted to documenting the on-going arrest and punishment of demonstrators, whose release or more humane treatment, they argued, may be secured through stiffer sanctions.

Asia Watch first documented the *quantitative* significance of political arrests since June 3: "Western diplomats interviewed in Beijing last November estimated that anywhere between 10,000 and 30,000 people had probably been arrested in China since the commencement of the crackdown" (pp. 10–11). Their "crimes," according to Asia Watch, consist of speaking critically of the government. In China, the charge is "counter-revolution," potentially a capital offense (p. 15). At least 40 of those arrested have already been executed (p. 7).

In order to document the *qualitative* significance of these arrests, Asia Watch explained *what it means* to be arrested for political offenses in China. Those arrested, they explained, are almost always convicted and sentenced to long terms of imprisonment, because there is no presumption of innocence in the Chinese judicial system and an acquittal is considered a "loss of face" for the government (p. 42). They described the conditions under which those who are arrested or convicted are imprisoned, including "gross overcrowding in cells, severely inadequate diet and widespread infectious diseases—and of frequent beatings and worse," such as prolonged isolation in solitary confinement (p. 30).

> The most common forms of torture used by police and other interrogating officials in China include vicious and prolonged beatings, often resulting in damage to the internal organs; applying ropes or handcuffs so tightly to prisoners' wrists that nerves are compressed and blood circulation is stopped, causing extreme pain and sometimes permanent loss of function; and, perhaps most widespread of all, applying electric batons (cattle prods) to sensitive parts of the body, including the face. (p. 34)

The Asia Watch report documents the qualitative significance of arrest and imprisonment both through general overviews of conditions and through the stories of individual prisoners, who supply an element of significance otherwise lost: the understanding that these conditions are suffered by individuals with names and feelings.

Asia Watch supported their case for sanctions by demonstrating that the benefits they attribute to them (securing the release of all political prisoners) are both quantitatively and qualitatively significant.

*The Advocate Must Demonstrate the Uniqueness of These Advantages.* To say that a proposed course of action is *advantageous* is to deem it superior *in comparison with other available courses of action.* Let us imagine that in a discussion in which you are deciding where to dine with friends this evening, Restaurant *X* or Restaurant *Y*, a friend speaks in glowing terms of the delicious lobster available at Restaurant *X*. That attribute would constitute a reason for choosing Restaurant *X* only if an equally delicious lobster is *not* available at Restaurant *Y*. It must be shown that the benefit is unique (at least to some degree) in order for it to constitute a reason to adopt the proposed course of action that entails it.

In order to demonstrate the uniqueness of an advantage attributed to the proposal, it is necessary to demonstrate why and to what extent the present system, or other competing alternatives, are unable to gain the advantage. In the case for women's suffrage outlined earlier, Alden demonstrated the uniqueness of advantages attributable to suffrage by comparing the proposal for enfranchisement with the then-current means by which women's interests could be secured—namely, through the protective actions of husbands. Alden concluded that such male protection is an inherently less satisfactory means by which to protect women's interests, in that women's interests may be at odds with those of their husbands, and that many women are not married. Women's suffrage, Alden argued, would offer *unique* advantages in the pursuit of women's interests because women are in the best position to know their interests and are most likely to be motivated to pursue them.

The claim that the present system is unable to gain an advantage attributable to a proposed course of action is called an inherency argument. For some inherent reason, advocates claim, the present system is unable to perform as well as the proposed one would. If you were to decide to transfer from your present university to another, it would be because you had identified some asset (such as a major program) of the new school that your current school lacked and would be unlikely to acquire. If you wish to pursue studies in computer science and your current university lacks a major program in that field, you might decide to transfer to another institution that possesses such a major. Even though your current university offers individual courses in computer science, you might decide that a major program would necessarily offer greater coherence and depth of study in the field. Thus, you might conclude that your current university is inherently inadequate with respect to studies in computer science, and that the competing university with a major program possesses certain *unique* advantages.

An inherency/uniqueness argument always involves *prediction*, as the advocate compares the future performance of the present system with the future performance of the proposed system. Which will achieve greater benefits? For what reasons?

When Ida B. Wells built her case for national anti-lynching legislation, she first dismissed as inadequate all present and possible recourses short of such legislation:

> Various remedies have been suggested to abolish the lynching infamy, but year after year, the butchery of men, women and children continues in spite of plea and protest. Education is suggested as a preventive, but it is as grave a crime to murder an ignorant man as it is a scholar. True, few educated men have been lynched, but the hue and cry once started stops at no bounds, as was clearly shown by the lynchings in Atlanta, and in Springfield, Illinois.
>
> Agitation, though helpful, will not alone stop the crime. Year after year statistics are published, meetings are held, resolutions are adopted and yet lynchings go on. Public sentiment does measurably decrease the sway of mob law, but the irresponsible bloodthirsty criminals who swept through the streets in Springfield, beating an inoffensive law-abiding citizen to death in one part of the town, and in another torturing and shooting to death a man who for threescore years had made a reputation for honesty, integrity and sobriety, had raised a family and had accumulated property, were not deterred from their heinous crimes by either education or agitation.
>
> The only certain remedy is an appeal to law. (Foner, 1975, pp. 73–74)

By explaining the inadequacy of alternative approaches (education and agitation), Wells demonstrated that the advantage (significantly diminishing the incidence of lynching) is *uniquely* attainable through national anti-lynching legislation.

*The Advocate Must Demonstrate That the Benefits To Be Gained by Adopting the Policy Outweigh the Costs.* If the previous four requirements may be termed *prima facie* burdens of the advocate – characteristics that must be demonstrated "on the *first* making" of the proposal, this fifth burden may be termed, as former national debate champion Rich Lewis has put it, an *"ultima facie"* burden borne by the advocate. "On its *last* making," at the conclusion of the debate, the advocate must have assured decision makers that the proposal will generate some net advantage, even after accounting for all arguments – including disadvantages – put forth by the opposition.

According to the formats of most policy debates, an advocate of the proposed policy both opens and closes the debate. The opening speech should provide a *prima facie* case for change, logically complete and compelling. In the final speech, the advocate should endeavor to demonstrate that the case for change *remains* logically complete and compelling as the debate concludes. On the other hand, the opposition attempts to demonstrate that the impact of their arguments through the course of the debate has been such that the anticipated *costs of the proposal outweigh its prospective benefits.*

## STRUCTURES OF POLICY OPPOSITION

Although the many effective strategies of refutation will be discussed in far more detail in chapters 4, 5, and 6, it may be useful at this point to outline the basic structures of arguments for the opposition that have their counterparts in the burdens of proof assigned to policy advocates.

If the ultimate objective of the opposition is to demonstrate that the costs of the proposal outweigh its benefits, the opposition may best proceed by arguing that: (a) The unique benefits attributable to the proposal are lower than claimed by its advocates; and/or that (b) The costs uniquely attributable to the proposal are higher than claimed by its advocates.

This two-track approach is pursued by use of specific types of arguments, each with its own logical burdens of proof and conventional structures for presentation. Excluding, for the moment, the presentation of a counterplan (discussed in chapter 6), the basic types of opposition arguments in a policy debate are:

1. The advantage is less significant than claimed;
2. The advantage is not unique;
3. The policy will fail to gain the advantages claimed; and
4. The policy will produce significant disadvantages.

*The Advantage Is Less Significant Than Claimed.*  The opposition's refutation of the significance attributed to a proposed policy's outcomes must center on one or both of the two dimensions of significance discussed earlier: The opposition may argue that the *quantitative* significance is less than claimed and/or the opposition may argue that the advantage is not so valuable as claimed – that its *qualitative* significance is lower.

Earlier, we discussed the proposal that a student interested in computer science should transfer from his/her current university (which has computer courses but no major program) to one that has a major program. The significance of the advantage presented by the new university program might be questioned. How *many* additional courses does the major program provide? A university that has a major program in a subject does not necessarily have many (if any) more courses in that subject than a university without a major. How important are the additional courses provided to the student's career plans? What difference does the credential of a completed *major* in computer science make (as opposed to being able to stress on one's resume that one has completed *x* courses in computer science)?

The actual advantage associated with transferring to the new school may be far less significant than originally supposed.

If the advantage claimed for a proposal lies in its ability to reduce a given problem (such as flag-burning), the opposition might argue that the problem is not so widespread as claimed (the incidence of flag-burning is low) and/or that the effects of the problem *when it occurs* are less dire than claimed (the opposition may even argue that flag-burning has its *merits* as a form of political expression – a strategy discussed in chapter 5). By reducing the dimensions of the problem that the policy addresses, the opposition reduces the advantage or benefits attributable to the policy.

Animal rights activists have lobbied for legislation to impose greater restrictions on the uses of animals in scientific research. Some animal liberation groups have staged nighttime raids on laboratory facilities, documented abusive treatments through film and photography, then publicized these instances of abuse. Opponents of the 1984 Improved Standards for Laboratory Animals Act, such as Dr. Glenn Geelhoed of

George Washington University, attempted to diminish the significance of such abuses in his testimony before the House Agriculture Committee:

> It cannot be denied that there have been incidences in some research institutions of non-compliance with existing animal care guidelines; but these have been isolated and few and far between, while strict compliance has been the rule in a very large national research program involving hundreds upon hundreds of institutions. (House Committee on Agriculture, 1984, p. 151)

Geelhoed argued that the actual significance of laboratory animal abuse is less than might be inferred from highly publicized examples. He attempted to direct the debate toward overall assessment of incidence, which he believes will demonstrate such abuse to be rare rather than common and therefore less compelling as a basis for new legislation.

At the height of the farm crisis in the mid-1980s, many analysts disputed the dire portrayals that captured the headlines. Rep. Henry Hyde of Illinois (1985) argued that the actual dimensions of the crisis were far less than claimed by advocates of federal bailouts for farmers:

> Last Spring, farm advocates claimed that 15% of American farmers would be unable to get financial aid for planting and would thus be forced out of business. The true figure was less than 5%, not grossly out of proportion to the 6% of nonfarm businesses that will fail this year. (p. 26)

In the last sentence, Hyde disputed not only the quantitative significance of the farm crisis, but its qualitative dimension as well: We should be less concerned about it, he argued, because it is hardly more of a financial threat than that faced by the average businessperson.

*The Advantage Is Not Unique.* The advocate of a proposal seeks to demonstrate that it is able to achieve what competing alternatives (particularly the present course of action) cannot. The opponent may seek to establish that the present system is likely to achieve much of the benefit claimed for the new proposal. In doing so, the opponent lessens the comparative (unique) advantage of the proposal.

If your current school were scheduled to begin a major program in computer science next semester, there would be less reason to transfer to a school that already has one.

In arguing that a claimed advantage for a proposed policy is not unique, the opponent compares the future outcomes of the proposed policy with the future performance and outcomes of the present system, arguing that the difference between them is less than the proponents have stated.

In speaking of a "present system," one refers to a dynamic rather than a static complex. Systems adapt and modify approaches, monitor and improve performances. In order to evaluate the probable outcomes of the present system, one must appreciate its *possibilities* and the ability and proclivity of those who manage the system to exploit its potential. In arguments against the proposed act for Improved Standards for Laboratory Animals, veterinarian Gerald von Hoosier of the University of Washington testified that:

> The current animal welfare act along with NIH standards is adequate to meet reasonable standards of care for animals in research. New legislation may not be necessary. In addition, there is no reason to believe that the new legislation would be enforced any better than present law, absent adequate support for APHIS. (House Committee on Agriculture, 1984, p. 128)

Von Hoosier attempted to demonstrate that a regulatory framework already exists with sufficient authority for the potential protection of laboratory animals. There is no unique advantage, he argued, that obtains to the regulatory authority prescribed in the proposed legislation. This means that any difference in the projected outcomes of the two systems would depend on superior enforcement of the new regulations, which he argued is unlikely.

Von Hoosier's argument demonstrates the natural affinity between inherency arguments (that there is no inherent reason that the proposed system should out-perform the existing one) and arguments that the proposal will prove unable to gain the advantages claimed for it.

*The Policy Will Fail To Gain the Advantages Claimed.*   The difference between the benefits expected from adopted policies and the actual outcomes of those policies is often immense. As policy analyst Susan Hansen (1982) has written, "the process of implementing policy is so difficult that we should be surprised when policies have *any* favorable accomplishments" (p. 27). The potential barriers to the success of legislative proposals are numerous and diverse. By documenting the barriers a specific policy proposal will face and their likely impact on the achievements of the proposal, opponents may substantially reduce the strength of the advocates' case.

After the terrorist bombing of Pan-American Airlines flight 103, legal scholars David Newman and Bruce Bueno de Mesquita argued on the Op-Ed page of the *New York Times* (January 26, 1989, p. A23) that President Bush should repeal Executive Order 12333, which stipulates that "No person employed by or acting on behalf of the U.S. Government shall engage in, or conspire to engage in, assassination." The authors maintained that repeal of the prohibition on assassination would give the United States a free hand to retaliate against terrorists: By leaving our options open, unconstrained by legal prohibition, terrorists would be deterred from attacking Americans by the threat of potential assassination.

But would the repeal of Executive Order 12333 actually leave the U.S. with a free hand to assassinate foreign nationals, unconstrained by legal prohibition? University of Illinois law professor Francis Boyle argued in response to this proposal (*New York Times*, February 9, 1989, p. A26):

> Irrespective of Executive Order 12333, Hague Convention IV (adopted in 1907) is a "treaty" of the United States that has received the advice and consent of the Senate and is therefore the supreme law of the land according to Article 6 of the United States Constitution, the so-called Supremacy Clause. But even if Congress were to enact a statute that expressly repealed the rule found in Hague regulation article 23(b), that would still not help U.S. Government officials allegedly responsible for assassinations during the course of their travels abroad. This is because the Nuremberg Tribunal of 1945 expressly ruled that the rules found in the Hague regulations had entered into customary international law as of 1939.

Boyle argued that it is not possible for the president (or the Congress, for that matter) to remove the legal prohibitions against assassination because they would remain enforceable under *international* law. "The repeal of Executive Order 12333," Boyle concluded, "would not change this."

This type of argument may be referred to as a "plan-meet-need" ("PMN") or, more properly, a "plan-meet-advantage" ("PMA") argument—an argument that the proposal will fail to gain some significant proportion of the benefits claimed for it by its advocates. The structure and logical burdens of a plan-meet-advantage argument are as follows:

1. **Aim.** Identify the specific aim/advantage of the plan—What beneficial outcome has been predicted for it by its advocates?
2. **Barrier.** Demonstrate some reason(s) why the plan will fail to achieve its stated objective—What barriers, obstacles, or interceding factors will prevent its success?
3. **Impact.** Specify the degree to which these barriers will reduce the *actual* benefits of the proposal—What is their impact on the claimed advantage?

In Professor Boyle's plan-meet-advantage argument, he identified the claimed advantage of Newman and de Mesquita's proposal to eliminate

U.S. laws prohibiting assassination: deterrence of terrorism due to the unconstrained ability of United States agents to engage in assassination. Boyle identified an obstacle to the achievement of this objective: Even if U.S. laws prohibiting assassination are removed, strong and enforceable international prohibitions will continue, as specified in the Hague Convention. Boyle claimed that this obstacle would completely negate the claimed advantage of the proposal, because U.S. leaders would remain as constrained in ordering assassinations as they are now. The impact of Boyle's plan-meet-advantage argument and Newman and de Mesquita's claimed advantage, he maintained, is total.

Plan-meet-advantage arguments need not totally eliminate the claimed advantage in order to have a significant impact in the debate, however. A plan-meet-advantage argument that substantially reduces (even if it does not *eliminate*) the claimed advantage will make it easier for the opposition to counterbalance the remaining advantage with costs or disadvantages attributable to the proposal.

Proposals to legalize cocaine and other drugs have gained some publicity and support in recent years, endorsed even by such conservatives as William F. Buckley, Jr. One of the principal advantages claimed for legalization is that it would reduce crime. Drug users are responsible for a high proportion of property crimes, committed in order to pay for drugs at the high prices forced by prohibition. Proponents of legalization argue that decriminalization would dramatically reduce drug prices, thereby lessening the number of crimes committed to pay for drugs. But Professor of Management and Public Policy James Q. Wilson (1990) has argued that the reduction of crime due to drug legalization would actually be far less than that claimed by proponents.

> Addicts would no longer steal to pay black-market prices for drugs, a real gain. But some, perhaps a great deal, of that gain would be offset by the great increase in the number of addicts. These people, nodding on heroin or living in the delusion-ridden high of cocaine, would hardly be ideal employees. Many would steal to support themselves, since snatch-and-grab, opportunistic crime can be managed even by people unable to hold a regular job or plan a regular crime. Those British addicts who get their supplies from government clinics are not models of law-abiding decency. Most are in crime, and though their per-capita rate of criminality may be lower thanks to the cheapness of their drugs, the total volume of the crime they produce may be quite large. Of course, society could decide to support all employable addicts on welfare, but that would mean that gains from lowered rates of crime would have to be offset by large increases in welfare budgets. (p. 25)

Wilson did not contend that there will be *no* reduction in crime if drugs are legalized. He simply argued that the reduction in crime would be significantly *less* than that claimed by proponents. By diminishing the likely benefits attributable to legalization, he rendered the proposal more vulnerable to the disadvantages he claimed elsewhere in his essay (dramatic increases in use, infant health problems and child abuse, human degradation, and violence).

The lower the benefits of a proposal, the easier it is to prove that the costs outweigh the benefits.

One special type of plan-meet-advantage argument is the circumvention argument, which claims that the policy will fail to gain the advantage claimed because of active efforts to evade or subvert its operation.

A circumvention argument must specify: (a) a motive powerful enough to produce significant evasion of the policy; (b) a means (or more than one) that may be employed by those with motives to evade the policy; (c) proof that the plan's enforcement provisions will fail to prevent circumvention by the means described; and (d) the impact such evasion would have on the ability of the policy to secure the advantages claimed.

Opponents of legislation that would restrict legal access to abortion argue that such measures would be circumvented through illegal abortion. Many women have powerful reasons (*motives*) to seek abortions, whether legal or illegal, including preservation of their current family's well-being, pursuit of their own education or career plans, or health risks associated with childbirth. Past experience with abortion prohibitions (prior to the 1973 *Roe v. Wade* decision of the U.S. Supreme Court) show that illegal abortions (*means*) were widely available and used despite legal penalties (*enforcement fails*). The impact of such circumvention has been calculated by several statisticians, as the National Abortion Rights Action League (1978) documented:

> Researchers from HEW's Center for Disease Control estimate that the number of illegal abortions has dropped from about 130,000 to 17,000 in 1975; during that period, annual deaths resulting from illegal abortions are estimated to have dropped from 39 to 4. In the absence of a liberal law, 7 out of 10 legal abortions now performed would take place illegally, according to Christopher Tietze, biostatistician for the Population Council in New York. (p. 23)

Because of successful circumvention of prohibitions against abortion, according to NARAL, 70% of abortions would continue even if such restrictive legislation were passed.

Through either the conventional plan-meet-objection argument or the more specialized circumvention argument, the opposition attempts to reduce the advantage claimed by policy proponents. The *actual* benefits of the policy, according to the opposition, will be significantly less than those originally ascribed to it.

*The Policy Will Produce Significant Disadvantages.* According to the National Abortion Rights Action League, the increase in illegal abortions that would accompany restrictions on the availability of legal abortion constitute far more than an "enforcement problem." Because illegal abortions are often conducted by non-physicians in primitive and unsanitary conditions with non-medical instruments ranging from coat hangers to knitting needles, increases in the incidence of illegal abortion would mean, according to NARAL, increased death, disease, and maiming of women. These would constitute disadvantages of a proposal to restrict access to abortion.

In general, disadvantages are the most important opposition arguments, with the possible exception of counterplans (which, as is explained in chapter 6, function logically as "opportunity costs" – a form of disadvantage). The three forms of opposition argument outlined earlier are all ways in which the opposition may *diminish* the advocates' claims for their proposal. In most debates, their impact will be partial, not total – leaving some residual of benefit attributable to the proposal.

Disadvantages, on the other hand, *counterbalance* the benefits claimed for the proposal. Remember that the ultimate obligation of the advocate is to demonstrate that the benefits of the proposal outweigh the costs. Therefore, the ultimate burden of the opposition is to demonstrate that the costs of the proposal outweigh its benefits – its disadvantages outweigh its advantages. The other forms of opposition argument may play important roles in the debate, but their real function is to diminish the estimate of benefits likely to be achieved by the proposal to such an extent that the disadvantages offered by the opposition outweigh them.

A disadvantage should include the following elements:

1. **Identify the specific aspect or action of the plan that will produce some ill effect.** In the case of the proposal to increase sanctions against China, this action would simply be the specific sanction imposed.

2. **Establish the *link* between the plan and some ill effect;** establish its causal relationship. It may be argued that increased sanctions against the Chinese would lead them to "shut their door" to the world, retreating into isolation as they did during the Cultural Revolution. Some observers, such as ex-president Richard Nixon, have argued that this effect could result as sanctions would strengthen the position of hardliners within the Chinese government who dissent from China's current "opening up." "China has 'gone it alone' in the past," Nixon warned, "and could do so again." (quoted in Ye, 1989, p. 30).

3. **Document the ill effect caused by the plan; demonstrate its significance or *impact*.** The significance of these ill effects should be weighed against the claimed benefits of the proposal. If China were to

close its doors, it has been argued, purges and further crackdowns would take place, as the Chinese government would no longer be constrained by the presence of foreigners and threat of foreign action. The result of sanctions may then be an *increase* rather than a decrease of political repression and human rights violations.

4. **Demonstrate that these ill effects are the *unique* results of the proposal; that unless we adopt the proposal, we would be unlikely to suffer these ill effects.** China, it might be argued, is currently embarked on a path of increased contact and interdependence with other nations and its hardliners are, for the moment at least, held in check. The imposition of stiffer sanctions, it might be charged, would uniquely alter this equilibrium. The most common way to demonstrate uniqueness of the causality scenario in a disadvantage is to identify some threshold or brink that has not yet been crossed, but will be by the action of the plan.

5. **Sometimes, it may be wise to *preempt* possible responses to the disadvantage.** This is not a *logical* requirement of the disadvantage but sometimes, as is described in chapter 4, is a *strategic* one.

A disadvantage is a form of causal argument. By adopting the plan, the opposition claims, some ill effect will be produced. The burdens and tests of causal arguments are explored in greater detail in the next chapter.

The most effective disadvantages are those that explicitly contextualize and surpass the advantages claimed for the proposal. Such a disadvantage is clearly stipulated as an "independent voting issue"; if it is won, then presumably the debate as a whole should fall to the opposition. As is explained in more detail in chapter 5, the clearest way to establish such a disadvantage is to build on the affirmative's own significance, claiming that the problem will be made *worse* instead of better if the affirmative's proposal is adopted.

A common use of this disadvantage strategy may be found in the so-called "Export Death" argument. Proposals to ban hazardous substances or businesses in the United States (such as dangerous chemicals, manufacturing processes, or unsafe consumer goods) often provoke the charge that companies subject to such bans in the U.S. will then shift their sales or operations to other countries. Because other nations may be more susceptible to damages caused by these products and processes (e.g., because of comparatively lax regulation), it may be claimed that the net result of domestic bans on products and processes is to *increase* the net damage inflicted by them.

American consumer advocates have mounted increasingly effective campaigns in recent decades to prohibit the manufacture and use of various agricultural pesticides and other pollutants. Yet, as Barbara Vagliano (1981) has observed in the *Journal of International Law:*

Increased environmental regulations in the U.S. have motivated domestic
manufacturing companies of hazardous substances to transfer entire plants
to the Third World, because the U.S. government has not exercised any
control over the facilities once removed. The transfer has resulted in the
continued manufacture of substances banned in the U.S. and the exposure of
foreign workers to hazards unacceptable in the U.S. (p. 350)

When increased safety regulation in the United States encourages
corporations to shift their operations elsewhere, the net result of the
safety regulations may be to increase the hazards of such manufacturing.
Political Scientist Robert Engler of Brooklyn College has observed that
"Third World nations ardently pursuing industrial and agricultural development are even less rigorous in evaluating potential risks from chemical
plants and imported chemicals" (Engler, 1985, p. 494). As a result, plant
operation in such nations may be even more hazardous than it is in the
United States. Engler cited the example of a Union Carbide pesticide
plant in Bhopal, India, which operated in open violation of poorly enforced
health and safety standards. In December 1984, a cloud of toxic gas
escaped from the plant, killing thousands of nearby residents.

The "Export Death" disadvantage argues that the net result of some
safety and environmental regulations in the United States may be to
*increase* hazards of the regulated products rather than reducing them. It
is a strategically effective disadvantage to such proposals because it
purports to fully account for and surpass their claimed advantages.

Disadvantages, however, need not attempt to "turn" the significance
claims of the affirmative. The ill-effects described in a disadvantage may
be *side*-effects of the proposal, affecting different sorts of conditions than
those covered in the proposal's advantages. A proposal to increase employment through massive public works programs may create the disadvantageous side-effects of additional resource-consumption, environmental pollution and global warming associated with industrial growth and rises in
personal income. A proposal to increase the scientific exploration of outer
space may have the disadvantageous side-effect of enhancing development
of "Star Wars" technology, thereby increasing the threat of nuclear war.

By constructing disadvantages, opponents seek to document the most
significant costs associated with adoption of a proposal.


## CONCLUSION

In order to establish a logically complete case in support of the proposition,
advocates must assume certain burdens of proof. Ultimately, proponents
of a policy must demonstrate that the benefits uniquely obtainable from

the adoption of that policy outweigh the costs. Opponents, conversely, attempt to prove the opposite. The burdens of proof assumed by each side take particular argumentative forms, each with their own logical structures and implicit responsibilities. These arguments must be supported by evidence and analysis, as we discuss in chapter 3.

# RESEARCH AND EVIDENCE

As debaters seek to gain the assent of an audience, they must support their claims with proof. "Proof," Wharton observed in *Criminal Evidence*, "is the basis for accepting a proposition as true" (Torcia, 1985, p. 3). Evidence is the means through which proof is established, the observations and testimony that may lead us to conclude that a claim has been substantiated.

An unevidenced claim is a mere assertion, and generally is discredited in debate. When faced with a controversial assertion, we naturally ask "But, can you *prove* that?" Scientist Thomas Huxley described this challenging impulse as a valuable habit of mind, "believing nothing unless there is evidence for it," and "looking upon belief which is not based upon evidence, not only as illogical, but also as immoral" (quoted in Foster, 1908, p. 53).

The ability to understand, develop, and support argumentative claims is gained through research. The functions of debate research are really threefold: to gather background information on the designated topic; to discover the most important issues and arguments related to the topic; and, finally, to gather evidence in support of one's own prospective arguments and in refutation of the arguments expected from one's opponents. Most research time should be devoted to the last of these three tasks. Locating the best available evidence with which to substantiate one's claims, however, is no easy matter and requires mastery of a systematic approach to the conduct of research.

## A STRATEGY FOR RESEARCH

The literature pertinent to almost any given debate topic is staggeringly voluminous. If a topic is important enough to be debated, it is likely to have been the subject of many published analyses and to involve many related topics that are also the subjects of extensive literatures. The debater will usually find it more difficult to cope with the task of researching a topic about which much has been written than a topic that has received less attention.

Efficient and productive research requires that the researcher proceed in a systematic fashion through the available resources.

*Do Some Background Reading Before You Begin To Research.* If the purpose of research is to produce the best possible arguments on a topic and sufficient evidence to prove them, one must begin by discovering what the issues and arguments *are.* This requires an understanding of how the controversy has developed, what the sides are, and with what basic arguments these sides have supported their positions.

*Brainstorm the Possible Arguments for Both Sides.* List the arguments you have gleaned from your background reading and add to them other strong arguments that *might* be made to support either side of the controversy. One must brainstorm *both* sides of the controversy because of the need in a debate not only to advance one's own arguments but to refute those of one's opponent.

Brainstorming works best when it follows the list of structures for case arguments and opposition presented in chapter 2. What specific policies or plans of action might the affirmative support in defense of the proposition? What advantages might they claim for these policies? How might they demonstrate that these advantages are achievable, significant, and unique? How might the opposition refute these claims? What counterpositions or counterproposals might the opposition support? What disadvantages might the opposition claim will result from the affirmative proposal?

Be as comprehensive as possible in brainstorming. By knowing all the available arguments, you will be able to choose the strongest for your side and anticipate and prepare to refute the probable arguments of your opponent.

It is crucial that the researcher brainstorm possible arguments *before* beginning to research. By knowing the arguments you hope to support or refute with evidence, you are able to select relevant readings and material within readings with greater efficiency. Knowing what you are looking for enables you to skip or skim irrelevant material and to be more alert for truly useful material. In the process of conducting research, the debater will doubtless encounter certain arguments that he or she has not brain-stormed. The potential importance of these arguments may be evaluated and they may be added to the brainstorm list for further research.

*Identify Research Needs and Resources.*   Having identified the poten-tial arguments for each side, prioritize: Which arguments do you most need to support or refute? There may be many reasons one could poten-tially offer in support of Athens as a permanent home for the Olympic games, for example, but which deserve serious consideration?

Having identified the most important arguments, one must ask: What sorts of evidence would be required to support them? If one were at-tempting to support the claim that the U.S. atomic bombing of Hiroshima inflicted enormous and cruel suffering on the city's inhabitants, one would wish to find evidence attesting to: the immediate casualty rates; the long-term death, disease, and disability figures; the horrible *experience* of the bombing and its aftermath; and possible distinctions between the degree and nature of suffering inflicted by this weapon and that inflicted by others.

After identifying what must be proven to support his or her arguments, the researcher must then ask: Where is such evidence most likely to be found? What kinds of publications would most likely provide such support? Under what subject headings would such publications be located? Al-though the general topic for the debate may be the bombing of Hiroshima, the researcher must have a more precise sense of the specific subject headings under which needed evidence may be located. The casualty statistics for Hiroshima, for example, might best be located by looking in a library card catalogue under the heading "Atomic bombing–medical effects," whereas the comparison of suffering inflicted by various weapons might best be located under the heading of "Military Ethics," in order to find books whose authors are most likely to address the issue. For the research needs identified in the case of the Hiroshima bombing, a re-searcher had best turn to the following resources:

For immediate casualty rates and long-term statistics, the researcher must locate the work of some organization or individuals who have compiled longitudinal health statistics. Because the researcher wants to know not only the best estimates of immediate casualties but also long-term casualties due to cancer and other radiation effects, the ideal re-source must be relatively recent. One such resource is the book *Hiroshima and Nagasaki: The Physical, Medical, and Social Effects of the Atomic Bombardment*, published in 1981 by the Japanese Committee for the Compilation of Materials on Damage Caused by the Atomic Bombs.

For some understanding of the experience of the atomic bombing and its aftermath, the researcher should turn to the accounts provided by bombing survivors, or *hibakusha*. Several collections of *hibakusha* accounts have been published. Such works as Richard Rhodes' *The Making of the Atomic Bomb* also draw on *hibakusha* accounts in their description of the bombing.

To explore the similarities and differences between the effects of the atomic bomb and those inflicted by other weapons (such as incendiary bombing), the researcher might best consult works on military ethics and international law that consider such distinctions. *The Ethics of War*, by Barrie Paskins and Michael Dockrill (1979), and Michael Walzer's *Just and Unjust Wars* (1977), for example, both consider such comparisons.

The effective researcher must know what evidence s/he is looking for and where–in what kind of publication, from what time period, and on what subject–it is most likely to be found. Later in this chapter, a list of the most useful library resources for most research is examined in more detail.

*Prepare a Bibliography.* Consult indexes (listed in the next section) and card catalogues for relevant sources. Photocopy or transcribe *selected* entries–those entries whose titles and dates suggest clear relevance to the specific arguments you are researching. Additional sources can be gleaned from most books and scholarly articles you research: Always check their notes and references for sources.

*Engage in Selective Reading.* Consult those portions of readings (through tables of contents, indexes, or quick scanning) relevant to your research objectives. You should be looking to support and refute particular arguments. Having such arguments clearly in mind enables you to read more efficiently, paying attention to what is important. You may, of course, encounter new and powerful arguments in your readings, which you had not previously considered and which should be added to your research agenda.

*Extract Useful Evidence.* Most evidence extracted in the research process is designed to be read in support of arguments used in a debate. An argumentative claim will be made, bolstered by evidence drawn from some authoritative source. Therefore, any single piece of evidence extracted should be concise, clear, and to the point.

Evidence may be recorded on index cards or, as is described in the next chapter, incorporated directly into argument briefs. Recording on index cards is more useful for the beginning debater and for research projects that have yet to be fully organized. Material recorded on index cards can be filed by subject and arranged (and rearranged) as arguments are designed. Each index card should contain a single quotation. Each quotation should be accompanied by a full bibliographic citation (or keyed to an accessible bibliography that contains the information): author's name; author's qualifications; name of source (book or magazine title); full date; and page number(s). At the top of each card a brief descriptive label (such as "Hiroshima death figures") should be written to identify the argument that this piece of evidence supports. These labels may be scanned for more rapid location of needed evidence cards.

Evidence cards should be filed according to the arguments they support. Once filed, the evidence cards become a resource that may be drawn on during the debate. An argument is heard, the relevant file subject heading is consulted, and the best evidence cards under that heading are used to support arguments in a subsequent speech. Evidence cards also form the basis for briefs and cases that may be prepared prior to the debate.

## SOURCES

Once one knows both the general subject of research and the specific topics and arguments for which one hopes to gather evidence, the most pressing question becomes: Where does one find such evidence? The basic sources of most debate evidence are books, government documents, newspapers, specialized journals, popular journals and magazines, and pamphlets. Each type of source has its strengths and weaknesses. Books, for example, may contain the most comprehensive treatments of issues, but involve relatively long lag times between events and publication and (apart from collections) are generally representative of only a single point of view. Each type of source also has its own indices. Books on a given subject, for example, may be located through a library card catalogue, the "Subject" index of *Books in Print*, or through computerized publications listings.

Understanding which sources are most likely to yield the information you need and how to locate these sources is the fundamental prerequisite for successful research.

### Popular Journals and Magazines

Popular periodicals provide relatively timely and accessible (if not often very comprehensive) information about current issues. They are indexed in several ways. *The Magazine Index* and, in some libraries, the *Public Affairs Information Service* (P.A.I.S.) index are available on-line for computerized searches by subject. The most widely available index is the

*Reader's Guide to Periodical Literature,* published in both monthly and annual volumes.

## Government Documents

United States government documents are an invaluable resource for research on national and international affairs. They are current (given a relatively short lag time between writing and publication), well-indexed, oriented toward policy decision making, and widely available. The national depository system for government documents includes over 1,400 designated libraries throughout the country, housed mostly at educational institutions.

There are three basic types of government documents that are useful in debate research: hearings of the U.S. Senate and House of Representatives; *The Congressional Record;* and the reports of various federal agencies, departments, and commissions. Each of these offers distinctive sorts of information and each has its own index.

*Hearings* provide transcriptions of testimony offered before House and Senate committees. They are normally devoted to the investigation of issues related to pending legislation. Unlike most other publications, hearings feature testimony from experts and interested parties on both (and sometimes several) sides of the issue. Therefore the debater is likely to find evidence in a given hearing to support his or her position on the issue. Three types of testimony are featured in hearings: prepared statements, read into the record or simply submitted by the witnesses to the committee; responses to questions of committee members; and additional materials submitted by the witnesses. These additional materials may include articles from other publications, charts and graphs, or relevant correspondence and other previously unpublished texts.

The most comprehensive and best organized index to congressional hearings is the *Congressional Information Service Index,* which also catalogues prints and reports generated by congressional committees themselves. The *CIS Index* is published in two volumes for each year. One volume provides an index listing of documents, the other provides abstracts of the documents' contents.

The index lists materials in several ways: by subject (such as "Child Abuse"); by names of witnesses and authors who appear in the documents; by the title of the publication; and by the name of the committee that conducted the hearing, among others.

The *Congressional Record* has its own index, listing speeches delivered on the floor of the House and Senate and other materials submitted for publication by members of Congress. *The Monthly Catalog of Government*

*Documents* includes not only selected Congressional hearings, but also reports released by committees and agencies of the Executive Branch.

## Newspapers

Newspapers provide several sorts of evidence not likely to appear in other sources. Major newspapers offer far more comprehensive coverage of most current events than appears in other sources. Indeed, most stories covered in a major newspaper appear in no other printed source. Newspapers also have a shorter lag time between the occurrence of events and the appearance of stories about the events.

Newspaper stories are drawn from three different types of sources: investigation and reporting generated by members of the newspaper's own staff, wire service releases (usually Associated Press, United Press International, or Reuters), and syndicated columns. Newspapers vary in the degrees to which they rely on these sources. Most local newspapers offer little original reporting on national or world events; such stories are normally drawn from the wire services.

Newspaper articles useful for debate research are best located through a combination of index searching and daily reading. Most major newspapers publish annual and monthly indexes to their articles, organized by subject. The *National Newspaper Index*, available in many college and university libraries, offers a joint index for articles appearing in the *New York Times*, *Los Angeles Times*, *Wall Street Journal*, *Washington Post*, and *Christian Science Monitor*. This joint index may be accessed through a microprocessor, which provides rapid location of entries and a printout of research citations. Once the researcher has these citations in hand, he or she must then locate the articles cited in the microfilmed back issues of the newspaper.

But every debater should also read at least one major newspaper daily. This allows the debater to keep up with the latest developments in areas likely to be important in debates and to avoid the time lag required for newspaper indexes and microfilm to be printed. Moreover, daily newspaper reading is an invaluable prod to the argumentative imagination—alerting the reader to new issues, case ideas, and connections between issues that would not otherwise be discovered.

## Specialized Journals

Specialized journals publish research pertinent to specific professions or academic disciplines. Medical journals publish results of medical experimentation, for example, or discussions of ethical or financial issues affecting physicians. Law reviews publish research and commentary on legal issues, cases, and principles.

Specialized journals differ from general periodicals in several ways. Specialized journals usually:

- Present original research and provide details regarding how the research was conducted (so that others in the field may seek to check the data, evaluate experimental designs, or even replicate the research);
- Offer unique presentations of material, not available elsewhere. Editors of most specialized journals insist that works accepted for publication constitute some sort of new and original contribution to the field;
- Often use technical language, geared to an audience of specialists in the field. The material in specialized journals is likely to be far more detailed than material geared to general audiences.

Indexes for specialized journals may be limited to a particular field or profession (e.g., *Index Medicus*), or embrace a larger range of disciplines, such as the *Social Science Index, Humanities Index,* or *Index to Business Periodicals*.

By understanding the very different types of materials available in different sources, the researcher may turn to those sources most likely to yield useful evidence in support of particular arguments.


## EVIDENCE

Evidence comes in many forms. A claim may be supported by reference to examples, scientific or personal observation, statistical analysis, or the opinions of experts. A debater's own unevidenced opinion is unlikely to be persuasive unless: (a) he or she has acquired eminence and expertise in the relevant field that will be acknowledged by the audience; or (b) the point is founded in "common knowledge," shared by speaker and audience alike.

Unless one of these two situations pertains, evidence must be drawn from the testimony and investigations of others who possess greater authority.

### Evidence From Authorities

Authoritative testimony is used to support claims that the debater cannot credibly assert on his or her own. In quoting someone, the debater implies that this person possesses credible expertise on the matter discussed. But what makes someone an "authority" on a given issue?

The mere fact that someone's statement has been published should lend it no special weight as evidence. Foster (1908/1932) admonished that:

> Most grown-up people get rid of the notion that whatever appears in print is true, but many cling to the equally absurd notion that the printing of a statement does give it some claim to dignity and credence. For the purposes of argumentation, let us here make this point emphatic: The mere fact that a statement appears in print lends not one atom to its value. Every assertion that is brought forward – though it may have been printed a thousand times and repeated a million times – must be challenged and tested before it can be of any value as evidence. (p. 59)

The credibility of a source depends on the ability to demonstrate his or her objectivity and relevant expertise in making the quoted statement. Evidence from authorities should be subjected to the following tests, which form the basis for argumentative challenges that may be used in debate.

*Is the Reference to Authority Definite?* A statement attributed to some authority gains credence because of the specific expertise of the individual who made it. That individual must be clearly identified in order for his or her expertise to be ascertained. Vague references to authority such as the following are common, but as Foster (1908/1932) declared, "worthless as proof":

"Scientists have concluded . . ."

"Many political observers agree . . ."

"A new study shows . . ."

"I could cite hundreds of authorities who say . . ."

The reference to authority must be definite and open to scrutiny.

*Is the Authority Capable of Giving Expert Testimony on the Matter at Hand?* Well-known people are not necessarily authorities and authorities are not necessarily well-known. Moreover, people with considerable expertise in one area may have no special authority whatsoever in another.

Why do we give special weight to the testimony of certain people on certain subjects, such as Julia Child on French cooking or Ann Lewis on the internal politics of the Democratic Party? "Not only because of their ability," as Foster (1908/1932) noted, "but because they have had special opportunities to know the facts whereof they speak" (p. 95). Julia Child's opinion on the Democratic campaign would be less valuable for evidentiary purposes, as would Ann Lewis' on vichyssoise.

As simple as this principle may seem, it is often compromised in the presentation of evidence. For more than a century, commercial advertisements have employed celebrity testimonials on behalf of their products. Sports stars, movie actors, musicians, former politicians, and other well-known celebrities extol the virtues of products (such as automobiles or breakfast cereals) utterly unrelated to the fields in which they may have some actual expertise.

Political opinions are also offered by sources outside their areas of real expertise. The pundits who make frequent appearances on television news and "talk" programs are liable to make widely publicized statements about almost anything, regardless of the limits of their own credentials in making such statements. The fact that they are "household names" does not always imply genuine authority.

Source qualifications are an essential part of the credibility of evidence. Such credibility must depend on the source's qualifications with respect to the subject matter at hand.

*Does the Authority's Statement Support the Claim?* Authoritative evidence consists of a statement made by one person used to support an argument made by another person. It is always wise to scrutinize the fit between the two and to ensure that the evidence says what it is claimed to say and proves what it is said to prove.

In his 1952 campaign for the vice-presidency, Richard Nixon was rocked by stories concerning a secret fund established for him by wealthy contributors. On September 23, Nixon issued a nationally televised speech to deny the three charges against him: (a) that the money went for his personal use; (b) that the fund was secretly collected; and (c) that contributors to the fund solicited favors from Nixon. In his efforts at self-vindication, he posed a tougher standard for himself than even the law required, "because it isn't a question of whether it was legal or illegal, that isn't enough." If any of these charges were true, he insisted, it would be morally wrong, even if legal. He then employed both personal testimony and authoritative evidence to dismiss these charges:

And let me say I am proud of the fact that not one of them has ever asked me to vote on a bill other than as my own conscience would dictate. And I am proud of the fact that the taxpayers by subterfuge or otherwise have never paid one dime for expenses which I thought were political and shouldn't be charged to the taxpayers.

Let me say, incidentally, that some of you may say, "Well, that's all right, Senator; that's your explanation, but have you got any proof? And I'd like to tell you this evening that just about an hour ago we received an independent audit of this entire fund . . . It's an audit made by the Price, Waterhouse, & Co. firm, and the legal opinion of Gibson, Dunn & Crutcher, lawyers in Los Angeles, the biggest law firm and incidentally one of the best ones in Los Angeles . . . And I'd like to read to you the opinion that was prepared by Gibson, Dunn & Crutcher and based on all the pertinent laws and statutes, together with the audit report prepared by the certified public accountants.

"It is our conclusion that Senator Nixon did not obtain any financial gain from the collection and disbursement of the fund by Dana Smith; that Senator Nixon did not violate any Federal or state law by reason of the operation of the fund, and that neither the portion of the fund paid by Dana Smith directly to third persons nor the portion paid to Senator Nixon to reimburse him for designated office expenses constituted income to the Senator which was either reportable or taxable as income under applicable tax laws."

Now that, my friends, is not Nixon speaking, but that's an independent audit which was requested because I want the American people to know all the facts and I'm not afraid of having independent people go in and check the facts, and that is exactly what they did. (in Ryan, 1983, p. 117)

But what did the legal opinion quoted by Nixon really prove? Nixon implied that it exonerated him from all charges; that it confirmed his personal denials of the three claims of unethical conduct lodged against him. But although the legal opinion offered by Gibson, Dunn & Crutcher may be relevant to the first charge (that the fund went for his personal use), it in no way supports Nixon's denials that the fund was secret or that contributors later sought favors from him. Furthermore, because it is simply an opinion on the *legality* of the fund, it fails to meet the higher standard of proof that Nixon himself had constructed ("it isn't a question of whether it was legal or illegal, that isn't enough") even for the first charge.

Nixon's trick is an all too common (albeit sometimes inadvertent) one: State an argumentative claim; read some evidence that sounds relevant; and pronounce the claim proved. Often, as in Nixon's speech, close scrutiny reveals a substantial gap between what is claimed and what is proved.

*Is the Authority Biased?*   In Nixon's defense of his expense fund, he relied on the reputations of Price-Waterhouse and Gibson, Dunn & Crutcher as objective, well-respected authorities with no stake in his electoral success. He offered their reports as credible and *independent* confirmation of his claims, signalling that he was unafraid "of having independent people go in and check the facts." Nixon recognized that his own testimony may have been suspect, because of his obvious self-interest in his own exoneration. He resorted to independent sources in order to defuse the charge of bias that might have been leveled against his personal accounting of the matter.

According to Robert Newman and Dale Newman (1969), "a bias, belief system, or perspective is a set of lenses which focuses the attention of an observer so that he perceives certain phenomena and disregards others, thus distorting reality" (p. 58). Such perceptual distortion may not be willful or recognized by those whom it afflicts; it may unintentionally influence the ways in which they perceive the world and, as a consequence, they may report about it in statements that may be used as evidence in a debate.

Bias varies in degrees and in the impact it should have on the evaluation of evidence. Although there is a sense in which all who have strong opinions on a given matter or even know a great deal about it are prone to bias (because human beings have a tendency to perceive things that confirm their beliefs and ignore those that do not), to dismiss as sources all those with such connections to the subject would be to unnecessarily impoverish the pool of evidence. In selecting a jury for the trial of Oliver North, potential jurors who had read or heard about the North case were dismissed for fear that they would be prejudiced. This left a jury pool consisting only of people so disconnected with the affairs of their own nation that they had heard and thought nothing about the most widely covered news story of the year.

Credibility is in the eye of the beholder. The perception that a given source has a bias or conflict of interest so substantial that it may invalidate or diminish the credibility of his or her statement is often a powerful source of refutation in debate.

There are three basic sources of bias that may lessen credibility. Newman and Newman (1969) have described these as: (a) having a material stake in the outcome of the dispute; (b) having an ego investment in the matter; or (c) having an ideological stake or perspective sufficient to distort one's judgment or expression.

People who will benefit in some material way from a particular outcome of a dispute may be seen as less credible when they present information to support that outcome. When the U.S. Surgeon General's report of 1963 concluded that cigarette smoking poses a significant health hazard, major tobacco companies formed their own scientific institute to study the claims. Unsurprisingly, scientists funded by the Tobacco Institute have consistently found there to be no causal relationship between smoking and ill health. These findings are less credible because they are produced by scientists who are dependent on the tobacco companies for their livelihood.

The drug Retin-A, originally designed as an acne medication, has been marketed in recent years as a wrinkle remover. The effectiveness and safety of Retin-A as a wrinkle remover has been demonstrated in a limited number of studies. When it was disclosed that the scientists who authored these studies and testified to the national Food and Drug Administration about their findings had in fact been funded by Ortho Pharmaceutical Company (the makers of Retin-A), the credibility of the studies was damaged.

Such biases may not be fully apprehended by the people subject to them. A doctor who testifies on behalf of a company that has underwritten his or her research may honestly believe that he or she has not been influenced by that relationship. Nevertheless, the demonstration that a quoted authority has a material interest in the issue will usually diminish the persuasiveness of the quoted statement.

Ego investments reflect the stake people have in maintaining their public reputations, but also the personal attachments people develop regarding policies they have helped create, agencies they have helped run, or studies they have conducted or championed. Most of us are prone to respond defensively when opinions, groups, or activities with which we have been involved come under criticism. "Those who originate ideas, who develop and publicize theories," wrote Newman and Newman, "acquire a parental affection for them," such that "subsequent confirmation of the theory will be exaggerated, disconfirmation played down." "Professors," they warned, "are especially susceptible to this disease" (p. 62).

Ideological bias appears even in highly reputable information sources, and is concealed at least in part by the frequent lack of ideological diversity in mass communications. As a result, modest differences of opinion among ideologically similar panelists on a television news show, for example, may give the illusion of balanced coverage. Investigative journalists Marc Cooper and Lawrence C. Solely (1990) conducted an extensive 2-year study for the University of Minnesota School of Journalism regarding the ideological range represented by experts appearing on network news programs.

> The role of these expert "news shapers" is to put complex national and world events into a context we can understand, to tell us what an event "really" means, or, often, to predict what course an evolving news story will take. And they claim to do it dispassionately, neutrally, objectively.
>
> After conducting a study of every network newscast from January 1987 through June 1, 1989, we found that correspondents and producers established a pattern of returning time and again to a very small group of the same experts. Indeed, our study found that less than one-fifth of all experts used accounted for more than half of the group's appearances on the air. And the cluster of experts most favored is remarkably homogeneous in its composition. They tend to be men rather than women, East Coasters rather than West, and Republicans (along with a few conservative Democrats) rather than critics of the political establishment. Also favored by television news

are ex-government officials (mostly from Republican administrations), and "scholars" from conservative Washington, D.C., think tanks who appear to be more steeped in political partisanship than in academic credentials. (p. 20)

People with strong and potentially distortive ideological convictions may regard themselves as utterly objective: Aspects of their belief systems that are questionable to others are simply "the way things *are*" in their own minds.

Source bias occurs in various forms and to various degrees. Detecting some measure of source bias does not usually *invalidate* the evidence (particularly since, as discussed earlier, *all* expert sources may be biased to some extent by perceptual distortions produced by the sheer depth of their involvement with the subject). Rather, the claim of significant bias is best used to lend comparatively greater weight to another, more credible source (who has presumably come to a different conclusion).

*Is the Authority Reluctant?* Reluctant testimony is drawn from sources who (intentionally or unintentionally) offer evidence *against* their own apparent self-interests. In the case of the doctors who testified regarding Retin-A after their research had been funded by the drug's parent company, the credibility of their testimony might be very *high* if they were to disclose *adverse* findings about the drug. In such an unlikely event, the doctors would be testifying in a way that is at odds with their self-interest by jeopardizing their continued financial support.

As Newman and Newman (1969) have written,

> *The greater the damage of his own testimony to a witness, the more credible it is.* The principle of reluctant testimony is ancient and esteemed in jurisprudence. It is assumed that sane individuals will not say things against their own interests unless such testimony is true beyond doubt. Thus, when Chinese Communists claim that a steel production quota has been overfulfilled, one must take it with a grain of salt. When, on the other hand, they state that the Red Guards are not obeying orders to go back to school, or that there is a food shortage in Shinsi Province, or that the enemies of the state are making trouble in Sinkiang, one can accept this as highly probable. Peking would probably dispense such damaging facts only if they are true. (p. 79)

In the continuing debate over whether the atomic bombing of Hiroshima was justified, an important role has been played by various forms of reluctant testimony. Many scientists who worked on the bomb and supported its use at the time have since changed their minds and engaged in public renunciation of their former positions. Because it is self-indicting (at least of their *former* selves), such testimony has a cachet of reluctance that may enhance its credibility. Convert testimony, however, may be suspect on other grounds (based on the very inconsistency of opinion it represents, as well as the notorious zealotry with which converts may express their new-found positions).

Excerpts from President Truman's personal diaries of the period, published after his death, have also yielded reluctant (if unintended) testimony. Of particular note is his diary observation prior to the bombing that he believed the Soviet entrance into the Pacific war would quickly produce a Japanese surrender *without the need for an American invasion.* "Fini Japs [sic] when that happens," he wrote. This statement is at odds with Truman's public justification of the bombing as necessary to gain surrender and prevent the need for a bloody invasion and has been widely used by latter-day opponents of the bombing precisely because it was made by the man who authorized the bombing.

Personal reluctance may be disclosed by a speaker to enhance his or her own credibility. In his defense of Great Britain's declaration of war against Germany in 1914, Gilbert Murray drew on his past reputation as an opponent of other wars to bolster his defense of this one:

> I have all my life been an advocate of Peace. I hate war, not merely for its own cruelty and folly, but because it is the enemy of all the causes that I care for most. . . . I opposed the war in South Africa with all my energies, and have been either outspokenly hostile or inwardly unsympathetic towards almost every war that Great Britain has waged in my lifetime. . . . I do not regret any word that I have spoken or written in the cause of Peace, nor have I changed, as far as I know, any opinion that I have previously held on this subject. Yet I believe firmly that we were right to declare war against Germany on August 4, 1914, and that to have remained neutral in that crisis would have been a failure in public duty. (Foster, 1908/1932, p. 97)

Murray made clear that his predilections are *against* the declaration of any war, thus making his support of Britain's declaration more remarkable and persuasive. An opinion reluctantly offered may be more credible than one offered in support of the speaker's own apparent self-interest.

These, then, are the five preliminary questions to be asked of evidence from authority:

1. Is the reference to authority definite?
2. Is the authority capable of giving expert testimony on the matter at hand?
3. Does the authority's statement support the claim?
4. Is the authority biased?
5. Is the authority reluctant?

These are, however, but preliminary challenges. Even credible authorities make statements susceptible to substantive challenges, particularly challenges supported by other authorities.

## EVALUATING STUDIES AND STATISTICS

Some evidence used in debate simply states an authority's conclusion on a given matter and relies on the high credibility of the source to gain acceptance of the argument. Generally, however, the most useful evidence supports the debater's conclusion by providing data – observations that the quoted authority is in a privileged position to make and draw implications from.

The two most common types of argumentative claims supported by evidence in debate are *generalizations* and claims of *causality*. For each, there are burdens that must be assumed by those who present them and challenges to be posed by those who would refute them.

### Generalization

A generalization is an inferential leap made from the observation of a limited set of verified instances to a more general conclusion. I may generalize from my experience in seeing a few films made by director $Z$ to the conclusion that director $Z$ is a poor filmmaker. My generalization may be faulty if I have improperly evaluated the films that I have seen or if the films by director $Z$ that I have not seen are markedly superior in quality.

Generalizations are frequently used to substantiate significance claims in debate. The Asia Watch report discussed in chapter 2 on conditions suffered by political prisoners in China, for example, is generalized from reports by individual prisoners. Not every prisoner was accessible to Asia Watch; not every case is documented. Instead, they offer reasons to believe that the experience of the individuals who *have* been able to report on their imprisonment are *representative* of the experience of most, if not all, other political prisoners.

The following sections discuss the three basic requirements that a generalization should meet.

*Instances Should Be Sufficient in Number to Support the Generalization.* If the first three Swedes that one meets smoke pipes, is it safe to conclude that all Swedes smoke pipes? Or, in a slightly more cautious statement, that the *typical* Swede is a pipe-smoker? We may, on the basis of this limited observation, only state with confidence that *some* Swedes smoke pipes. Any further generalization would be unwarranted.

Foster (1908/1928) likened such tendencies to that of an affluent and protected "child who believes that all people have enough to eat, that all dogs are gentle, and that all children have nursemaids" because s/he has experienced nothing else (p. 101). Yet sampling size errors are common enough in scientific studies, often prompted by the expense and difficulty of maintaining larger projects.

*Instances Should Be Representative.*   In order to justify a generalization from a sample to a larger population, one must believe the members of the sample population to be representative of the larger group. The Nielsen Ratings attempt to document which television shows are most watched by the general U.S. population. They are used to set advertising rates for programs and are highly influential in determining which television shows will remain on the air. Yet these powerful generalizations are based on surveys of the viewing habits of fewer than 2,000 households. Although the sample *size* is sufficient for generalization within an acceptable margin of error (comparable to those of the Gallup and Harris opinion polls), the *representativeness* of the Nielsen sample has been criticized. Minorities (especially Blacks and Hispanics), for example, are less likely to be asked to serve as Nielsen households and more likely to refuse if asked (Gitlin, 1983, pp. 49–52).

In the midst of the great wave of immigration to the United States at the end of the 19th century, U.S. Census authorities concluded, based on their 1890 surveys of prison inmate populations, that "the tendency toward criminality among the foreign-born was twice as great as among the native population." There were shown to be 1,768 prisoners per million of the foreign-born population in the United States, compared with 898 per million of the native-born population.

The difference, however, was entirely a figment of problems in comparison based on unrepresentative sampling. Young and middle-aged adults are far more likely to be imprisoned than children or the elderly, and during this period the proportion of adults among the foreign-born was markedly higher than among the native-born population. The demographics of the two population groups were not comparable. When demographically *comparable* groups of the two populations were compared, the results were quite different. A comparison of the number of male prisoners in 1890 per *million males of voting age* showed that the tendency toward imprisonment among native-born males was nearly *three times greater* than that for foreign-born males (Foster, 1908/1932, p. 195).

Racism continues to be fueled by faulty generalization in the form of stereotyping today. Consider the widespread (but false) notion that young African-American males are more prone to violence than their White counterparts. This notion has been given credence by prominent politicians, the news media, and law enforcement agencies, based largely on data produced by the U.S. Federal Bureau of Investigation. According to the FBI's *Uniform Crime Reports,* Blacks commit over half of the nation's murders, rapes, and negligent manslaughters, yet constitute only 13% of the population (Stark, 1990). The relative rate of incarceration for Black youths and White youths is 44 to 1. Such figures have supported damaging stereotypes of young Black males as violent threats to society.

After careful analysis of the data collection process, however, these figures and generalizations are less convincing. As Professor Evan Stark (1990) of Rutgers University has observed:

> The problem with using this information to draw conclusions is that its primary source–data on arrests and imprisonment–may itself be the product of racial discrimination. Our picture of black violence may be more a reflection of official attitudes and behavior than of racial differences. (p. A21)

Rates of arrest and imprisonment offer but one imperfect indicator of how many crimes have been committed and who has committed them. Most crimes are not reported and for many reported crimes, no arrest or conviction is gained. National surveys of crime victims may provide a better indicator of what crimes have actually been committed and by whom, because many victims respond to the survey who do not report crimes to the police. Data from the National Crime Survey provides a very different profile of the relative rates of violent crime by Blacks and Whites.

> According to the FBI, for example, the proportion of blacks arrested for aggravated assault in 1987 was more than three times greater than the proportion of whites. But the National Crime Survey, based on victim interviews, found that the actual proportion of blacks and whites committing aggravated assault in 1987 was virtually identical: 32 per 1,000 for blacks; 31 per 1,000 for whites. (Stark, 1990, p. A21)

What accounts for the discrepancies between the FBI figures and those produced through victim surveys? Victims appear to be more likely to report violent crimes involving Black perpetrators, and Black criminals who have committed the same offense as Whites are seven times more likely to be charged with a felony, according to Stark's research.

The cases reported in FBI data are not truly *representative* of the racial profile of criminals and are therefore a faulty basis for generalization about criminal proclivities of the different races.

*Exceptions Should Be Accounted For.*   The more absolute the generalization, the more susceptible it is to refutation through negative instances. When John Ruskin proclaimed that none of Shakespeare's characters is a hero (Foster, 1908/1928, p. 106), he issued an implicit challenge for an opponent to identify a single exception. The existence of but one exception, one hero among Shakespeare's characters, would prove Ruskin's generalization unwarranted. Ruskin could, however, account for a few exceptions by qualifying his claim (e.g., "few of Shakespeare's characters are heroes").

Foster (1908/1932) recommended the "habit of seeking exceptions" as a "staunch protection against hasty generalization, not only because of the tendency to overlook contradictory evidence, but also because the commonplace 'exceptions' may really be far more numerous than the conspicuous cases employed as proof" (p. 104).

The generalization should thus conform to the following three requirements:

1. Its instances should be sufficient in number to support the claim;
2. Its instances should be representative; and
3. Exceptions should be accounted for.

## Claims of Causality

Many of the most important claims in policy debate are about causes and effects. The affirmative team must demonstrate that their proposal will produce (or cause) certain benefits. If the action of their proposal is to remove or curtail some threat (e.g., banning the use of Pesticide $X$, or requiring that warning labels be placed on rock music recordings that contain violent lyrics), at least three levels of causal claims are involved:

1. The object of curtailment causes harm (pesticide $X$ causes cancer; violent lyrics provoke real violence by listeners);
2. Something causes continued use of the object despite its threat (farmers use Pesticide $X$ because it is cheap and effective; young listeners are attracted to violent lyrics); and
3. The proposal will cause the threat to be reduced or eliminated (banning Pesticide $X$ will reduce the incidence of cancer; warning labels will lessen violence among potential listeners).

All defenses of a proposition of policy ultimately rest on the proof of causal claims. Economist Julian Simon of the Cato Institute, for example, has urged that the United States increase the number of immigrants it accepts from other nations. His case for doing so rests on a claim of cause and effect: "More immigration can cut the [budget] deficit. . . . Increased immigration," he argued, "would augment the pool of young, skilled workers who pay high taxes and use few governmental services and hence swell the public coffers" (Simon, 1990, p. A33).

This argument is essentially identical to that made by Wattenberg and Zinsmeister (1990), as discussed in chapter 2. Unlike Wattenberg and Zinsmeister, however, Simon supported each step of his causal reasoning with statistical data and analysis. Immigrants, he demonstrated, tend to be substantially younger on average than the native population. Only 4% of immigrants are age 60 or older, whereas 15% of the current U.S. population is 60 or older. Younger workers will contribute more in taxes while consuming fewer government benefits (such as Social Security or Medicare payments). Therefore, he argued, increased immigration will cause the budget deficit to diminish.

Claims of causality have been at the heart of renewed efforts in the United States to expand the use of capital punishment. The most important effect claimed by proponents of the death penalty is deterrence: Executions of those who have been convicted of serious crimes, they argue, will prevent others from committing them. Chapter 1 described the refutation of this causal claim by Amnesty International, listing their reasons why the death penalty would *not* produce a deterrent effect. But in order to gain public acceptance of their position, opponents of capital punishment must do more: They must be able to successfully refute the major studies through which proponents have bolstered their causal claim. In their report, *When the State Kills . . .* , Amnesty International (1989) refuted the most influential and widely publicized of these studies, that conducted by economist Isaac Ehrlich:

> One of the few studies purporting to show that the death penalty does have a clear deterrent effect (and therefore often cited by those favouring the death penalty) was that of Isaac Ehrlich, a United States (US) economist. He used a statistical method known as "regression analysis" to examine the possible effect of executions and other variables on homicides in the USA as a whole between 1932 and 1970. During that period, and especially in the 1960s, homicides increased while executions declined. In an article published in 1975, Isaac Ehrlich concluded that his investigation had indicated "the existence of a pure deterrent effect of capital punishment" and suggested that "an additional execution per year over the period in question may have resulted, on average, in 7 or 8 fewer murders."
>
> This study has been extensively criticized on methodological grounds. Although Isaac Ehrlich's research included a number of variables likely to affect the homicide rate, he had omitted others which might also have done so, such as the increasing availability of guns. Crime in general had increased during the 1960s, but the rate of growth in homicides was less than that of other crimes against the person. The decline in executions could not have affected homicide rates in places where the death penalty had already been

abolished or fallen into disuse, yet the growth in homicides during the 1960s was as great in states that previously did not carry out executions as in those that previously did.

A panel comprising criminologists, statisticians, political scientists, psychologists, economists and other experts, established by the US National Academy of Sciences in 1975 to provide "an objective technical assessment" of studies of the effects of sanctions on crime rates, reported in 1978 that Isaac Ehrlich's analyses provided "no useful evidence on the deterrent effect of capital punishment". More broadly, the panel also found that "the current evidence on the deterrent effect of capital punishment is inadequate for drawing any substantive conclusions."

Some research has even suggested that executions may temporarily result in more homicides. Two US researchers analysed monthly homicide rates in New York State between 1907 and 1963, incorporating a wide range of controls. They concluded that there had been, on average, two additional homicides in the month immediately after an execution. They suggested that this momentary rise in homicides might be due to a "brutalizing" effect of executions, similar to the effect of other violent events such as publicized suicides, mass murders and assassinations. A month-by-month analysis of executions and first-degree murders in Chicago from 1915 to 1921 produced similar findings.

The authors refute Ehrlich's causality claim by arguing that:

1. Countercauses (such as increasing availability of guns) were omitted from Ehrlich's study and may account for the effects he discovered;
2. Anomalies (such as the fact that homicide rates increased at the same levels in states that had not previously committed executions as in those that had and then abandoned the practice) indicate that variables other than capital punishment are responsible for homicide rates;
3. A prestigious panel of experts reviewed and dismissed Ehrlich's findings; and
4. Other credible studies have produced findings opposite to those of Ehrlich (increased executions may *increase* homicides).

Claims of causality are of equal importance to the opposition in debate. In addition to refuting the causal claims of the affirmative, the opposition generally makes causal claims of its own. A disadvantage is a claim that adoption of the proposal will cause certain ill effects (e.g., "Increased immigration will cause job displacement among current residents"). In offering a counterplan, the opposition also relies on causal claims that: (a) An alternate proposal will generate (cause) greater benefits than will the affirmative's plan; and (b) Adoption of the affirmative's plan will cause these benefits to be sacrificed.

The causal claims of both sides in a debate should be subjected to certain tests, which form the basis of forceful refutation:

1. Could any other cause be responsible for the observed effect?
2. Is the assumed cause adequate to produce the effect?
3. Was the operation of the assumed cause prevented by any other forces? (Adapted from Foster, 1908/1932, p. 131)

Each side in any debate must understand the logical requirements of causality claims and be prepared to refute the causality claims of the adversary.

## WEIGHING EVIDENCE

On most important issues in any debate, *both* sides are likely to be able to generate strong arguments supported by authoritative evidence. The primary question to be addressed in extension of the arguments is, therefore: How should the audience decide between the two?

In 1989, a team of medical researchers from Harvard made headlines around the world when they announced their findings that, by taking an aspirin every other day, men are significantly less likely to be stricken by a heart attack. In November of that year, however, the headlines reported the contradictory findings of a study published by Dr. Anlia Paganini-Hill of the University of Southern California. Not only did aspirin not reduce the risk of heart attack, she claimed, but it increased the risk of kidney cancer and heart disease. Which study should be believed?

The chief author of the Harvard study, Dr. Charles Hennekens, defended the superiority of his study by comparing the methods by which the two studies were conducted. The California study, he observed, was based on observations of a group of elderly members of a retirement community. The subjects themselves decided whether or not to take aspirin and when, then answered questionnaires about their use patterns. Hennekens contrasted this procedure with that employed in his study, in which the participants (all of whom were physicians) were assigned to take either aspirin or a placebo, with neither subjects nor researchers knowing which was which until the study was over.

In order to defend his study as more reliable, Dr. Hennekens explained how the different results of the two studies might be explained by the differences in their procedures.

Dr. Hennekens said it was crucial in such studies to make sure that results were not skewed by unanticipated factors that might lead some participants to choose to take aspirin regularly. For example, results might be misleading if those who decided to take aspirin were more likely to be heavy, to smoke more cigarettes or to have high blood pressure than those who decided not to take aspirin. Analyses to correct for those kinds of factors were not reported by the California team. (Altman, 1989, p. 8)

Hennekens focused on a crucial difference between the two studies – whether the subjects may decide when to take the aspirin or are administered it on a regular basis – and explained why it might distort the findings of his rival.

Inexperienced debaters may shy away from direct comparison of evidence. When an opponent raises an argument supported by evidence, the inexperienced debater may simply respond with counterevidence supporting the opposite view and think the job has been done. In such an instance, the job of deciding which evidence is better is left entirely to the audience. No wise debater would take such a gamble; he or she would instead *compare* the two bodies of evidence and explain why the evidence supporting his or her own side is superior to that offered by the opponent.

Weighing the quality of one body of evidence against another is difficult, and often pursued incorrectly. Certain obvious differences between bodies of evidence (such as the *quantity* of evidence submitted or the *dates* of the evidence) may be seized upon for comparison, yet frequently offer little real guidance in choosing between them. Having twice as many pieces of inferior evidence does not constitute superior proof. A more recent piece of evidence may or may not be more valuable, depending on whether or not relevant conditions have *changed* in the period since the earlier evidence was issued.

In order to resolve conflicts between bodies of evidence, it is best to:

1. Explain *why* your evidence is superior;
2. *Account* for the differences between them (e.g., differences in methodology, definitions, statistical flaws, or characteristics of the authority cited); and
3. If one body of evidence cannot be clearly established as superior to another conflicting body of evidence, explain how this impasse should affect the evaluation of the debate.

James Q. Wilson (1990) employed this last technique in the conclusion of his case "Against the Legalization of Drugs." He acknowledged the existence of persuasive evidence used by his opponents to downplay the ill effects of legalization (such as increased drug use) and to claim sizable benefits (such as decreased crime). In the course of his argument, Wilson denied these claims for legalization and supported his denials with strong evidence and reasoning. Still, at the end of the dispute, he recognized that his audience might yet entertain doubts about which side's evidence is most convincing and therefore constructed a reason why, faced with uncertainty produced by conflicting evidence, his side should prevail.

> No one can know what our society would be like if we changed the law to make access to cocaine, heroin, and PCP easier. I believe, for reasons given, that the result would be a sharp increase in use, a more widespread degradation of the human personality, and a greater rate of accidents and violence.
>
> I may be wrong. If I am, then we will needlessly have incurred heavy costs in law enforcement and some forms of criminality. But if I am right, and the legalizers prevail anyway, then we will have consigned millions of people, hundreds of thousands of infants, and hundreds of neighborhoods to a life of oblivion and disease. (Wilson, 1990, p. 28)

Wilson resolved the evidentiary conflict by comparing the risks associated with each side being right or wrong. Given such uncertainty regarding the effects of legalization, he asks his audience, can we afford to take the risk that its proponents are wrong?

Because evidence is the building block of arguments and arguments from the two sides in a debate clash, many debates are likely to present conflicts of evidence that somehow each side must seek to resolve.

## ETHICAL USES OF EVIDENCE

When a debater introduces evidence into a controversy, he or she does so premised on the audience's confidence in the debater's honest representation of these materials. Care in the accurate representation of evidence is a matter of personal honor; the value of debate (and, indeed, all forms of scholarship) depends on the good faith of its participants in abiding by certain standards of evidence. The perception that a debater has violated ethical standards governing the use of evidence may reverberate beyond the specific violation. Once a debater is discovered to have engaged in hyperbole on one matter, for example, his or her representation of other matters may become suspect. This is, of course, damaging both to the reputation of the debater and to his or her prospects for success in the debate.

In presenting evidence, one should invite and enable scrutiny of one's sources.

*Full Bibliographic Citations Must Be Provided on Request.*   All pieces of evidence read in a debate, whether in the form of evidence cards, briefs, or portions of a scripted speech, must be accompanied by full bibliographic citations (including name of publication, full date, and page number). In the early 1950s, Senator Joseph McCarthy caused a national sensation by claiming to have evidence of "numerous known-communists" employed in the U.S. State Department (although the actual number of communists he claimed to exist changed from speech to speech). At press conferences, he would wave sheets of paper that he claimed contained the names, yet these sheets and the sources of the information they supposedly contained were never revealed nor subjected to critical scrutiny.

Full citations are essential because they enable others to better evaluate the quality of the source and to confirm the accuracy and context of the evidence you have quoted from it.

*The Original Dates of Reprinted Materials Should Be Cited.*   As previously noted, the date on which an authoritative statement was issued may sometimes be important to the assessment of evidence. Sometimes, however, statements originally made on one date are quoted or reprinted in another publication at a later date. In anthologies that compile essays from various sources, for example, an essay originally published in 1988 might be reprinted in a 1992 book. If in quoting from this essay, the date of the statement were cited as 1992, this would be inaccurate and unethical.

*Source Qualifications Must Be Provided for All Authoritative Testimony.*   Arguments supported by authoritative testimony should carry no more weight than an unevidenced assertion unless the authority cited is credible. This credibility depends on the source's qualifications to make the quoted judgment. In entering a piece of evidence into the dispute, the debater assumes a responsibility to submit that evidence and its source to scrutiny.

*Evidence Must Not Be Quoted Out of Context.*   When an author's statement about some subject is cited in a debate, that statement should represent the author's actual opinion about the matter in question. Authors often summarize positions with which they disagree, then later refute these positions. In Christopher Hitchens' (1987) book, *Imperial Spoils,* he summarized the controversy surrounding demands that the British Museum return the marble friezes that Lord Elgin removed from the Greek Parthenon in the early 19th century. Although Hitchens favored return of the marbles to Greece, he explained the reasons his opponents have offered for retaining them. Thus, he identified the argument that return of the marbles would set a precedent for denuding the collections of other museums. This was not, however, Hitchens' *own* view, and he subsequently refuted it. To quote Hitchens' statement that the return of the marbles would set a bad precedent as if it were his own would be a serious misrepresentation, unethically using Hitchens' credibility as an authority to support a position diametrically opposed to his own.

The actual context of evidence must be preserved.

*The Substantive Integrity of Quoted Material Must Be Preserved.* There is sometimes a temptation to "improve upon" a quotation gleaned from research by making the author's claim a bit stronger, less ambiguous, or otherwise more supportive of one's own position. Debaters may find the qualifiers (through which a source seeks to limit or hedge a claim) frustrating. Particularly in the reporting of scientific findings, authorities are generally careful to qualify claims, using such phrases as "it is possible that ... ," or "*one* explanation is ..." or "assuming that $x$ is not so, then ..." to introduce a note of proper scientific caution.

It may be tempting to remove such qualifiers in the process of quotation. Any such "improvements," however, are unethical distortions that overstate the degree of certainty with which the original claim was made.

*Do Not Make False Claims About the Evidence.* Evidence does not make arguments in debate; it supports them. The debater must interpret the evidence, explain its meaning and impact on the debate. Such interpretations are prone to abuse, especially in the form of hyperbole, in which the strength or significance of evidence is exaggerated. Thus, a piece of evidence citing "worrisome economic indicators" becomes "proof" that "we are on the brink of a recession" or evidence documenting that "many citizens of Hiroshima were employed in military industries" becomes "proof" that "Hiroshima was a military base."

Not only is hyperbole unethical, as a willful misrepresentation, but it also backfires. When detected by an audience or judge, an exaggerated claim on one point may undermine the credibility of the speaker on other matters.

A similar problem often arises when a debater in one speech refers to a piece of evidence read in a prior speech. In recounting tales of fishing trips, the fish one has caught tends to become larger with each retelling. So it is in debate, when a piece of evidence cited in one speech may be described in subsequent speeches as more significant or certain than it really was.

These guidelines for the ethical presentation of evidence simply state the assumptions that listeners must make in order to give a piece of evidence credence (e.g., its contextual accuracy) and the obligations (such as the provision of full bibliographic citations) that advocates must shoulder in order to permit full scrutiny of the ideas and information that form the substance of debate.

## CONCLUSION

Through research we gain a more thorough understanding of the issues we debate and the authoritative support we need in order to make our arguments more convincing. Participation in debate teaches a strategic approach to research that will prove invaluable in other scholarship—an approach that is based on advance understanding of the topic, informed choices among available resources for research, selection of relevant data, and the ability to organize and use materials gleaned from research in the construction of arguments.

Because each side in a debate may be expected to have bolstered its case with evidence gained through research, debaters must be able to assess and refute the evidence used by their opponents. All evidence, a debater soon learns, is not created equal. Authorities differ in their expertise and objectivity; statistical analyses differ in the care with which data is collected and interpreted. Debaters must learn to weigh conflicting evidence and explain why one is better than the other or, if this is not possible, to explain the implications of such uncertainty.

# ARGUMENT ANTICIPATION AND BRIEFING

## ANTICIPATION

Before you debate against an opponent, you should debate against yourself. Adopt the viewpoint of your opponent and think strategically from the opponent's perspective. Examine your position from the critical perspective of your adversary. It is only by coming to know the strongest arguments and strategies that your opponent *might* make in support of his or her position that you will truly be prepared to debate. The process of argument anticipation is the cornerstone of strategic planning for debate and the key to the success of most outstanding debaters.

In preparing for the 1988 nationally televised debate between the candidates for the office of vice president of the United States, Senator Lloyd Bentsen's campaign staff drew up lists of issues they thought might arise in the debate. Having done so, the campaign staff members framed these issues as questions and rehearsed for the debate by asking them of Bentsen. His answers were then discussed, as the staff members wondered: "What other answers might be made?" "Which of these are the *best* answers?" and "How could we best support these answers with examples and other evidence?"

In addition to answering the individual questions, Bentsen also wished to emphasize certain basic themes in the debate. Two themes, or overarching arguments, were deemed to be of particular importance: that he was far more qualified than his opponent (Senator Dan Quayle) to assume the office of president should that become necessary; and that his views and record on a variety of issues were in accord with that of his running mate, Michael Dukakis (a point of some contention during the campaign and one that Bentsen's campaign staff believed might be used as a strategic ploy by Quayle in the debate). Therefore, in selecting the best responses to individual issues, Bentsen's campaign staff looked for ways in which to connect them with the larger themes he hoped to stress.

Although neither Bentsen nor Quayle took notes with them to the podium for the debate, both had made great efforts beforehand to anticipate and prepare to counter the arguments, evidence, and strategies that the other might employ. The Bentsen staff, for example, had studied recordings of many of Quayle's campaign speeches. One of the things they discovered was that Quayle often quoted and referred to the late (Democratic) president, John F. Kennedy, particularly in order to compare Quayle's youth and relatively short career in the Senate to those of one of America's most popular presidents. According to staff member Robert Shrum, this Quayle tactic angered Bentsen and in their briefing sessions prior to the debate, they plotted a strategy to counter it.

The opportunity to use this strategy came when, in response to a question regarding his qualifications for the office, Quayle responded by saying: "I have as much experience in the Congress as Jack Kennedy did when he sought the Presidency." Bentsen then rebuked him: "Senator, I served with Jack Kennedy. I knew Jack Kennedy. Jack Kennedy was a friend of mine. Senator, you're no Jack Kennedy." Quayle was stunned, and found himself unable to generate a substantive response. Bentsen's became the most quoted line in the campaign and lent weight to the chief issue pressed by the (ultimately unsuccessful) Democratic ticket. But although it appeared to be spontaneous, Bentsen's devastating comment was in fact the result of successful anticipation prior to the debate. He and his campaign staff were able to predict an important argument that Quayle would make and prepare a response that not only snuffed the issue, but resonated with the larger theme Bentsen hoped to stress: comparative qualifications for the Office.

Debate is in some ways similar to chess. Players who contemplate one move at a time will almost always lose to players who have been able to look several moves ahead. The best players will map out the various moves available to them, foresee the moves the opponent could make in response to each, the alternative moves that might be made in response to *those*, and so on.

Anticipation is equally important in debate. For every argument one plans to make, the following questions should be answered: "What will *they* say when I say that?" and "What will *I* say *then?*"

The strategic and intellectual advantages of thorough anticipation are several-fold. Fundamentally, it is only by coming to understand the strongest case that can be made for one's opponent that one can have genuine confidence in one's own position. As John Stuart Mill (1859/1947) declared in *On Liberty:*

> The greatest orator, save one, of antiquity, has left it on record that he always studied his adversary's case with as great, if not still greater, intensity than even his own. What Cicero practiced as the means of forensic success, requires to be imitated by all who study any subject in order to arrive at the truth. He who knows only his own side of the case, knows little of that. His reasons may be good, and no one may have been able to refute them. But if he is equally unable to refute the reasons on the opposite side; if he does not so much as know what they are, he has no ground for preferring either opinion. (p. 36)

## Strategic Value of Anticipation

As Mill recognized in his commendation of Cicero's example, there are also great strategic advantages to such anticipation. A prominent lawyer once emphasized this strategic advantage by taking Cicero's suggestion one step farther: "If I have only one side of the case to study before the trial," he pleads, "let it be that of my opponent." Why? Because debates are clashes between competing positions; successfully refuting one's opponent's claims enhances the status of one's own position. Your own best arguments will be for naught unless they can be shown to be superior to those of your opponent. The most successful debaters are those who have anticipated the strongest arguments their opponents might employ and who have prepared still stronger responses to deliver against them.

In England, as in the United States, the battle for women's suffrage raged for decades in the lecture hall, the pub, the legislature, the home, and elsewhere. In a lecture delivered at the New Hall in Tavistock, on March 11, 1871, suffragist Millicent Garret Fawcett addressed the "Electoral Disabilities of Women." Although she was an advocate of women's suffrage, she structured her speech (and, correspondingly, her preparation for the speech) around a list of "the principal arguments urged against the removal of electoral disabilities of women." She began by describing the 13 most important arguments used by her opponents and presumably embraced by at least some in her audience:

1. Women are sufficiently represented already by men, and their interests have always been jealously protected by the legislature.
2. A woman is so easily influenced that if she had a vote it would practically have the same effect as giving two votes to her nearest male relation, or to her favorite clergyman.

3. Women are so obstinate that if they had votes endless family discord would ensue.
4. The ideal of domestic life is of a miniature despotism: one supreme head, to whom all other members of the family are subject. This ideal would be destroyed if the equality of women with men were recognized by extending the suffrage to women.
5. Women are intellectually inferior to men.
6. The family is woman's proper sphere, and if she entered into politics, she would be withdrawn from domestic duties.
7. The line must be drawn somewhere, and if women had votes they would soon be wanting to enter the House of Commons.
8. Women do not want the franchise.
9. Most women are Conservatives, and, therefore their enfranchisement would have a reactionary influence on politics.
10. The indulgence and courtesy with which women are now treated by men would cease, if women exercised all the rights and privileges of citizenship. Women would, therefore, on the whole, be losers if they obtained the franchise.
11. The keen and intense excitement, kindled by political strife, would, if shared by women, deteriorate their physical powers, and would probably lead to the insanity of considerable numbers of them.
12. The exercise of political power by women is repugnant to the feelings and quite at variance with a due sense of propriety.
13. The notion that women have any claim to representation is so monstrous and absurd, that no reasonable being would ever give the subject a moment's serious consideration. (Lewis, 1987, pp. 101–102)

Fawcett then proceeded to refute each in turn. All of these arguments and sentiments had been heard and read in the public discussion of the suffrage issue. Fawcett's comprehensive list of her opponents' arguments reflected her preparation to meet them, having marshalled the strongest possible responses to each.

As Fawcett recognized, not all of these arguments were likely to be used by any one speaker of the other side (Arguments 2 and 3, for example, being contradictory). It is nevertheless wise to prepare to meet such arguments, even if they do not arise in a given debate. If one is prepared to meet the strongest objections one *might* face, one will be able to advocate the position with greater confidence. As William Trufant Foster (1908/1932) explained:

It does not matter, for purposes of finding the issues, what your opponent may or may not say on the question. The issues are there irrespective of any opponent, and if you find them all, you will not be surprised by any relevant argument your opponent may present. (p. 16)

In an actual debate, Fawcett would also have been likely to encounter some unexpected arguments, examples, or variations on familiar ones.

Even the best efforts to anticipate an opponent's arguments in advance of the debate will usually fail to predict at least *some* of the arguments that are actually made or the precise ways in which they are supported. But anticipation is of great value even in these instances. Having anticipated and prepared to answer *some* arguments that the opponent actually makes in the debate, one is able to devote more attention during the debate to the arguments that had *not* been anticipated, or that have been argued in ways somewhat different from those anticipated.

Fawcett's preparation to meet and defeat her opponents was centered around an examination of the controversy from *their* perspective. In addition to the strategic advantages of such preparation for debate, it also helped her understand and address the possible (and unspoken) reservations her audience might hold.

## The Process of Anticipation

The process of anticipation should be a central feature of the preparation for any debate. Several steps that should be taken to ensure that this process is as efficient and comprehensive as possible are discussed here.

*Understand the Origin and History of the Question.*   Topics selected for debate normally reflect a preexisting controversy. These topics may have arisen from specific recent events. For example, the question of whether the United States should extend its designation of China as a "Most Favored Nation" for international trade arose in 1990 because of the Chinese government's human rights abuses in the treatment of dissidents in Tiananmen Square (June 1989) and afterward. In preparing to debate the question of continuing "Most Favored Nation" trade status, one should be prepared to discuss the charges against the Chinese government that gave rise to the dispute, the historical successes and failures of sanctions against other nations, and the standards employed in previous decisions to award or rescind "Most Favored Nation" status to trade partners, for example.

*Define the Terms of the Question.*   As discussed in chapter 2, one must locate the key terms in the proposition and determine the various ways in which these key terms might be defined. Understanding the origins and history of the controversy will help you to identify alternate definitional approaches and to defend particular definitions as superior in the context of the preexisting dispute.

If one is preparing to defend the proposition, he or she has the ability to select a definition, construct a case based on that definition, and anticipate and prepare to refute the arguments one expects to be made against that case. If, on the other hand, one is preparing to oppose the proposition, one must often be prepared to meet a variety of cases based on a variety of possible definitions of key terms.

A narrowly drawn topic (such as the "Most Favored Nation" status argument) minimizes the uncertainty for the opposition as to what sort of case they will meet (and, as a result, generally produces better debates). A more broadly drawn topic, such as "Resolved: that illicit drugs should be legalized," requires (unless some clear understanding has been reached by the two sides prior to the debate) that the opposition prepare for a huge and diverse range of potential interpretations. Because the nature of the "illicit drugs" is not specified in the topic, the affirmative might or might not argue for the legalization of any given drugs (e.g., marijuana, cocaine, LSD, heroin) prone to abuse. Moreover, because the term *drug* also includes pharmaceuticals, the affirmative may choose to recommend the legalization of such drugs as RU-480 (the so-called "abortion pill") or an experimental AIDS medication in addition to or instead of the "recreational" drugs that would first come to mind. Finally, because the term *legalization* may be defined to include or exclude limits on legally permissible quantities and sales to minors, for example, the opposition must be prepared to debate an enormous range of possible permutations, uncertain as to which of its prepared arguments will prove relevant in any given debate. Alternatively, the opposition may craft argumentative strategies (such as the claim that legalization of a drug increases its use) that will apply generically to most, if not all, potential cases for the proposition.

*Identify the Main Issues of the Controversy.* In preparation to debate a more narrowly drawn proposition, such as "Resolved: that the atomic bombing of Hiroshima was justified," brainstorming may begin by simply identifying the major arguments for each side. In all the thousands of books and articles written on both sides of the Hiroshima question for the past half-century, the major arguments for each side boil down to the following positions:

## FOR THE PROPOSITION

1. The atomic bombing saved lives by shortening the war and eliminating the need for an invasion of Japan.
2. The bombing provided just retribution for war-time actions of the Japanese.
3. The bombing was necessary to check Soviet expansion, by:
   A. Ending the war before the Soviets could claim more spoils; and
   B. By demonstrating U.S. power to the Soviets and a willingness to use it, thus enhancing deterrence.

4. The bombing enhanced prospects for international control of atomic weapons in the immediate post-war period, providing a demonstration of the bomb's destructiveness.

## FOR THE OPPOSITION

1. Superior alternatives existed to the bombing (e.g., non-lethal demonstration, negotiation, etc.)
2. The bombing of Hiroshima was an unjustified attack on civilian non-combatants.
3. The bombing employed an immoral weapon, cruel and unusual in its effects.
4. The bombing was unjustified because it was the product of tainted decision making (tainted by racism, improper consideration of important issues, or other factors).

Although there are many individual arguments on the Hiroshima topic, virtually all fit within one of the eight basic claims just listed. Knowledge of this list enables more efficient research and strategic planning. One could now begin the process of asking: "How would they support that?" "What could we say against that?" and "What will they say in response?"

Use the list of components for the case structures of both sides (provided in chapter 2) to brainstorm the arguments that might be made. If the question is a broader proposition of policy (such as "Resolved: that the United States should significantly increase its exploration of outer space") for which many different policy interpretations might be made, begin by imagining what specific courses of action might be endorsed and by identifying all of the potential benefits that might be claimed from each of them. For what appear to be the strongest case approaches, then brainstorm possible lines of response to the advantage claims and the potential disadvantages that might be attributed to the policies.

This list of arguments for the two sides serves several functions: It allows one to choose the strongest possible approach from among the various argumentative alternatives; it enables preparation to refute the arguments one's opponent might make; and it provides a list of specific subjects for efficient research.

*Research the Arguments You Anticipate Meeting or Making.* Although the process of research is explored in more detail in chapter 3, it is important to note at this juncture the role that research plays in the process of argument anticipation and at what point in the process of preparation one should undertake research. One should *begin* the task of research (as opposed to preliminary background reading on a topic) with a clear list of arguments that one wishes to support or refute with evidence. This enables the processing of far greater amounts of information through knowledge of what is argumentatively useful and pertinent and what is not. If you discover an argument in the literature that you had not previously thought of, you may evaluate its relative merit and decide whether or not to incorporate it into your position and research.

*For Topics That Are Debated More Than Once, Keep an On-Going List of Arguments Used Against You.* In most debates, you will face some argument or approach that you have not anticipated or heard before. If you will debate the topic and case again, add these arguments to your list of those to research and prepare for. This is obviously of particular importance when these arguments have been effective against you. One should never lose to the same argument twice. If you *do*, even after having prepared the best possible responses, it is probably time to reconsider the viability of your position.

*After Anticipating Your Opponent's Arguments and Preparing Your Responses, Ask Yourself: "How Will They Respond to My Responses?" and "What Will I Say Then?"* Normally, the debate will not end when you have responded to the anticipated argument of your opponent. They will then respond in turn, and you must be prepared to extend your arguments in the face of these objections. In preparation for this task, experienced debaters often hold back a powerful example, piece of evidence, or synthetic analysis for presentation in the rebuttal extensions of an argument, a process called *sandbagging*.

The systematic approach to argument anticipation is especially important when preparing to debate controversial matters of public policy, for which a clear argumentative history has been established in the public domain. Speakers who address the issue in later public debates are obliged to know and understand the major arguments used by others before them, because their audiences and opponents are likely to be aware of these previous discussions. In recent years, for example, many have argued that the ban imposed in 1988 on federal funding of fetal tissue transplantation for use in the treatment of Parkinson's disease and other disorders should be lifted. Those who advance this proposal should be aware of the primary argument that has been leveled against the procedure: that it will increase the incidence of abortion to supply the needed tissue. This was the stated rationale of the Reagan administration in imposing the ban on federal funding in 1988 and of the Bush administration (as expressed by Secretary of Health and Human Services Louis Sullivan) when they extended the ban in 1989.

In writing an essay advocating that the federal government lift the ban on funding for fetal tissue transplants, political columnist Charles Krau-thammer (1989) anticipated that some readers might argue that this might increase the incidence of abortion. He therefore prepared several strong counterarguments against this potential objection:

1. There is no evidence from 1987 (the last year in which funding for tissue transplants was permitted) that even a single abortion was moti-vated by the procedure;
2. The incidence of abortion did not *fall* in 1988, after the ban was imposed;
3. Even if the transplantation research did provide some inducement to abortion that, as with the potential inducement to suicide provided by the ability of suicides to donate their organs, "the inducement is so marginal that by any reasonable moral calculus it is far outweighed by the very tangible good that comes" from the procedure.

Thus, Krauthammer has prepared to answer one of the strongest and most likely objections he can anticipate being raised by opponents.

**Spikes**

But Krauthammer did more than prepare responses to the "increased abortion" argument. He crafted his own position in such a way as to weaken the applicability of the objection to his specific proposal. This strategy, which was described in chapter 2 as a "plan spike," is of general utility: The strongest positions in debate are those that have been forged in response to an opponent's strongest *potential* arguments. Knowing that there is a potentially devastating response to an argument one contem-plates making enables one to *change* the argument before presenting it, so as to minimize the effect of that potential response. In defense of a proposition of policy, one should endeavor to fashion the proposal in such a way as to avoid potential disadvantages, so far as possible.

In order to weaken the impact of the "increased abortion" argument, Krauthammer began by asking *why* the procedure *might* increase abor-tions – what incentives might conceivably be provided by the procedure for women to abort? One must come to understand the substance and reasoning of the potential objection before one can adequately address it. Having determined the potential incentives for increased abortions under a program of fetal tissue research, Krauthammer sought to eliminate these incentives through careful design of his proposal. He built into his proposal certain procedural safeguards for fetal tissue transplants that greatly weaken the force of the "increased abortion" objection: no payment for donation of fetal tissue (thus eliminating any monetary incentive to abort); no designation of recipients by the donor (thus eliminating any incentive to abort based on the medical needs of relatives or friends); and no discussion of the possibility of tissue donation with the women until *after* she has already decided to abort (so that the transplantation procedure does not figure in the woman's decision). Thus, Krauthammer joined the debate having considered his opponents' strongest objection and having tailored his position to defuse it.

When a policy has been crafted to obviate a potential objection, the clause through which this is achieved is called a *spike*. In volleyball, a spike shot occurs when one side has been able to anticipate the trajectory of the other side's shot and smash it back to them at great velocity from above the net. In debate, the spike similarly reflects one side's anticipation of the other's potential objection and preparation to return it with force.

## Preemptions

There is a temptation when one has anticipated the likely arguments of an opponent to attempt to preempt them before they have been made. Such preemption is usually introduced by saying, in effect, "My opponent is going to come up here and tell you that. . . ." Having described the predicted argument, the speaker then proceeds to argue against it, hoping to set up a critical screen through which the audience will then filter the opponent's argument if it is actually made.

There are some instances in which this strategy of preemption is sound. If one is arguing in a monologue (as in the case of Krauthammer's essay on fetal tissue research) or oration, one may not have the opportunity to hear or respond to the objections or doubts that an audience may harbor to one's own arguments. Krauthammer must imagine what objections his readers might raise and refute them in advance. The necessity for preemption also exists to some extent in legal advocacy, where opposing attorneys may find it strategically advisable to describe and criticize each other's cases in the opening arguments rather than waiting until the closing statements (after the opponent's arguments have been supported at length through submissions of evidence and questioning of witnesses) to refute them.

Another instance in which anticipatory preemption may be sound strategy is that in which the speaker faces an audience predisposed against his or her position and already familiar with opposing arguments. In this special case, the debater is really debating against the audience as well as against a formal opponent. If the debater in such a situation fails to raise and address the major objections to his or her position, even in an opening speech, these objections will form a silent rebuttal in the audience's minds to every argument the speaker makes. Until they can be set aside, the speaker can make no progress. Harvard professor George Baker

(Baker & Huntington, 1905), the great systematizer of American academic debate, advised that if the audience is predisposed against the debater and "familiar with the arguments of an opponent, the refutation should be placed first in order to remove the objections that the audience must surely have in mind and to put them into a more favorable attitude toward" the speaker's own case (p. 181).

In general, however, preemption of an opponent's arguments through advance refutation is a *strategic blunder*. Apart from the few instances just described, refutation based on anticipation is best left until *after* the opponent has actually made the argument in the debate. There are several reasons for this:

1. Advance refutation may give the opponent new ideas. Because one would presumably try to preempt the strongest arguments an opponent might raise, there is always the danger that one may be providing the opponent with arguments that had not occurred to him or her and are stronger than those that had.

2. If the preemptive arguments are very strong, they may deter the opponent from making the objection at all. Although this may sound desirable, it in fact is not. *It is in your interest to see that your opponent raises the arguments that you are best prepared to defeat.* To frighten your opponent away from making these arguments is to force your opponent to generate new and creative objections that you may not have anticipated. Some wily debaters go so far as to tempt their opponents to make certain arguments (usually by fashioning some apparent "weakness" in their case or support), just so they can soundly defeat the objection when raised or, better yet, use it for their own purposes.

3. Preemption gives the opponent an advantage in argument extension. By giving the best responses to an argument before the opponent's argument has been given, one affords the opponent an additional speaking opportunity in which to counter these responses.

Thus, although preemption of an opponent's arguments is sometimes useful in special circumstances, it is generally an unwise strategy. A more strategic use of anticipation and advance preparation for refutation may be found in briefing.

## BRIEFING

Having anticipated the arguments one's opponent is likely to make, one should then brainstorm possible responses to these arguments and gather evidence to support these responses. The strongest responses and evidence should be gathered together on *briefs*. A brief is an outlined set of arguments on a specific issue, each supported by reasoning and/or evidence. During an actual debate, the debater may consult his or her briefs in responding to an argument, selectively drawing from the arguments and evidence they contain.

Briefs are widely used in public political debate. Candidates preparing to participate in the American presidential debates have routinely relied on "briefing books" that anticipate and respond to the questions that may be raised in the televised encounter. The success of Ronald Reagan in the 1980 presidential campaign debates has been partly attributed by some analysts to the fact that his campaign staff had obtained a copy of President Jimmy Carter's briefing book before the debates, thus enabling the Reagan staff to prepare their own responses. (Fairlie, 1983, p. 28)

Briefs are especially important for participants in an on-going controversy, where arguments are likely to recur and to require in-depth analysis. In the contemporary abortion controversy, each side has grown quite familiar with the other's major arguments and examples and developed sophisticated responses to deal with them. Speakers representing the Right-to-Life organization, which seeks to restrict access to abortion, can anticipate most of the counterarguments they will face in any public debate because they have studied the previous speeches and writings of their opponents. In fact, not only do they know the arguments that their opponents will use, but in many cases they know the precise examples and study data that will be used to support these arguments. As a result, they are able to prepare, support, and refine the strongest possible answers to these anticipated claims and evidence. For example, in its films *The Silent Scream* (1985) and *Eclipse of Reason* (1988), the Right-to-Life filmmakers address their opponents' claim that opposition to abortion is based primarily on religious faith by marshalling scientific testimony from physicians and by employing the recently developed technology of ultra-sound imaging to depict the fetus as a human being sufficiently developed to deserve legal protection.

The opponents of the Right-to-Life organization are also devoted to the task of anticipating and preparing for the crucial issues in the dispute. One of the leading groups in *support* of abortion rights, the National Abortion Rights Action League (NARAL), has long supplied its spokespersons with information and arguments to help its spokespersons face the arguments of its opponents or to answer questions likely to be raised by audience members. NARAL has prepared two kinds of briefing books for its spokespersons:

1. **Concise response briefs,** designed for speakers who must face many potential issues and questions in a given encounter. The concise response

brief attempts to list as many of the opposition's arguments as possible, and to state succinctly the best one or two responses to each of them; and

2. **Detailed analysis briefs,** designed for speakers who need to prepare for individual issues in more depth. The detailed analysis brief will pertain to a single argument likely to be raised by an opponent, outline multiple responses to it, and marshall the best available evidence to support these responses.

NARAL's principal concise response brief is a five-page pamphlet titled *Choice, Legal Abortion: Arguments Pro & Con.* It lists 54 arguments, strategies, and examples that their opponents have relied on and offers succinct responses to each. As shown in Fig. 4.1, the opponents' arguments are stated in concise and recognizable fashion, phrasing them as the opponent might. The suggested NARAL responses are listed next to each opposition argument. This format allows the NARAL speaker to scan the

| *Anti-Choice* | *Pro-Choice* |
|---|---|
| **32** Abortion causes psychological damage to women. They suffer guilt feelings all their lives. | The Institute of Medicine of the National Academy of Sciences has concluded that abortion is not associated with a detectable increase in the incidence of mental illness. Some women experience depression and guilt feelings, but a higher percentage of new mothers suffer post-partum depression. That some women experience guilt is no reason to make abortion illegal for all. |
| **33** More women die from legal abortion than ever did from illegal abortion. Abortion is not as safe as natural pregnancy. And abortion greatly increases the incidence of miscarriage in future pregnancies. | Right-to-lifers only show concern for women's health when they can use it in their propaganda; they invent or exaggerate risks and document them with old figures from other countries. The Centers for Disease Control said the risk of dying from childbirth is 13 times that for abortion. CDC researchers have also concluded that today's abortion procedures will not adversely affect a woman's future reproduction, and have said, "the reality is that legalized abortion has had a definite impact on the health of American women (by providing them with a safer way to terminate their pregnancies than by either illegal abortion or childbirth)." |
| **34** There are too many late (after 12 weeks) abortions. Women shouldn't wait so long. | 91% of abortions are done in the first 12 weeks of pregnancy, and only 4% after 16 weeks. Tests showing birth defects are not done until the 16th week, and some women do not discover they're pregnant until this time. Most late abortions are done for health reasons. Ironically, restrictive laws pushed by right-to-lifers, such as mandatory parental involvement and cutoff of Medicaid for poor women's abortions, cause delay and lead to increased numbers of late abortions. |
| **35** The Supreme Court ruled that abortion on demand is legal for the entire nine months of pregnancy. | The Supreme Court ruled that states may prohibit abortion in the third trimester, unless a woman's life or health is endangered. Only .9% of abortions are performed after 20 weeks, and none after 24 weeks. After 24 weeks, an emergency condition, e.g. toxemia, of the woman could end in an induced premature birth, with survival of both mother and infant as its goal. |
| **36** With the central nervous system already developed, the baby is capable of feeling intense pain when it is killed in abortion. | The brain structures and nerve-cell connections that characterize the thinking and feeling parts of the brain are not completed until between the 7th and 8th months of gestation. Only after 30 weeks do the brain waves show patterns of waking consciousness when pain can be perceived. The reflex actions that are present before this stage do not indicate ability to feel pain. Abortions virtually never occur after 24 weeks. |
| **37** Fetuses aborted late in pregnancy and born alive are left to die or are killed by doctors. | Abortions near the point of viability are performed only in extreme medical emergencies when the woman's life is threatened. A tiny fraction of these cases result in live-born infants, who are given all care necessary to sustain their lives. |

*38*  We oppose amniocentesis and other medical techniques which are used to diagnose birth defects. These are "search and destroy" missions that can lead to abortion. Even imperfect human beings have the right to live.

Less than 3% of such tests result in abortion. The tests permit parents who know they are at risk of bearing a baby with birth defects to conceive, assured that if the test results are positive, they can abort and try again for a healthy baby. Before this technique was available, at-risk parents often aborted all pregnancies. It is heartless to deny parents access to medical technology that permits them to avoid giving birth to an incurably ill or severely retarded infant.

*39*  Doctors make large profits from legal abortion. Abortion has become a multimillion dollar industry. No wonder the medical profession opposes the "human life amendment."

Illegal abortions were big business, as back-alley practitioners were able to extract huge fees from desperate women. Organized crime syndicates ran the notorious "abortion mills." Doctors earn less for abortion than for prenatal care and childbirth, yet RTL uses the word "industry" for abortion providers in order to make this aspect of medical practice seem dirty. Only a small percentage of physicians perform abortions, yet most support legal abortion in the interest of good medical care.

**FIGURE 4.1.**   A concise response brief (Copyright © 1983 Westchester Coalition for Legal Abortion. Reprinted with permission).

left-hand column for an opponent's argument and then find at a glance the answers to it.

Although this format is adequate for the preparation to speak in most public forums, it would not provide sufficient depth of analysis to sustain a more focused discussion of a single issue or small range of issues. NARAL has thus developed a second set of briefing materials to prepare its speakers for such occasions. In many situations, the debate will not focus on abortion as a whole, but rather on a specific topic or legislative initiative, such as the requirement that minors seeking abortions gain parental consent or that access to abortion for specific reasons (such as sex selection or birth control) be prohibited. NARAL's detailed analysis briefs are contained in the booklet *Who Decides? A Reproductive Rights Issue Manual* (January 1990). In this brochure, NARAL identifies the leading issues and legislative initiatives that its spokespersons are likely to be called upon to address. For each of these issues and initiatives, NARAL's strategists have briefed what they believe to be the strongest responses and, when necessary, have cited authoritative evidence to support the responses.

One of the forms of restrictive abortion legislation for which NARAL has briefed responses is the move considered in the Alabama state legislature and elsewhere to make "abortion for the purposes of birth control" illegal. The NARAL brochure suggests three main lines of response:

**I. Attempts to outlaw abortions for sex selection or what is misleadingly labeled "birth control" are only anti-choice smokescreens to disguise the true goal of opponents of choice: to deprive all women of the right to decide whether or not to have an abortion. These proposals are a crude public relations ploy to trivialize the personal and serious reasons women choose to have abortions.**

– The decision whether or not to have an abortion involves deeply personal questions of values, religion, and conscience, and an intensely personal evaluation of a woman's overall life situation and responsibilities. For most women, the decision to have an abortion cannot be reduced to a single, simply stated reason, but reflects the complex realities of their lives.[5] . . .

5. Aida Torres and Jacqueline Forrest, "Why Do Women Have Abortions?" *Family Planning Perspectives*, vol. 20 (New York: Alan Guttmacher Institute, 1988): 169.

**II. The "birth control" label is used to give the false impression that because abortion is legal, women act irresponsibly and use abortion as an alternative to using contraception. In fact, the majority of women who choose abortion do so not as their primary means of birth control, but because their primary means of birth control failed.**

–The majority of women who obtain abortions were using a contraceptive method during the month in which they became pregnant.[9]

9. Stanley Henshaw and Jane Silverman, "The Characteristics and Prior Contraceptive Use of U.S. Abortion Patients," *Family Planning Perspectives*, vol. 20 (New York: Alan Guttmacher Institute, 1988): 158, 165.

–Fewer than 10% of women obtaining abortions say they have not used contraceptives, and of these, the vast majority are young unmarried women, particularly teens, who may only recently have begun having sexual relations.[10]

10. Henshaw and Silverman, "The Characteristics and Prior Contraceptive Use of U.S. Abortion Patients," pp. 165–66.

–During the first year that a couple uses a diaphragm or condoms as their method of birth control, about one woman in seven will nevertheless become pregnant; even among couples who use the Pill–the most reliable birth control method short of sterilization–one in sixteen women will become pregnant.

The rate of unintended pregnancies likely to occur during the first year of use of the following birth control methods is:[11]

11. Elise Jones and Jacqueline Forrest, "Contraceptive Failure in the United States, (Revised Estimates from the 1982 National Survey of Family Growth)," *Family Planning Perspectives*, vol. 21 (New York: Alan Guttmacher Institute, 1989): 109.

| | |
|---|---|
| oral contraceptives | 6.2 pregnancies/100 couples |
| condoms | 14.2 pregnancies/100 couples |
| diaphragm | |
| | 15.6 pregnancies/100 couples |
| the "rhythm" method | 16.2 pregnancies/100 couples |
| spermicides | 26.3 pregnancies/100 couples |

–The birth control methods with the lowest rates of unintended pregnancies are either irreversible, like sterilization, or have the highest risks of injury and disease, and may therefore be medically inappropriate for many couples.[12] For many women, preexisting health conditions may increase the risk or difficulty of using some contraceptive methods.

12. Howard Ory, M.D., Jacqueline Forrest and Richard Lincoln, *Making Choices: Evaluating the Health Risks and Benefits of Birth Control Methods*, (New York: Alan Guttmacher Institute, 1983).

**III. Once *any* reason for having an abortion is deemed unacceptable – including a reason such as sex selection that rarely, if ever, is a woman's actual reason – *all* women could be forced to publicly justify their reasons for seeking an abortion. As in the days of hospital screening committees and illegal abortions, a woman could be subjected to a humiliating official inquisition into the most intimate details of her life to prove that her reasons satisfy the governmental criteria. Consultation would be replaced by cross-examination.[13]**

13. Gene B. Sperling and Walter Dellinger, "Anti-Abortionists' Semantic Scam," *New York Times*, Feb. 7, 1990, p. A25.

– Prior to 1973, many states required any woman who wanted to have an abortion first to go through an arduous and demeaning process of testifying before and gaining the approval of a screening committee. If such approval were necessary today, anti-choice groups could be expected to try to pack the screening committees with doctors who would deny all requests.

– Any restriction – regardless of its scope – could cause all women to suffer this gross invasion of privacy. Whether the restriction involves a general ban on abortion with narrow exceptions (such as rape, incest, life and health), or it involves a reason that rarely, if ever, is a woman's actual reason (such as sex selection), any such "reasons" restriction could cause every woman to have to publicly reveal, support and defend her most intimate reasons for choosing to have an abortion.

Such detailed analysis briefs prepare NARAL speakers to address difficult issues. A NARAL spokesperson might use such a brief as background for lobbying a legislator, to prepare for testimony before a legislative committee, or to prepare for a public speaking appearance or televised debate. The briefs supply NARAL speakers with what the organization believes to be the strongest arguments and the specific facts, figures, and citations with which to support them. The NARAL briefs are revised periodically to include new issues and to incorporate more recent research.

Briefs are equally useful in academic debate. In order to best defend their case on a prepared resolution, debaters should make a list of all potential objections to their case and brief responses to each. These briefs should gather the best arguments and the evidence necessary to support them. Similarly, those preparing to *oppose* a set resolution should have brainstormed potential cases through which it might be supported, and briefed arguments against those potential cases.

The following is a sample brief constructed by a debater preparing to defend the proposition, "Resolved: that the atomic bombing of Hiroshima was justified." Opponents of the bombing frequently argue that there were superior alternatives to the destruction of a city. Because the development of the atomic bomb had been kept secret, the Japanese had no idea of the threat they faced. Some opponents have suggested that the United States should have offered a non-lethal demonstration of the atomic bomb by dropping it on Mt. Fuji, Nikko Forest, or some other uninhabited but visible area of Japan. This demonstration, opponents of the bombing argue, might have induced the Japanese to surrender without the loss of hundreds of thousands of lives in the atomic bombings.

A supporter of the bombing might prepare to answer this argument through the following brief:

### DEMONSTRATION = INFERIOR ALTERNATIVE

**1. A demonstration would fail to produce surrender.**
A. Any non-lethal attack would be less convincing than the real thing. When the demonstration proposal was considered, physicist Ernest Lawrence reported that "Oppenheimer could think of no demonstration that would be sufficiently spectacular to convince the Japs [sic] that further resistance was useless" (quoted in Wyden, 1985, p. 161).
B. Japanese would suspect trickery. Nobel laureate Isidor Rabi, quoted in Wyden (1985, p. 150): "Only the destruction of a town would be 'incontrovertible.' Who would evaluate a demonstration? The Emperor? He would never understand that new principles of physics had been mobilized. His warlords? They would suspect a ruse."
**2. Demonstration would jeopardize the military mission.**
A. It would sacrifice the "shock value" of a surprise attack, making the military mission less likely to produce surrender.
B. A demonstration would alert the Japanese defenses. If held in Japanese territory, it would give them a chance to defend against it. Arthur Holly Compton, Nobel prizewinner in physics, Chair of the National Academy of Sciences' committee on military use of atomic energy:

> If a bomb were exploded in Japan with previous notice, the Japanese air power was still adequate to give serious interference. An atomic bomb was an intricate device, still in the developmental stage. . . . If during the final adjustments of the bomb the Japanese defenders should attack, a faulty move might easily result in some kind of failure. Such an end to an advertised demonstration of power would be much worse than if the attempt had not been made. (quoted in Wyden, 1985, p. 160)

Staging a demonstration would have risked the success of the real bombing if it remained necessary.

C. Demonstration would have made the real bombing less shocking, hence less likely to produce surrender. Physicist Arthur Holly Compton: "If such an open test (over Japanese territory) were made first and failed to bring surrender, the chance would be gone to give the shock of surprise that proved so effective" (quoted in Wyden, 1985, p. 161).

**3. A demonstration would have taken more time to arrange, costing more lives by the delay.** Journalist Peter Wyden (*Day One*, 1985, p. 153): "Extra people would also die as a result of the delay inevitably caused just by making arrangements for a demonstration, even if the end of the war were to be postponed by only a couple of weeks." The U.S. should not be expected to suffer more casualties itself in the hopes of saving the lives of its enemies.

This brief outlines some of the strongest responses that have been made to the demonstration option, and identifies the authorities who voiced these objections in the actual decision-making process or in subsequent analyses. A debater using this brief should be prepared to "customize" its presentation in an actual debate: adapting the arguments and evidence on the brief to the specific circumstances of the debate at hand. Factors that necessitate adaptation include:

1. **The amount of time the opponent has spent on the argument.** If the opponent has simply said "We should have provided a non-lethal demonstration of the bomb by blowing up Mt. Fuji. The Japanese might have surrendered before we had to blow up Hiroshima" it would probably be unwise for the defender of the bombing to read the entire brief outlined earlier. If the defender used all of the brief, s/he would likely be forced to neglect some other argument by overkilling this one. Select the strongest and most succinct arguments from the brief that may be used when time is short;

2. **The particularities of the opponent's arguments.** Not every argument on this brief will be relevant to every way in which the demonstration option may be presented. For example, if the opponent were to argue that a demonstration should have been held on some U.S. territory rather than in Japan, argument 2B would be less powerful (it would be more difficult for Japanese defenders to thwart the demonstration), but argument 1B would be made more powerful—the Japanese might be more likely to suspect trickery if the demonstration were held in U.S. territory. The defender should adapt the presentation of arguments from the brief, deleting those that are irrelevant and explaining the specific relevance of others.

There are obvious strategic advantages in the construction of briefs.

Briefs may improve the quality of the arguments and evidence used in the debate. Because briefs are assembled in advance of the debate, more care can be taken in the selection of arguments used and in the research and selection of the best possible evidence to support them.

Another advantage, however, is often overlooked: Briefs save preparation time during the debate itself and *enhance* creative adaptation to new arguments. Instead of spending time during the debate constructing and supporting arguments that could have been prepared in advance, the debater who has composed thoughtful briefs prior to the debate is able to devote more attention during the debate to the analysis of *unanticipated* arguments or evidence and to making specific adaptations of prepared arguments to the specific contingencies of the debate.

Nevertheless, the use of briefs does entail certain potential liabilities. Once briefs have been composed on a given issue, there is a temptation to use them inflexibly, without regard to the specific nuances of the opponent's argument or evidence. Debate and public speaking are sometimes intimidating experiences, and an inexperienced debater may seek refuge behind the printed page, reading instead of debating.

But briefs should facilitate thinking in debates, not foreclose it. Similarly, problems with inflexible application of briefs are not necessary. The brief should be a *starting point* for refutation of an argument. Its arguments should be adapted to the specific instance at hand: excised when irrelevant or augmented when necessary. The brief should not be used as a substitute for creative thought during the debate itself, but rather as a way of freeing up preparation time to enable *more* creative and spontaneous analysis during the debate, looking for new insights, connections, and strategies. Briefs should, moreover, be an expression of the debater's *own* thoughts and strategic planning. Reading a brief composed by someone else compromises the intellectual value of debate and usually renders the brief-reader less able to adapt, extend, and selectively employ the arguments on the brief.

The proper use of briefs varies according to the nature of the debate. In a technical debate before an expert judge, a Congressional committee hearing, or a dispute conducted before a municipal planning board, for example, the speaker may wish to carry fully developed briefs to the podium and use them as speaking notes. This is especially true when the nature of the dispute is technical and when the advocates are expected to support their arguments with authoritative evidence. If a city planning board is considering several alternate designs for the construction of a new public library, an advocate for a specific design should be prepared to provide specific design details, backed by reputable cost estimates, environmental assessments, and studies of other similar facilities, for example.

In such a situation, briefs enable precise responses to questions and the accurate citation of the best available evidence to support them.

In other forms and forums of debate, however, reliance on briefs as speaking notes would be inappropriate. This is particularly true in public presentations, where less emphasis is placed on the reading of authoritative evidence and more attention is paid to the speaker's personal knowledge and analytical abilities, credibility, and persuasiveness. In such circumstances, it may be counterproductive to rely on prepared issue briefs. In a debate between political candidates, for example, a person who spoke from prepared issue briefs might signal that s/he has been prepared by "handlers" and is unable to respond to the issues on the basis of his or her own knowledge.

Issue briefs are nevertheless very valuable in preparing for public appearances and debates. The NARAL speakers may not take their briefing books to the podium with them, but they have used the briefs *in advance of the debate* to prepare for their appearance. Similarly, Senator Bentsen and most other major political candidates have relied on issue briefs in strategic planning and practice sessions *prior* to their debate, even if they do not carry them to the speaking platform. Advance briefing facilitates the understanding of an opponent's strongest arguments and the plotting of strategic responses to counter them.

# REFUTATION

Debaters often feel the need to disagree with every statement made by an opponent. Refutation becomes almost reflexive, as the debater contends every point. By so doing, the debater will often miss the most important opportunities for strategic gains: those instances in which your opponent's arguments may be *granted* and put to use in support of your side.

The first impulse on hearing an opponent's argument should *not* be: "How can I beat that argument?" Instead, the following questions should be asked on hearing an opponent's argument, and asked in this order:

1. Can I *use* that argument or evidence to support *my* position?
2. If I cannot use it, must I refute it? Is it relevant and consequential to the decision?
3. If so, does an argument I have already made on another issue adequately answer this one?
4. If not, how can I beat that argument?

## STRATEGIC AGREEMENT

Let us begin by discussing the circumstances in which a debater might profitably answer "yes!" to that first question, attempting to accept and *use* an opponent's arguments and evidence against them. This is a refutational strategy that requires a perspective on the overall positions of the two teams, employing strategic agreement with an opponent's *arguments* as a means of defeating the opponent's *position*. The principle is a simple one: **When possible, convert an opponent's arguments or evidence to your own uses.**

Some of the Asian martial arts, such as *aikido*, offer unusual advice on how one might deal with an attack or thrust from an opponent. In Western-style boxing, one might dodge, deflect, or simply absorb the adversary's blow. In other martial arts, however, the adversary's own power is used against him or her. Instead of meeting the blow, the expert will use the adversary's own momentum in the attack to carry him or her off-balance.

The 6th-century B.C. writings of Lao Tzu reflect this principle, as he admonished his readers to "yield and overcome."

> Under heaven nothing is more soft and yielding than water.
> Yet for attacking the solid and strong, nothing is better;
> It has no equal.
> The weak can overcome the strong;
> The supple can overcome the stiff.
>
> (Feng & English, 1972, p. 78)

This principle is of equal value in verbal battle.

**The strongest evidence and arguments in any debate are those that are coopted from one's opponent.** Such coopted evidence and arguments are damaging to the opponent because they clearly show him or her to have been outflanked, they demonstrate agreement rather than clash on the arguments in question, and most importantly, they are rather difficult for the opponent to refute, being his or her own statement.

There are several ways in which an opponent's own arguments and evidence might be turned against him or her. These cooptations may occur at the level of individual arguments or general positions. In either case, they are powerful strategies of refutation.

*Exploit Contradictions, Inconsistencies, and Unintentional Concessions.*   A contradiction exists when two mutually exclusive statements of fact are made by the same advocate. If one statement is true, the other cannot be. An inconsistency may refer not only to conflicting statements of fact, but also to philosophically incompatible claims.

Arguments made by an opponent should be analyzed not only in isolation but in relation to each other and to the larger context of the debate. Among the critical questions that should be asked of an argument made by the opponent are the following: "Is this argument consistent with the overall position or philosophy of the opponent?" and "Does this argument conflict with other individual arguments the opponent has made?"

When Representative Patricia Schroeder argued before an audience at Harvard Law School (March 16, 1987) for the reduction of U.S. troops stationed in Europe, she examined the various objections to troop reduction that had been raised by opponents. Assistant Secretary of Defense Richard Perle was among the most vocal opponents to this proposal, claiming that troop reductions would jeopardize European security in the event that a pending treaty for the reduction of intermediate nuclear forces (INF) was passed. Schroeder dismissed Perle's objection by *embracing* a contradictory claim that he had also made in the same speech.

> Richard Perle came before the Armed Services Committee last week to say that troop withdrawal was particularly bad if an INF Treaty is signed. At the same appearance he also pointed out that we would handle a ban on intermediate range nuclear missiles by placing the same number of warheads on short range missiles. Since short range missiles can go up to 600 miles, such a transition ensures that, insofar as the use of tactical nuclear weapons in response to a Soviet blitzkrieg is necessary, the military equation will remain about the same. (in Johannesen, Allen, & Linkugel, 1988, p. 249)

A common misconception regarding contradictions is that once a conflict between two arguments of a single advocate has been discovered, the proper thing for a judge or audience to do is to dismiss both. This makes no sense, however. If I say in successive sentences that "It is raining outside" and "It is not raining outside," the fact that they contradict does not mean that *both* statements are false. Generally, the respondent should choose which of the two conflicting statements is true (and, if possible, coincides with or is less damaging to the respondent's own position). The best strategy for exploiting a contradiction between two of an opponent's arguments is to embrace the less threatening argument in order to dismiss the more threatening one. Thus, when Rep. Schroeder exposed the contradiction in Richard Perle's arguments, she *embraced as true* (although not necessarily desirable) his claim that multiple warheads on short range missiles will functionally replace those cut from intermediate range forces, in order to defeat his argument that the prospect of an INF Treaty would make troop reduction dangerous.

Even the most skilled and careful advocates sometimes make contradictory and inconsistent claims. In the U.S. Supreme Court's 1989 ruling in *Texas v. Johnson*, overturning the defendant's conviction for burning an American flag, Chief Justice William Rehnquist wrote a lengthy but inconsistent dissent. Justice Rehnquist argued with great passion for the veneration of the flag as a unique and powerful symbol of our nation's ideals. He also claimed, however, that the act of burning a flag "conveyed nothing that could not have been conveyed and was not conveyed just as forcefully in a dozen different ways." These two claims, as Justice Brennan politely commented in a footnote, "sit uneasily" next to each other (quoted in Hertzberg, 1989, p. 4). If the flag is a uniquely powerful evocation of national ideals, then presumably its destruction poses a uniquely powerful challenge to those ideals or their achievement in practice. Moreover, if as Rehnquist argued, displaying the flag is an act of political speech (symbolically evoking patriotic ideals), then presumably so is burning it (providing a symbolic critique of those ideals).

Why do contradictions and inconsistencies occur? Mainly because of the temptation to use every possible argument on a given issue, without sufficient regard to the compatibility of these claims. This is particularly likely when two or more advocates speak on the same side of an issue, without sufficient prior coordination of their arguments. The alert respondent should search for contradictions and inconsistencies between the arguments of the two advocates and, in preparation for the debate, should anticipate likely inconsistencies.

But the arguments of an opponent need not be contradictory or inconsistent in order to be useful for the other side. Particularly when they have not fully contemplated the implications of their arguments, speakers may make claims or read evidence which can be "captured" or put to use by the other side, sometimes with devastating results. In the ongoing debate over the morality of bombing Hiroshima, for example, two prominent claims by opponents of the bombing are that: (a) Hiroshima was densely populated with civilians, therefore an impermissible target; and (b) The bombing was fueled by American genocidal race-rage, thus the product of immoral intentions. One answer frequently made to the first charge is that most "civilians" were engaged in the war effort, as home-based factories produced war materials, farmers raised food for the military, women raised future soldiers, and even the aged drilled for defense against invasion. But this answer (Japanese "civilians" were legitimate military targets) to the first claim of immorality may *strengthen* the *second* claim (genocide), because it amounts to a rationale for killing all Japanese. An opponent of the bombing should identify and explain the impact of this connection.

Whatever strategy is used to turn the opponent's arguments against them, one practical rule should be followed: The opponent's words or evidence should be *quoted*, specifically and accurately. In taking notes on the opponent's speech, the exact wording of the key phrase in the argument or evidence (along with a citation of the authority who produced it) you hope to turn to your benefit should be quoted whenever possible. The phrase should be set off with quotation marks to indicate that it *is* the exact wording of the opponent, and this fact should be made clear to the judge or audience in your subsequent reference to it.

*Accept the Opponents' Base Value, Standard, or Criterion and Use It Against Them.* Too often, the opposing sides in a debate are left comparing apples and oranges. Each side claims to maximize a different value that must somehow be compared to that of the other side. In the global battle over destruction of tropical rain forests, for example, an argumentative stalemate has long existed between developers and environmentalists. Developers claim economic benefit for desperately impoverished regions from the selling of rain forest timber and from conversion of the land to other purposes (such as cattle ranching). Environmentalists, on the other hand, claim that the destruction of the rain forest ruins an unique and intrinsically valuable ecosystem, threatens many species of flora and fauna, disrupts indigenous peoples, and contributes to global climatic changes. How does one weigh one set of values against the other?

Recently, some environmental advocates have adopted a new strategy. Instead of merely countering the developers' values with other values that must somehow be weighed against them, some environmentalists have sought to argue against the destruction of the rain forests *on economic grounds*. Their argument is that more revenue can be gained from an acre of rain forest left standing than from the deforestation and conversion of the same acre. They calculate the revenues to be gained from the production of nuts, rubber, and other goods from the standing forest, then (after computing the monetary costs of clearing the forest) compare this figure with the revenues to be gained from the felled timber and from agricultural or cattle production on the cleared land. Their conclusion that the former figure is *greater* than the latter has been used to bolster preservation appeals made to local governments.

Thus, these environmentalists' have accepted the value criterion of the developers and turned it against them. By the developers' own standard, these advocates claim, the rain forest should be preserved, not destroyed.

In their best-selling book *Getting to Yes: Negotiating Agreement Without Giving In*, Roger Fisher and William Ury (1981/1983) of the Harvard Negotiation Project outlined a strategy for resolving even the most bitter disputes. Disputes become bitter and difficult to resolve, they explained, because the disputants are tied to positions that seem unreconcilable. Fisher and Ury suggested that this impasse can often be broken if the disputants "focus on *issues*, not positions" and generate mutually acceptable *criteria* for evaluating the result of the negotiations, insisting "that the result be based on some objective standard" (Fisher & Ury, 1981/1983, p. 11).

Although debate is by nature a form of positional negotiation, Fisher and Ury's model of "principled negotiation" (negotiation that proceeds from basic principles that have been accepted by both sides) is of great strategic value. In debate, either side may strategically embrace the value criterion of the other side, thus forging a common principle by which the competing positions of the two sides may be evaluated. "Behind opposed positions," wrote Fisher and Ury (1981/1983), "lie shared and compatible interests, as well as conflicting ones" (p. 43).

In 1853, the American navy led by Commodore Perry forced Japan to open itself to foreign commerce. In the decade that followed, public sentiment against foreigners was rallied with the appeal to "Revere the Emperor; expel the barbarians," whereas those who supported greater contact with the West urged the Japanese to "Revere the Emperor; open the country." Although the positions of the two forces were quite different, their value criterion was the same: Which policy would better show reverence for the Emperor? When the Emperor himself became a strong public advocate of Westernization in 1871 (cutting his topknot, donning Western clothes, and eating beef), support for Westernization was consolidated.

Embrace of an opponent's basic values or interests is not always, of course, wise strategy. **It is in your strategic interest to embrace the value criterion of your opponent when you can demonstrate the superiority of your position or policy according to that criterion.**

President Reagan employed this argumentative strategy with great success in his public defense of his administration's increases in military spending against the campaign for a nuclear freeze. The proposal to freeze the American nuclear weapons arsenal at current levels gained enormous popular and legislative support from 1980–1982. Freeze proponents such as Dr. Helen Caldicott and Randall Forsberg sought to awaken Americans to the dangers posed by weapons escalation by breaking through the "psychic numbing" through which most people shielded themselves from thinking about the terrible consequences of nuclear war. The Reagan administration, in its most successful strategy against the freeze proposal, embraced the notion that nuclear war is awful and that the avoidance of nuclear war should be the standard by which the competing policies should be evaluated. Using the slogan "peace through strength," members of the administration argued that the best way to avoid nuclear war was to *build up* American nuclear forces. Such a buildup, President Reagan argued, would not only deter the Soviets but would induce them to negotiate, which would result in *reduced* rather than frozen levels of arms. A "build-up," he argued, was the best way to produce a "build-down." This argumentative strategy allowed the administration to embrace the ideal of the freeze movement ("peace"), to coopt the freeze movement's portrayals of nuclear holocaust, and to shift the debate from *ends* to the *means* by which shared ideals might best be achieved.

When the ABC television network in 1983 aired "The Day After," a fictionalized account of the effects of a nuclear attack on the United States, it had been preceded by great publicity. Advance reviews portrayed the film as a powerful attack on the Reagan administration's policies, showing the dangers of the military buildup that was underway. Influential supporters of the President's policies lambasted the network for airing what they perceived as one-sided propaganda. Sensitive to the outcry, ABC scheduled a panel of experts to discuss the film following its broadcast. Secretary of State George Schultz was the first panelist to speak. Instead of condemning the film as other opponents of the freeze campaign had done, he *embraced* its portrayal of nuclear disaster, saying, in effect, "That's exactly our point!" Schultz argued that the goal of the Reagan administration was to prevent events like that shown in "The Day After" from ever occurring.

The Reagan administration's policy of coopting ground from the freeze campaign proved highly successful, as freeze activist Pam Solo (1988) has observed in her history of the movement, *From Protest to Policy*. By 1982, despite the fact that he was presiding over the largest peacetime military buildup in American history, polls revealed a sharp rise in the percentage of Americans who believed that the President wanted to reduce arms levels (Solo, 1988, p. 104). In March 1983, President Reagan unveiled his proposal for a Strategic Defense Initiative ("Star Wars") for shooting down incoming missiles that proved a death knell for the freeze campaign, again by coopting its arguments and appeals. As Solo (1988) noted:

> While the Freeze helped to break down the "psychic numbing" for many, its focus on survival may have contributed to the effectiveness and the appeal of Reagan's "Star Wars" solution. The President addressed the fears, accepted popular disbelief in deterrence theory, and offered a "vision of the future which offers hope." He envisioned a world free from the threat of nuclear war by making nuclear weapons obsolete. Making civilians the targets for nuclear weapons was "immoral," according to the President. Standing on the moral ground built by the Freeze movement, Reagan proposed the psychological fix as well as the technical fix. (p. 135)

Thus, President Reagan accepted the ideals and values of his opponents and used them to gain support for his own programs.

One sphere of argument in which this strategy can often be employed with great success is that of **topicality**, the question of whether or not the specific policy upheld by the affirmative is sufficiently linked to the debate resolution. Disputes over topicality frequently degenerate into a competition between lists of alternate standards for determining topicality and dueling definitions. Because it is difficult to demonstrate that one definition is clearly superior to another and even more difficult to demonstrate that a given definition is wholly unreasonable, most topicality arguments are messy and indecisive.

The strategy of strategic agreement may prove to be a useful substitute or complement for simple disagreement. If on the affirmative and responding to a topicality indictment, you should ask yourself: Can my policy *meet* the standards or definitions my opponent has outlined? If, as is often the case, the policy can be construed to meet the opponent's standards and definitions, the topicality challenge becomes moot. Note that the affirmative speaker need not even fully accept the opponent's standards in order to demonstrate that the policy meets them. The affirmative speaker, having so demonstrated, is then free to provide other, arguably superior standards or definitions.

If you are on the opposition, and attempting to prove that the policy defended by the affirmative is insufficiently linked to the debate resolution, you should begin your preparation by asking: Does the affirmative's plan really meet their own definitions? Surprisingly, there is often room for substantial dispute on this matter. The affirmative may also be held more strictly to a definitional standard that they themselves have established, making the opposition's indictments more telling.

Despite its occasional strategic advantages, agreement with the central value or criterion upheld by one's opponent is a risky venture. When humorist Art Buchwald sued Paramount Pictures for failing to credit or compensate him when it used his ideas to make the movie *Coming to America* (starring Eddie Murphy), the central issue in the case was whether in fact the movie was "based upon" Buchwald's work. The attorneys for both sides were asked by the judge to define the phrase "based upon." "To the astonishment of most observers," wrote one reporter, "Draper [the attorney for Paramount] conceded that any substantial similarity in theme, story, plot, or character would justify the finding that the film was based upon Buchwald's concept" (Masters, 1990, p. 42). Because Buchwald's attorneys were fully prepared to meet these criteria, Paramount's attorney's acceptance of them sealed their fate and Buchwald won his suit.

You should only accept the value or criterion of your opponent when you are confident that it can be turned to your advantage: When you can demonstrate that you better achieve the conceded value or criterion and/or that your opponent has run afoul of the conceded value or fails to meet the agreed-upon criterion.

*Accept the Effect Claimed by Your Opponent, but Re-value It.* In policy debate, each side argues about the effects produced by competing policies. If your opponent advocates a policy and claims it will have a particular effect that is beneficial, you are faced with several options: You may deny that the policy will produce the desired effect; that the desirable effect, even if achieved, is outweighed by other disadvantages; or, as discussed in the last section, you may argue that the policy, instead of maximizing the desired effect, will lessen it. All three of these options generally involve at least conditional acceptance of the effect as truly beneficial. But another option exists: One may accept the opponents' claim that their policy will in fact produce the effect claimed, but argue that this effect is bad, not good. Conversely, if the opponent is arguing that a given policy produces ill effects (as in a disadvantage), the respondent may accept the causal reasoning, but argue that this effect is good, not bad.

This re-valuation may take one of two basic forms: The respondent may (a) reverse the evaluation of the effect in its *immediate* context, or (b) reverse the evaluation of the effect in a *larger or more long-term* context. Let us imagine that in learning to ice skate, you have attempted a dangerous maneuver, fallen, and been bruised. This apparent misfortune might be revalued in its immediate context if, for example, your fall induced an attractive fellow skater to come to your assistance, thus providing the pretext for a desirable meeting that might otherwise not have occurred. Your fall on the ice might be revalued in a larger context if the pain you experienced in doing so persuaded you to be more cautious in the future, thus avoiding even greater potential injury. In either way, one might be convinced that your fall on the ice was for the best.

## Re-Valuation in the Immediate Context

The strategy of re-valuating a given effect within its immediate context, portraying it as good rather than bad or bad rather than good, plays a significant role in many disputes. One example may be found in the debate that has raged during the past decade regarding the replacement of "The Star-Spangled Banner" as the national anthem of the United States. Responding to considerable popular sentiment, bills have been introduced in the U.S. Congress to abandon "The Star-Spangled Banner" in favor of "America the Beautiful" as the nation's anthem. Many sporting and other public events have already made this substitution for their opening ceremonies. One of the principal reasons offered is that "The Star-Spangled Banner" is an unwieldy tune, exceedingly difficult to sing.

> The tune is a constant stumbling block. Technically, it covers a span of a twelfth – that is, an octave plus a perfect fifth. Not only is it difficult for the

general public to sing, but it has repeatedly caused trouble even for professional opera singers. Some people assert that this problem could be solved by
selecting the right key for performance. But the point is that *all* 12 possible
keys are poor. No matter what the key, the tune goes either too high or too
low (and both, for some people). (Titcomb, 1985, p. 11)

In responding to this argument, essayist Daniel Mark Epstein chose to
accept the claimed effect ("The Star-Spangled Banner" is hard to sing), but
to re-value it as good, rather than bad.

"The Star-Spangled Banner" is a sublime anthem, democratic and spacious,
holding at least one note for every American. The tune is a test pattern not
only for the voice but for the human spirit. The soul singer, the rock star, and
the crooner—all are humbled by the anthem. We have heard world-famous
tenors and sopranos choke upon the low notes and cry out in pain at the high
ones. We have seen the great Mahalia Jackson tremble. . . . The anthem
perfectly suits our collective spirit, our ambition and national range. So it
ought to be sung by a crowd of Americans, to guarantee that all of the notes
will be covered. . . .
    This leads us to the next argument against "The Star-Spangled Banner":
that it is too difficult for schoolchildren to sing. An editorial in the New York
*World* of March 31, 1931, answered this charge with logic and eloquence.
"What if schoolchildren could sing it? We should be so sick of it by now that
we could not endure the sound of it, as the French are sick of the 'Marseil-
laise.' The virtues of 'The Star-Spangled Banner' are that it does require a
wide compass, so that schoolchildren cannot sing it, and that it is in three-
four time, so that parades cannot march to it. So being, it has managed to
remain fresh, not frayed and worn, and the citizenry still hear it with some
semblance of a thrill, some touch of reverence." (Epstein, 1986, p. 14)

Epstein employed several re-valuations of the "hard-to-sing" quality of
"The Star-Spangled Banner":

1. Because it is so difficult, it humbles all before it—even professional
   singers—and humility is the *proper* attitude one should have in
   singing the anthem;
2. Precisely *because* it is hard for any one person to sing it, "The
   Star-Spangled Banner" encourages singing *by a crowd,* which
   better fits "our collective spirit, our ambition and national range";
3. Because it is hard to sing (and, hence, sung less often), it has
   remained fresh and moving.

Each of these arguments grants the condition claimed by the opponent
("it is hard to sing") but attempts to re-value this condition as good, not ill.

## Re-Valuation Within a Larger Context

The strategy of re-valuating claimed conditions or effects by locating them within a larger or more long-term context has been employed in many policy and moral disputes. The basic move in this strategy is to accept that the effect claimed is indeed bad in its immediate context, but to claim that this evil or suffering promotes some greater good.

During and after World War II, considerable controversy arose over the use of "area bombing," aimed at civilian targets. Such bombing was a prevalent tactic in the Japanese attack on China, German raids on Great Britain, and later in American and British attacks against Germany and Japan. The bombing of civilians was denounced by many as barbaric.

In the following excerpt from one of his weekly columns for the London *Tribune*, George Orwell (1944/1968) attempted to re-value the claimed atrocity of bombing civilians.

When you look a bit closer, the first question that strikes you is: Why is it worse to kill civilians than soldiers? Obviously one must not kill children if it is in any way avoidable, but it is only in propaganda pamphlets that every bomb drops on a school or an orphanage. A bomb kills a cross-section of the population; but not quite a representative selection, because the children and expectant mothers are usually the first to be evacuated, and some of the young men will be away in the army. Probably a disproportionately large number of bomb victims will be middle-aged. (Up to date, German bombs have killed between six and seven thousand children in this country. This is, I believe, less than the number killed in road accidents in the same period.) On the other hand, "normal" or "legitimate" warfare picks out and slaughters all the healthiest and bravest of the young male population. Every time a German submarine goes to the bottom about fifty young men of fine physique and good nerve are suffocated. Yet people who would hold up their hands at the very words "civilian bombing" will repeat with satisfaction such phrases as "We are winning the Battle of the Atlantic." Heaven knows how many people our blitz on Germany and the occupied countries has killed and will kill, but you can be quite certain it will never come anywhere near the slaughter that has happened on the Russian front.

War is not avoidable at this stage of history, and since it has to happen it does not seem to me a bad thing that others should be killed besides young men. I wrote in 1937: "Sometimes it is a comfort to me to think that the aeroplane is altering the conditions of war. Perhaps when the next great war comes we may see that sight unprecedented in all history, a jingo with a bullet hole in him." We haven't yet seen that (it is perhaps a contradiction in terms), but at any rate the suffering of this war has been shared out more evenly than the last one was. The immunity of the civilian, one of the things that have made war possible, has been shattered. Unlike Miss Brittain, I don't regret that. I can't feel that war is "humanised" by being confined to the slaughter of the young and becomes "barbarous" when the old get killed as well. . .

War is of its nature barbarous, it is better to admit that. If we see ourselves as the savages we are, some improvement is possible, or at least thinkable. (pp. 151–152)

In the first paragraph, Orwell attempted to re-value the act of killing civilians in its *immediate* context, by arguing that as bad as it may be, it is better than " 'normal' or 'legitimate' warfare (that) picks out and slaughters all the healthiest and bravest of the young male population." It should be re-valued as acceptable so long as killing more soldiers on the battlefield remains the likely alternative.

In the second and third paragraphs, however, Orwell attempted to re-value the killing of civilians by placing it within a *larger* context in which its evil will serve some greater good. He argued that it is the immunity of the civilian (safe at home while hirelings or conscripts fight the battles elsewhere) that makes war possible. Such immunity, Orwell claimed, encourages "jingoism" (bellicose super-patriotism) in which safe civilians clamor for war. He implied that by shattering the immunity of the civilian, the jingos must face the consequences of their actions and, as a result, the probability or duration of war may be reduced. It is the very tragedy of civilian bombing, he argued, that will make war less likely.

Following the Vietnam War, a similar argument was often made concerning the military draft. Although some argued that the draft should be abolished because it was a much-resented form of involuntary servitude that disrupted education and career plans, others argued that it was precisely because of these ill effects that it should be retained. By making a large segment of the population vulnerable to these undesirable effects, it was argued that the draft served as a popular check on military adventurism. People subject to the draft (and their families) might be less likely to support policies that might cause them to be drafted. Another Vietnam, the respondents claimed, was far more likely when it would be fought by hired volunteers. Thus, the admitted evils of the draft make greater evils less likely.

The strategy of re-valuing an opponent's claimed effect by placing it within a larger or more long-term context is especially powerful because it completely coopts the opponent's argument. Using this strategy, the respondent is able to accept the opponent's claim that the effect has been produced by the designated cause *and* accept the opponent's evaluation of this effect in its immediate context. The respondent is thus able to say: "So far as it goes, my opponent's argument is correct . . . but it does not go far enough." The clash between positions is joined at a higher level of abstraction than that conceived of by the opponent.

Late in the development of the atomic bomb, significant debate and dissent erupted among the scientists at Los Alamos as to whether they should continue their work. Physicist Robert Wilson organized a meeting of 50 of the dissident scientists to discuss their principal questions: Why should they continue working on the bomb when the defeat of Germany (the foe against whom the United States was racing to complete the bomb) was imminent? Was it morally justified to unleash this "terrible object" on the world and change it forever? (Wyden, 1985, p. 148).

Dr. Robert Oppenheimer, the leader of the laboratory, stood before the dissidents and offered an ingenious response, as described by Wyden (1985):

> The United Nations was going to be organized in a few months, he (Oppenheimer) noted. It would be crucial for the bomb to be demonstrated beforehand. The results would be made public, or so Oppenheimer seemed to take for granted. People around the world would learn of its unimaginable destructive potential. They would be so awed that the statesmen would ban it forever. But if the bomb did not become a reality soon, the wily military would keep its existence secret until the next war and unleash it then. Therefore it was crucial that the men at Los Alamos continue to work as hard as they could. (p. 148)

Oppenheimer's argument used the very fears of the scientists about the "terrible object" they were creating to induce them to continue their work. Admitting their contention that the bomb and its effects were evil, Oppenheimer persuaded the scientists that by *demonstrating* this evil, they would produce good, encouraging the international control of the weapons and diminishing the chance that they would be used in the future. The argument that, if not developed and demonstrated during World War II, atomic weapons might be used in a future war, gained added significance because by the time of that future war, the atomic weapons would likely be more numerous and more powerful, thus producing far greater destruction. According to Nobel laureate Patrick M.S. Blackett:

> What they (the scientists) feared was that the bombs would *not* be used in the war against Japan, but that the attempt would be made to keep their existence secret and that a stockpile would be built up for an eventual war with Russia. To those who feared intensely this latter possible outcome, the dropping of the bombs and the publicity that resulted appeared, not implausibly, as far the lesser evil. (in Fogelman, 1964, p. 104)

Thus, Oppenheimer and others effectively employed the argumentative strategy of re-valuation by placing an admitted evil (using the atomic bombs against Japan) within a larger or more long-term context in which it may be seen as serving some greater good (promoting international control) or preventing some greater evil (a more destructive future atomic war against the Soviets).

## Turnarounds

One of the most common uses in policy debate of the last two strategies discussed (embrace of an opponent's base value and revaluation of an opponent's claimed effect) is the *turnaround*. A turnaround is an argument that attempts to turn a disadvantage claimed against one's policy into an advantage, transforming a reason offered to vote *against* one's proposal into a reason to vote *for* it. Because disadvantages are the most potent form of negative argument in a policy debate, turnarounds represent a potential bonanza for the other side.

Disadvantages claim that (a) enactment of the proposal will cause some effect, and (b) that this effect will be significantly undesirable. Turnarounds may be lodged against either part of the disadvantage, the link or the impact. For example, let us assume that a new law has been proposed requiring that all new oil tanker ships be built with double-hulls to protect against accidental oil spills. Opponents might well pose a disadvantage: The requirement of double-hulls would be costly and these costs would be borne by consumers, many of whom would be forced to choose between paying them and meeting other essential expenses.

A proponent of the double-hull requirement might argue either of two turnarounds. Against the link (double-hulls will drive up prices) the proponent might claim that this cost is far less than the cost of cleaning up projected oil spills, costs which would be passed along to the same consumers. The proponent would thus be arguing that instead of costing these consumers **more** than they would otherwise spend, the double-hull requirement would cost them **less.**

Alternatively, a turnaround might be argued against the claimed impact of the disadvantage. The proponent might accept the link (double-hulls *will* drive up consumer prices more than would otherwise occur), but argue that this is good, not bad. One possible reason is that higher prices encourage energy conservation. Given a competition between oil use and other necessities, most consumers could and would cut their fuel consumption. Cutting fuel consumption would yield a number of important benefits, such as improvement of air quality (and a concomitant lessening of diseases associated with pollution).

Thus, a disadvantage lodged against the proposal may be transformed into an advantage, a reason to vote for the double-hull requirement rather than against it.

The two turnaround strategies discussed here should sound familiar.

Turning the link of a disadvantage employs the strategy of accepting the opponent's base value criterion and employing it to show the superiority of one's own position. Turning the impact of a disadvantage is a strategy of revaluation: accepting a causal claim made by one's opponent, but arguing that the effect is good, not bad (or vice versa).

Debaters employing the strategy of the turnaround or other efforts at strategic agreement must be careful not to contradict themselves. In turnaround arguments, this usually takes the form of a "double-turn," in which the proponent foolishly attempts to turn *both* the link and the impact of a disadvantage. The folly of such an approach may be revealed through the example of the cost disadvantage attributed to double-hull tanker requirements. If the proponent of the requirement, in responding to the disadvantage, were to argue *both* that the proposal would make prices *lower* than they would otherwise be *and* that higher prices are good because they encourage conservation, the proponent would have thereby presented a new *dis*advantage against his or her own proposal. A wise opponent would concede *both* turnarounds and conclude that the double-hulled tanker requirement should be rejected because, by the proponent's own admission, it will diminish energy conservation by producing lower energy costs than would otherwise occur, leaving the proponent no room for response consistent with her or his positions.

The concept of strategic agreement challenges the instinct of debaters to "shoot anything that moves." One's own position may be helped, not hurt, by accepting the opponent's argument and converting it to one's own purposes, whether by exploiting a contradiction, inconsistency, or unintended concession, by accepting an opponent's base value criterion as a gauge of the superiority of one's own position, or by re-valuing a condition or effect claimed by the opponent. Thus, the first impulse of any debater on hearing an opponent's argument or evidence should be: How can I *use* that to my advantage?

## NEED I REFUTE IT?

Even if an opponent's argument does not seem convertible to your purposes, that does not necessarily mean that you should refute it. One should next pose another critical question: *Need I refute it?* Often, for example, an adversary's case will contain many statements that provide background information *about* the issues in dispute, but are not themselves in dispute. There are also many instances in which some part of your opponent's case may be relevant to the way your opponent *anticipated* that the debate would unfold, but turns out not to be central to the dispute as you have actually presented it. Finally, there are issues in almost every debate that, although fiercely contested, should ultimately have no great bearing on the outcome of the dispute. Even if conceded by one side or the other, they should not be critical factors in decision making.

The strategic advantage involved in knowing what issues are and are not of real consequence in the dispute is substantial: Knowing what issues are *not* central allows you to devote more attention to those that *are*. There is also a defensive function involved. Being able to explain why some of your opponent's arguments are irrelevant to the important issues of the dispute, especially if your opponent is winning those arguments, helps defend against the possibility that those arguments will wrongly be considered decisive by the judge or audience.

There are two basic ways in which a debater may explain why a given issue should be irrelevant to the outcome of the dispute: (a) By designating *extraneous and admitted matter*, contentions of one's opponent that will not be disputed, and (b) through *hypothetical concession*, in which the debater explains why a given argument should not prove decisive in the debate even if it were to be conceded.

## Extraneous and Admitted Matter

Extraneous matters are those that have no real bearing on the dispute at hand. Identifying such matters requires that the debater have a clear understanding of the issues on which the debate actually pivots. Extraneous matters should then be swept aside to focus attention on the heart of the matter. As Foster (1908/1932) admonished: "Irrelevant matters should be shown as such and excluded from the issues and from the argument proper whenever there is danger of mistaking them for real issues" (p. 36).

Admitted matters are those claims made by advocates for one side in the debate that the other side has decided not to contest. These matters may be relevant to the dispute (e.g., when a historical background to the issues has been provided), but are not themselves at the center of the dispute. The main reason for admitting such matters is not, through strategic agreement, to convert them to one's own purposes, but rather to clear the way for discussion of the central issues, and to sweep aside arguments of one's opponent that, however convincing in themselves, should not determine the outcome of the debate.

The great 19th-century lawyer and orator Daniel Webster often began his courtroom and debate speeches by distinguishing those matters *not* at issue from those that were. This tactic is demonstrated in his famous speech *In Reply to Hayne*, delivered on the floor of the U.S. Senate in 1830:

> What he contends for is, that it is constitutional to interrupt the administration of the Constitution itself, in the hands of those who are chosen and

sworn to administer it, by the direct interference, in form of law, of the states, in virtue of their sovereign capacity. The inherent right of the people to reform their government I do not deny; and they have another right, and that is to resist unconstitutional laws, without overturning the government. It is no doctrine of mine that unconstitutional laws bind the people. The great question is, **Whose perogative is it to decide on the constitutionality or unconstitutionality of the laws?** On that the main debate hinges. (1890, pp. 80–81)

Webster defused his opponent's arguments by admitting their most impassioned principle: It is not at issue. He then redirected attention to what he believed was the heart of the dispute.

The designation of admitted matter is especially important in legal argument. Most criminal cases feature extensive testimony on the physical layout of the crime scene, the nature of the crime itself (as in the pathologist's report on the physical injuries of a crime victim), and other matters. These matters may or may not be matters that the defense chooses to contest. The defense in one homicide case may find it important to dispute the claimed time of death (perhaps to establish an alibi for the defendant), whereas the same detail may prove irrelevant to the defense's case in another. Similarly, while the prosecuting attorney in most cases will offer arguments why the alleged crime is a heinous one, the defense may choose to dispute this claim (as in the defense of a political protestor against the charge of burning an American flag) or, in other cases, to accept it. Irish barrister John Curran (1750–1817), in his defense of Patrick Finney against the charge of high treason, found it wise to admit to the seriousness of the crime with which his client had been charged.

I confess I cannot conceive a greater crime against civilized society, be the form of government what it may, whether monarchical, republican, or, I had almost said despotic, than attempting to destroy the life of the person holding the executive authority; the counsel for the Crown cannot feel a greater abhorrence against it than I do; and happy am I, at this moment, that I can do justice to my principles, and the feelings of my heart, without endangering the defense of my client. (Cited in Foster, 1908/1932, p. 41)

Again, Curran separated what is truly in dispute from that which is not. In the process, he deflated the importance of an argument on which his opponent has spent considerable time and on which his opponent has waxed eloquent.

The tactic of setting aside admitted matter is one that replicates the judging process. A judge or audience of the debate must sort through the issues, determine which are important to the outcome of the dispute and which are not, and resolve the dispute accordingly. U.S. Supreme Court

Justice Harry Blackmun, in his opinion for the majority requiring universities to disclose confidential materials in their personnel files when challenged by lawsuits alleging discrimination, followed this method in explaining the Court's decision:

> We readily agree with petitioner that universities and colleges play significant roles in American society. Nor need we question, at this point, petitioner's assertion that confidentiality is important to the proper functioning of the peer review process under which many academic institutions operate. The costs that ensue from disclosure, however, constitute only one side of the balance. As Congress has recognized, the costs associated with racial and sexual discrimination is a great if not compelling governmental interest. Often, as even petitioner seems to admit, disclosure of peer review materials will be necessary in order for the commission to determine whether illegal discrimination has taken place. Indeed, if there is a "smoking gun" to be found that demonstrates discrimination in tenure decisions, it is likely to be tucked away in peer review files. (Blackmun, 1990, p. 136)

By admitting certain matters in his or her speech, a debater seeks to exert some influence on the arbiter's decision as to what issues are truly important. This tactic of narrowing the issues runs contrary to instinct; there is a persistent temptation to admit nothing and dispute everything. Yet, so long as the admitted matter is not central to the pivotal issues of the debate (and is *shown* not to be central), its admission will enable you to sweep away arguments in which your opponent has invested unwisely and to turn the spotlight of the debate on the matters that should resolve it in your favor. As Foster (1908/1932) advised: "Admit all that you can safely admit, but no more" (p. 41).

## Hypothetical Acceptance

Hypothetical acceptance of an opponent's argument really amounts to a figure of thought: The judge or audience is asked to imagine what the debate would be like if you *were* to concede a given argument. The purpose of the hypothetical concession is to demonstrate that the argument is not decisive; to show that even if you were to concede argument $x$, your side should prevail in the dispute.

In the political debate over potential restrictions on the use of tobacco products, for example, opponents have argued that such measures would have a severe economic impact on certain regions of the United States. A proponent might respond by saying: "Even if I were to concede that great economic hardship would ensue, such hardship would certainly not justify the deaths of hundreds of thousands of people each year from tobacco-related illness." If the economic hardship argument were the major issue raised by the opponents, such a hypothetical concession might make clear the balance of interests at stake in the dispute. The speaker might then proceed to *refute* the claim that significant economic hardship will ensue from restrictions on tobacco use.

There are several important differences between this tactic and those discussed earlier. In the hypothetical concession, no attempt is made to convert the opponent's argument to one's own use. Furthermore, unlike the waiving of irrelevant or admitted matters, the hypothetical acceptance does not amount to a true concession. One is not conceding the argument, but simply evaluating the proper outcome of the debate if it were to be conceded. Having done so, the debater may proceed to dispute the point.

The hypothetical concession is most useful in the final rebuttal, when the debater sorts out the many issues in the debate and explains why his or her side should win the dispute.

In answer to the second question, the debater should ask upon hearing an opponent's argument – "Need I refute it?" – two instances have been outlined in which the debater might well answer "No." The debater may choose to waive off irrelevant and admitted matter, thus narrowing the dispute to the issues that matter most. The debater may alternatively choose to employ a hypothetical concession to make clear why a certain argument by the opponent, no matter how persuasively presented, should ultimately be inconsequential for the decision. Normally, the debater employing the hypothetical imperative will say, in effect, "I really don't *need* to refute this argument" but, having demonstrated this, will then proceed to refute it anyway, in order to make the victory even more convincing.

## THE PROCESS OF REFUTATION

After determining that an opponent's argument (a) cannot be converted to one's own purposes and (b) must be refuted, the question then arises: How best can I refute it? Although successful refutation depends on insightful analysis of the particular characteristics of the argument being scrutinized, following certain general procedures and methods of refutation will facilitate such analysis and help ensure that it is effectively communicated in the debate.

The process of refutation, as discussed earlier, should begin long before the actual debate with the systematic anticipation of what an opponent might say. As Harvard professor George Pierce Baker (Baker & Huntington, 1905) observed in the late 19th century, "one may often know as well as one's opponent the possible cases for his side" (p. 172). By coming to know and understand the opponent's possible cases and arguments, one can develop the strongest possible counter-arguments and briefs.

Beyond preparation, a second essential preliminary to refutation is selection. Refutation requires selectivity as to: (a) which points should be refuted, (b) in what depth, and (c) in what order. It is rarely possible or desirable to refute every single statement that an adversary makes. As Baker instructed, "Not everything which your opponent says is surely worth answering, probably not any large part of it" (p. 174). Particularly in a public debate, the attempt to cover too many minor points may distract attention (both the audience's and your own) from more important points.

Similarly, one should be selective in the depth in which issues are discussed. You may possess a dozen possible answers to a single point raised by your opponent. One would nevertheless be foolish to present all of them unless the issue were a pivotal one. To do so would lessen the attention accorded other issues. Instead, select your strongest and most succinct answers.

Third, one must select the order in which an opponent's points should be refuted. Normally, the basic structure for debate on a given set of issues is provided by the speaker who first presents those issues. Thus, discussion of issues relevant to the government (affirmative) case will generally follow the outline of contentions established by the first affirmative speaker. When the opposition raises issues not directly stemming from the affirmative's case structure (such as disadvantages to a proposed policy or a statement of the opposition's counterphilosophy or counterplan), the discussion of those issues will usually follow the order in which these points were originally raised.

Following a set order for the discussion of issues is more important in technical contest debate than in public debate, where comprehensiveness in refutation is less common. For a general audience, it is more important that debaters discuss the most significant points of the other side and establish clear general themes that can be recalled by the audience without the benefit of notes. Complicated coverage becomes confusing in a public debate; comprehensive coverage risks losing sight of the forest for the close inspection of individual trees. Even in more technical debate with expert arbiters, it is always advantageous, particularly in closing arguments, to lift one's head out of the thicket of individual arguments and provide a simple synthetic vision of the debate that restructures the discussion and decision-making process.

Speakers may choose to deviate from the established order in which issues have been introduced for the purposes of synthetic analysis. These overviews of the debate should be identified as such, and normally are presented at the outset of one's speech.

Speakers will generally find it advisable to offer a *preview* of their speech in the introduction. This preview (or "roadmap") may include a brief overview of your case, a list of the main arguments you will present, and a description of the order in which you will cover your own points and those of your opponent.

## Opportunities for Refutation

Refutation may focus on any of several aspects of a given argument. Each of these aspects is discussed elsewhere in the text in more detail, as are the lines of refutation appropriate to each.

1. **The *relevance* of the opponent's point.** The opponent's argument may be indicted on the grounds that it begs the question, misrepresents your case, or is based on a misunderstanding of the issue.

2. **The *reasoning* behind the opponent's argument.** Normally such indictments concentrate on the presence of some logical fallacy in the opponent's reasoning, such as:

- the use of undefined or misleading terms;
- circular reasoning, in which the arguer "supports" a claim by restating it, as in former U.S. Presidential candidate William Jennings Bryan's statement that "There is only one argument that can be made to one who rejects the authority of the Bible, namely, that the Bible is true"; (cited in McDonald, 1980, pp. 165–166).
- an internal inconsistency in the opponent's argument or evidence;
- a non-sequitur, in which it is claimed that the arguer's claim "does not follow" from the reasons offered for it;
- faulty generalization, a flawed conclusion drawn improperly from a given instance;
- faulty claim of causation, an improper attribution of a cause-and-effect relationship; or faulty analogy, the improper claim of similarity between one example or situation and another.

3. **The *evidence* used to support the opponent's argument.** As described in chapter 3, an argument may be refuted on the basis of the evidence provided (or not provided) for it on any of a number of grounds, including:

- reliance on an unproven assertion, the lack of authoritative evidence where it is required;
- use of an unqualified source for an evidentiary claim, a source who lacks the credentials necessary to lend authority to the quoted statement;

- source bias, an indictment of the objectivity and credibility of the quoted expert;
- faulty observation, an indictment of the means by which the source has gathered the data to support his or her conclusion;
- faulty generalization or claims of causation;
- the presence of significant internal qualifiers in the evidence (e.g., "in some cases" or "has been known to . . .") that weaken the claim.

4. **The *link between evidence and argument*.** There is often considerable disparity between the claim of a debater and the actual conclusion of the evidence offered as support for that claim. Debaters frequently succumb to the temptation of overclaiming or exaggerating their evidence. This may happen either in the initial presentation of an argument or in rebuttal references to an argument made in an earlier speech. In refutation, it is important to scrutinize the "fit" (a) between the argument label and the supporting evidence (because labels are often dramatized for effect) and (b) between a debater's description or summary of what a piece of evidence says and what it *actually* says.

5. **The *principle* behind the opponent's argument.** An argument may be refuted not only on the basis of its substance or support, but on the basis of the unstated assumptions behind it. As we discuss in greater detail in chapter 7, this process of refutation is especially useful in the conduct of moral and philosophical disputes.

## Presenting Refutation

Refutation of a given argument should be presented in five basic steps, normally in the following order:

1. ***Locate* your opponent's argument.** Before describing the argument you are about to refute, orient the listener by directing his or her attention to the place of the argument in the debate. This location cue may be quite specific. If there is an explicit organization to the opponent's arguments, such as the presentation of three major contentions, identify which of the three points you are about to address.

Location cues provide another important function as well: They signal a clear transition as you move from the coverage of one argument to another, as in the simple statement, "Now let's turn to my opponent's second argument." Location cues are sometimes referred to as signposts, markers that allow the judge or audience to understand what portion of your opponent's case or your own is now under discussion.

2. **State your opponent's argument.** Refutation is directed at the discrediting of a specific argument offered by one's opponent. In order for

the referent to be clear, your opponent's argument should be clearly and succinctly identified. The description of an opponent's argument should be as brief as possible (ideally no more than three or four words), while still enabling the judge or audience to know precisely what argument you are addressing. In debating the topic "Resolved: that the atomic bombing of Hiroshima was justified," one common argument for the opposition is that "The atomic bombing of Hiroshima was a barbaric attack on innocent civilians." In answering this argument it should be referred to in a simpler fashion, such as "Civilians" or "Bombing Civilians." Do not describe or elaborate your opponent's argument beyond the minimum required to identify it for your listener. To do more not only wastes your time, but also reinforces the loaded rhetorical garments in which your opponent has clothed the argument (such as the terms *barbaric* and *innocent* in the aforementioned original argument label).

If your objection is aimed at some specific part or aspect of the opponent's argument, you must identify not only the relevant general argument of your opponent, but also the specific target of your attack. This is especially important if you intend to indict some element of the reasoning or specific piece of evidence with which your adversary has supported his or her argument. Refutation only gains its fullest effect when its target is in clear focus.

3. **State your objection or answer to the opponent's argument.** Offer a concise title and explanation of your argument. Each response should be briefly titled or labeled before it is explained or supported. This label makes clear what you are trying to prove, eases the audience's understanding and/or recording of your point, and makes the argument easier to remember and refer to later.

Even if you are relying on expert testimony to support your argument, first state the point of your argument in your own words, rather than letting the evidence "speak for itself." Properly used, evidence *supports* arguments, rather than making them.

4. **Support your argument.** As discussed in chapter 3, arguments may be supported with reasoning and with various forms of evidence. Evidence read in a debate should be cut to the point, keeping the relationship between argument and evidence in clear focus.

5. **Explain the *impact* of your refutation.** After presenting and supporting your argument, you must explain the importance of what you have done. In refutation, you should first make clear what impact your argument has on the argument of the opponent, which it was designed to rebut. This impact may be total (if your argument is accepted, the opponent's should be completely discounted) or partial (the original impact of the opponent's argument is diminished but not eliminated).

For arguments that may prove decisive in the outcome of the larger dispute, the impact of your argument should be explained not only with respect to the specific argument of the opponent that has been refuted, but with respect to the debate as a whole. After refuting an argument, explain the effect on your opponent's case of that refutation. What is the significance of winning this argument? How should it affect the outcome of the debate? Why? As Baker and Huntington (1905) advised:

> Do not pass on to something else, secure that your opponent's case is hopelessly weakened or demolished. If doubt be in the least possible, emphasize, showing briefly just what you take to be the effect on your opponent's case of what you have done and the consequent result for your own views; in other words, make clear the exact state of the two sides as you finish a piece of rebuttal. (p. 178)

These five steps should be followed in all oral debate for the presentation of refutation, and are often employed in written argument as well.

1. *Locate* your opponent's argument;
2. *State* your opponent's argument;
3. State your objection or answer to the opponent's argument;
4. *Support* your argument; and
5. Explain the *impact* of your refutation.

It is important to remember that counterargument and counterevidence *alone* do not constitute refutation. True refutation requires clash, in which your arguments are *compared* with those of your opponent. Whose evidence is better, and why? Whose reasoning on a point is superior, and why? The critique of the structure and support of your opponent's argument is a necessary component of the establishment of your own.

The following case study provides a useful illustration of systematic refutation in actual practice.

## Case Study in Refutation: Return of the "Elgin" Marbles

The Parthenon has stood atop the Acropolis in Athens for nearly 2,500 years. It was constructed in the 5th century BC at the height of Athens' power, a period in which much of the rubric of Western culture, in philosophy, politics, science, and art, was assembled. The Parthenon has long been regarded as the symbol of this cultural achievement, a dramatic illustration of the principles of balance and symmetry that dominated Greek aesthetics. Despite wars, occupation, and natural disasters, it has remained remarkably intact.

In 1799, Thomas Bruce, Seventh Earl of Elgin, was appointed British Ambassador to the Ottoman Empire that occupied Greece for centuries. In 1802, he obtained written permission from the Turkish government to make casts and drawings of the sculptures and to "remove some pieces of stone with inscriptions or figures." Lord Elgin proceeded to remove 50 slabs and 2 half-slabs of the Parthenon's marble friezes and then shipped them to England. In 1816, Elgin sold the marbles to the British government, which placed them in the British Museum where they remain today.

Controversy over the removal of the marbles began almost immediately. The government's purchase of them was fiercely debated in the House of Commons in 1816. When Greece gained its independence from the Turks in 1821, they demanded return of the marbles – a demand that has been revived periodically ever since and one that has always enjoyed considerable support from many British. Demands for the marbles' return have been pressed with renewed vigor since the appointment of Melina Mercouri as Greek Cultural Minister in 1981. Within Britain, the case has been most forcefully advocated by writer Christopher Hitchens in magazine essays and his comprehensive 1987 overview of the controversy, *Imperial Spoils: The Curious Case of the Elgin Marbles.*

Hitchens (1983) argued that the friezes should be returned (a) because they are of central importance to Greek culture. "The briefest of conversations with a Greek will show that feeling about the friezes runs very deep," he wrote, "Their presence in London is felt as a crude amputation of the country's greatest shrine" (p. 129). Furthermore, he argued, the friezes should be restored to the Parthenon (b) as a matter of artistic integrity:

> . . . there is only one Parthenon frieze. And its actual home, the building with which it was designed to harmonize, is still standing. One does not have to be an expert on Greek sculpture to know that its essence is balance and symmetry. . . . The Marbles would look much better in the building for which they were intended – which is now itself undergoing a very dedicated work of protection and conservation. (1983, p. 12)

Finally, Hitchens argued that the Marbles should be returned (c) as a matter of simple property right. They were removed illegally, he argued, and should be returned to their rightful owners. Elgin "bought them from the Turkish regime of occupation," he observed, and "seems to have cheated even them," in that the license he obtained from the Turks for the preparation of casts and minor excavation does not seem to have authorized removal of the friezes. "Clearly," moreover, "no deal struck between Lord Elgin and the representative of a usurping foreign power is binding on the Greeks" (1983, p. 12).

Hitchens realized that the proposal he made for the return of the marbles was not a new one, and that it continued to face substantial opposition from many quarters–the British government, the British Museum, curators of other museums who fear similar demands, and many others. The basic arguments in the controversy have remained fairly consistent for nearly two centuries, and the arguments in favor of retaining the Marbles continue to be very persuasive for many. Hitchens realized that the prospects for his proposal depended on the clear, thorough, and forceful refutation of his opponents' arguments. In order to provide such refutation, he reduced the many individual arguments made by those who oppose return of the marbles into six basic objections. Hitchens then proceeded to refute each in turn, taken "at their strongest."

The six basic arguments of the retentionists are:

1. The removal of the marbles to Britain was a boon to fine arts and the study of the classics.
2. The marbles are safer in London than they would have been in Athens.
3. The marbles are safer in London than they *would be* in Athens.
4. Lord Elgin acted in the spirit of a preservationist.
5. The return of the marbles would set a precedent for the denuding of great museums and collections.
6. The Greeks of today are not authentically Greek and have no title, natural or otherwise to Periclean or Phidian sculpture." (Hitchens, 1987, p. 85)

These objections strike at different parts of the case for return of the marbles. Arguments 1, 2, and 4 are defenses of the original removal of the marbles, offering justification for Elgin's actions. They embrace the notion of the aesthetic significance of the friezes urged by proponents of their return and offer grounds for arguing that removal *enhanced* their aesthetic influence and better ensured the continued ability of later generations to view and appreciate them.

Argument 6 denies the legal basis of the Greek claim to the marbles, denying that they are the rightful owners to whom possession should be restored.

Arguments 3 and 5 are disadvantages to the proposed return of the marbles, the former an appeal to the value of the marbles themselves (their physical integrity would be endangered by return) and the latter a claim that the return of the marbles would endanger the collections of *other* museums by establishing a dangerous precedent.

Let us examine Hitchens' refutation of the three most important of these arguments, the first, third, and fifth.

The first argument, that the marbles have been a boon to the study of fine arts and the classics in Britain, rests on the undeniable premise that the marbles have been seen by millions of people in their London location and that they have proven immensely influential in architecture, literature (particularly on the works of Byron and Keats), and the study of ancient Greek civilization. After summarizing these lines of support for the argument, Hitchens refuted it:

> There is no argument against those who say that more people have seen the marbles as a consequence of their having been taken from Athens. The same could be asserted if the frieze was now a permanent exhibit at Disneyland. All that may be said with certainty is that both the act of removal and the act of installation in London led to some great efforts, for and against, in poetry and prose. Who can say what might be generated, in this line, by the reunion of the marbles with their parent building? At any event, we should not be losing the verses of either Byron or Keats. It may be moot whether the elevation of English taste was sufficient reason for the prying loose of the Parthenon's sculpture in the first place. . . . (pp. 88–89)

Hitchens' response made use of several of the tactics discussed in this chapter. He began by admitting two parts of the opponent's argument: The removal to London *has* enabled more people to see the marbles and their removal and installation *has* proven inspirational for artists and others. He then refuted the *conclusion* of the opponent's argument (that these facts warrant retention of the marbles) by arguing that:

1. Popular access is an insufficient criterion in itself for determining where artworks should be located (he used the example of a popular amusement park, Disneyland, to disprove the standard's viability). Hitchens identified the *principle* behind the opponent's argument (artworks should be located in the places where the most people will see them) and challenged the principle by taking it to its logical extreme;

2. The inspirational effect of the marbles on British fine arts *in the past* is no reason to block their return *now*. These effects have already taken place, and the poetry of Byron and Keats will not disappear with the marbles' return. Hitchens here argued that the opponent's point, although pertinent to the question of whether the marbles should have been taken in the first place, is irrelevant to the question of their proposed return;

3. If the opponent's principle (that the decision should be made so as to maximize artistic inspiration) is *accepted*, Hitchens noted, it becomes another reason to return the marbles, because "the reunion of the marbles with their parent building" may inspire people anew. Return of the marbles may thereby *increase* their influence on literature, rather than

reducing it. He thus converted the opponent's argument to his own use; and

4. Hitchens implied (albeit rather obliquely) that the value of the marbles for artistic inspiration is less important than the cultural value of retaining them in their rightful location. Here he compared two competing value claims, his and the opponent's, and reinforced his vision of each with colorful language. Artistic inspiration becomes "the elevation of English taste," a swipe at English culture; the removal of the marbles is described as a "prying loose" which, although literally true, underscores Hitchens' view that the act was one of thievery. In Hitchens' reformulation, the question becomes whether the "elevation of English taste was sufficient reason for the prying loose of the Parthenon's sculpture."

The third main argument forwarded by opponents of the marbles' return is that they are safer in London than they would be in Athens, particularly from the significant air pollution which Athens suffers. All strategically minded debaters must recognize which arguments of the opponent are the strongest, posing the greatest potential challenge. Hitchens identified the pollution argument as "undoubtedly the strongest argument for the retentionists" (Hitchens, 1987, p. 93).

Again, Hitchens began his refutation by conceding the basic premise on which the opponent's argument was constructed: Athens *is* highly polluted, despite recent increases in emission controls. He based his refutation on the following counter-arguments:

1. There has been a vigorous and successful program to protect the buildings of the Acropolis from the pollution of Athens, including the use of oxidation-resistant titanium supports for the structures, restriction of public access to some areas of the temples, and removal of endangered sculptures to the climate-controlled Acropolis Museum. The British Museum itself, Hitchens noted, has praised the Acropolis preservation efforts. Hitchens thus diminished the significance of the pollution threat to the artworks of the Acropolis themselves, rather than attempting to deny the general pollution problems of Athens;

2. Hitchens then disputed the principle ("artworks should be kept where they are most free from environmental pollution") that underlies the opponent's argument.

> The "environmental" case for retention ignores the fact that Athens is the historic and aesthetic environment for the marbles. In its most extreme form, this argument would justify the removal of the entire Acropolis to a giant vault in London or Glasgow or New York. (Hitchens, 1987, p. 96)

Finally, let us examine Hitchen's refutation of Argument 5, that the return of the marbles would establish a precedent that would threaten to strip other museums of their collections. This argument is, as noted earlier, a disadvantage based on a causal claim. The argument is a prediction of future costs (denuding other museums' collections) that may be incurred if the Parthenon marbles are returned. British museums are filled with artifacts taken from many countries, seized in war or from former British colonies, or gathered in archeological expeditions. Return of the marbles might fuel demands for the return of these artifacts to their countries of origin.

Hitchens refuted this claim with three principal arguments:

1. Past returns of artifacts have not created the predicted snowball of demands.

> The British Museum and the British Crown have on occasion made unobtrusive restitutions. One might cite the Ethiopian manuscripts that were returned in 1872; the shrine, sceptre and orb of the Kings of Kandy returned to Ceylon in the 1830s after being removed by Sir Robert Brownrigg in 1815; the bronzes returned to Benin in 1950; the Mandalay Regalia returned to Burma in 1864. . . . The British Museum agreed in principle to the return of a portion of the beard of the Sphinx, purloined by a British soldier, as a "loan" in 1985. The sky, one has to say, did not fall.

Hitchens here attacked the causal theory on which the argument is based. If, as opponents of the marbles' return claim, return of some artifacts will produce snowballing demands for the return of others, why then did this not occur in past instances of restitution?

2. The return of the "Elgin" marbles would set no precedent because they are unique. The argument from precedent is based on the assumption that similar cases will be treated similarly. If the "Elgin" marbles are *not* similar to other museum holdings, then presumably they need not be treated similarly. Hitchens argued that the "Elgin" marbles are unique because of their central importance to the culture from which they were taken, because the descendants of the culture from which they were taken (the Greeks) exist today (whereas "there are no Assyrians, Hittites, or Babylonians to take up the cry of precedent"), and because the marbles were not taken as spoils of war ("whereas much of the glory of the various British museums is colonial or military in origin"). Thus, return of the marbles would not necessarily set a precedent for the return of other artifacts that do not possess these characteristics.

3. The "dangerous precedent" argument is an inappropriate standard for judging moral action. Here Hitchens disputed the very concept of the disadvantage. The real decision we must make, he insisted, is whether the proposed action (returning the marbles) is morally *right* or not. He quoted essayist F.M. Cornford to dispute the argument of precedent:

> The Principle of the Dangerous Precedent is that you should not now do any admittedly right action for fear you, or your equally timid successors, should not have the courage to do right in some future case, which *ex hypothesi*, is essentially different, but superficially resembles the present one. *Every public action which is not customary either is wrong, or, if it is right, is a dangerous precedent. It follows that nothing should ever be done for the first time.* (p. 101)

Hitchens thus ridiculed the claim of dangerous precedent as an inappropriate standard by which to judge action. If the proposed action is found to be morally right in itself, it should not be rejected because it may present us with future moral choices of a similar nature.

Thus, Hitchens not only provided a case for return of the marbles, but strengthens his case through a thorough review and thoughtful refutation of the strongest opposing arguments.

## PERSPECTIVE

Successful refutation requires more than persuasive responses to the individual arguments of an opponent; it requires that these responses be fitted into some clear position that competes with and can be judged superior to that of the opponent. If one stands very close to a painting, one may admire the brushwork and the composition of individual details. But in order to appreciate the painting as a whole, one must stand back and examine the composite interrelationship of its individual elements. Particularly in a rebuttal speech, the debater must paint "the big picture" of the debate so that the listener may apprehend how the many individual arguments fit together and why, on the basis of this composite view of the arguments, his or her side should win.

The ability to offer a clear explanation of why your side should win the debate is among the most rare and important skills in disputation. Far too often, debaters simply extend their arguments and leave it up to the listener to determine how these arguments fit together and how they compare with those of the other side. When they lose, such debaters may be exasperated at what they regard as the inability of the arbiter to see the "obvious" merit of their case. But the fault is theirs. It is the debaters' responsibility to provide a clear perspective on the dispute. The debater who fails to meet this responsibility gambles that the arbiter will assemble the many issues in the debate in the fashion that the debater desires but has not expressed. Gamblers usually lose.

There are three essential elements to the process of assembling the "big picture."

*Clearly Contrast the Competing Positions.*    This contrast should incorporate all major arguments in the debate and explain how these individual arguments weigh in the balance between the two sides.

*Establish a Common Scale of Measurement With Which to Evaluate the Two Sides.*    Conflict in debate often rests between value claims that are difficult to compare. If a policy risks some lives in the prospect of gaining more freedom for many, for example, which set of values should prevail? In a later chapter, we explore in more detail the strategies by which such value conflicts may be resolved. The key to most of these strategies is the construction of a common scale or set of criteria by which to evaluate both positions. By establishing a common scale, "unresolvable" conflicts become subject to settlement.

For nearly a century, a debate has raged in higher education regarding the propriety of the "lecture method" for instruction. Opponents of lecturing claim that it negates critical thinking, as students passively receive knowledge rather than gaining it for themselves through reading, analysis, and disputation. "Over-indulgence in being lectured-to," warned Cambridge historian Arthur Quiller-Couch (1928), "is the primrose path to intellectual sloth, the more fatally deceitful because it looks virtuous" (p. 34). Proponents of the lecture method, on the other hand, generally cite its efficiency in transmitting much information to many people in a limited period of time. Students require lectures, they argue, to provide the necessary base of knowledge in a particular field.

Too often, the debate between these two positions is left as an unresolved conflict between two disparate educational ideals: development of analytical abilities (by de-emphasizing lectures) and information acquisition (through lectures). Yet either side could re-fashion the debate according to common criteria. Proponents of lecturing could argue that, in the modern university system, it is lecturing that makes nonlecture-based systems of instruction successful. The personnel efficiency of lectures in introductory courses (where many students are taught by a single instructor) makes it possible to offer more discussion seminars with low student--teacher ratios. Moreover, they might argue, by providing a shared base of knowledge, lecture classes improve the quality of discussion in upper division seminars. Thus, if one values such nonlecture-based educational experiences as small discussion seminars, they might argue, one should *support* the lecture system.

The development of a common scale of measurement depends on the establishment of a single set of criteria with which to evaluate claims that are sometimes very different, "apples and oranges," as the saying goes. Despite the supposed difficulty of choosing between apples and oranges, we do so all the time. When we desire a piece of fruit, we rarely eat *both* an apple and an orange. We generally choose between them according to certain criteria that identify our specific needs or desires of the moment: If we are selecting a piece of fruit that is to be consumed while riding in an automobile, we might select the apple as less messy; if seeking a piece of fruit to share with others, we may decide that the orange lends itself more easily to division. Resolving disputes between competing values, whether literally or figuratively "apples and oranges," depends on the construction of objective criteria or standards by which *both* can be evaluated.

The tactics of strategic agreement discussed earlier in this chapter are potent ones precisely because they contribute to the establishment of a common scale of measurement through which the dispute may be resolved.

*Explain Why Your Side Should Win.*   Debates are not won by tallying up the numbers of points won by each side, but rather by determining whose points should prove decisive. If I am considering buying a brand X car, even if the sales representative convinces me that it has a dozen admirable but minor features (e.g., reclining seats, right side mirror, attractive paint job), I will nevertheless reject the proposal that I buy the car if I am convinced that there is a single major risk (such as a poor maintenance record) of greater significance than the combination of the many small benefits.

Particularly in rebuttals, it is often valuable to begin one's speech by isolating and addressing the decisive issue(s) in the debate. When Abraham Lincoln was a practicing lawyer, he once employed this tactic in defending a client charged with murder. The trial was a complicated one, involving much testimony and many issues. Yet Lincoln at last cut through the tangle of issues, arguing that the case against his client ultimately rested on the testimony of one witness, who claimed that a full moon enabled him to actually see the fatal blow struck. Lincoln then produced an almanac to show that on the night of the murder there was no moon at all (Baker & Huntington, 1905, p. 175).

It is usually wise to place such synthetic overviews of the debate at the beginning of one's speech, especially in rebuttal. This underscores the importance of the observation, according it a superordinate status. It also ensures that this presumably decisive argument will receive sufficient speaking time for full development. In a debate with time constraints, introducing such an argument at the end or in the main body of one's speech risks running short of time. If the synthetic observation is presented at the outset of one's speech, it should be recapped in concise form in the conclusion, thus leaving it with the audience as the principal lens through which to view the debate.

A synthetic overview of the debate can be used to restructure the debate, cutting away less important details and rearranging the remainder according to the synthetic vision. Justice John Marshall Harlan did precisely this in his famous opinion for the majority of the U.S. Supreme Court in the case of *Cohen v. State of California.* Cohen was convicted of "offensive conduct" during the Vietnam War in 1968 for wearing a jacket emblazoned with a vulgar epithet directed against the draft. Explaining the Court's decision to overturn the conviction, Harlan began by engaging in a review of extraneous issues: "In order to lay hands on the precise issue which this case involves, it is useful first to canvass various matters which this record does *not* present" (in Barnet & Bedau, 1987, p. 252). Having done so, he arrived at the true heart of the matter:

> Against this background, the issue flushed out by this case stands out in bold relief. It is whether California can excise, as "offensive conduct," one particular scurrilous epithet from the public discourse, either upon the theory of the court below that its use is inherently likely to cause violent reaction or upon a more general assertion that the States, acting as guardians of public morality, may properly remove this offensive word from the public vocabulary. (in Barnet & Bedau, 1987, p. 255)

Harlan had thus sorted through the many complicated issues of the case and found them all subordinate to a single question: Does California have the right to excise the epithet from public discourse? Having established this as the basic burden of proof borne by the State's counsel, Harlan identified the two possible ways in which they might justify the action, then dismissed each in turn as inconsistent with Constitutional guarantees of free speech. Each potential rationale for State action, he argued, is "inherently boundless," threatening proscription of more ordinary political and even non-political discourse.

In his conclusion, Harlan returned to the "big picture" he had painted of the case:

> It is, in sum, our judgment that, absent a more particularized and compelling reason for its actions, the State may not, consistently with the First and Fourteenth Amendments, make the simple public display here involved of this single four-letter expletive a criminal offense. Because that is the only

arguably sustainable rationale for the conviction here at issue, the judgment below must be *Reversed*. (Barnet & Bedau, 1987, p. 257)

When attempting such a synthetic analysis, it is important to explain *why* the issues you have isolated are in fact the decisive ones. It is not sufficient to exclaim that "The debate all comes down to this point" or "My opponent's argument rests on this single strut" without supporting these claims. Make clear how you have arrived at this critical judgment. Your claim that the debate should be viewed or resolved in a particular way is an *argument*, and as such is subject to dispute.

## CONCLUSION

Properly executed refutation consists not only of the line-by-line disputation of individual arguments, but of clash initiated within a broader strategic design. This broader design should inform the debater's decision regarding what should (or should not) be said regarding an opponent's argument. Debaters should decide when it is useful to *accept* an opponent's argument rather than disputing it; employing the opponent's own argument in order to refute their *position* in the debate. Debaters must be selective in deciding which arguments to refute and which may safely be ignored or waived as admitted matter. Once the decision has been made to refute an argument of the opponent, the debater must decide which parts of the argument to dispute and in what depth. Finally, the debater must be able, particularly in the final speeches, to reveal the pattern of his or her strategy. Moving from the microscopic level of individual arguments to the macroscopic level of the debate in its entirety, the debater should unveil the "big picture" of the round.

# COUNTERPOSITIONS AND COUNTERPLANS

A debate is a dispute between advocates of competing viewpoints or policies. They "compete" in that the audience or judge is forced to choose between them; to choose one approach or point of view is to reject the other. Unless we are forced to choose between them, there is really no ground for disagreement. A *good* debate, furthermore, depends on the existence of two or more viewpoints that are not only mutually exclusive, but *attractive*. As ethicist William Henry Roberts (1941) has observed:

> We never choose between what we want and what we do not want. When the issue becomes clear between happiness and misery, satisfaction and disappointment, we do not hesitate or debate. Nothing occurs that we can fairly call choosing. (pp. 7–8)

In a true debate, each side has merit, the question is: Which side has more? It therefore behooves each side, the opposition as well as the affirmative, to make clear what its position is and what there is to commend it.

The opposition in a debate should provide more than simple refutation of the adversary's individual arguments. Just as the affirmative (or government) side in a debate offers a case in support of the resolution, the opposition should ideally present a countercase to the resolution, a coherent explanation of what position the audience should hold *if not* that promoted by the affirmative. In a murder trial, the counsel for the defense usually attempts not only to deny that the defendant committed the homicide, but to answer the question, "If s/he didn't, then who *did?*" A common defense strategy is to present one or more plausible alternate suspects, thereby creating a reasonable doubt that the defendant is the guilty party.

In a policy debate, the presentation of both case and countercase should include the defense of a policy ("What should we do?") and of an underlying rationale or philosophy that the policy embodies. In a policy debate, the opposition always (at least implicitly) *defends* a policy, even if they are not fully aware of it. If we do not choose to adopt the affirmative's proposal, we will necessarily do something else, whether we continue on our current course or follow some other alternative. To say that the United States should not have dropped the atomic bomb on Hiroshima is to say that we should have done something else. The opposition may reasonably be expected to specify what that something else *is*.

The policy defended by the opposition may consist of nothing more than the present system. In debating the topic "Resolved: that the United States should expand its immigration quotas to accomodate the increased number of Jews leaving the Soviet Union," the opposition would probably defend the *existing* immigration quotas. Some opponents of a bill before the U.S. Congress in 1990 to *require* that employers provide unpaid leave time for employees who wish to care for members of their immediate families who are seriously ill argued that we should instead retain the present system in which employers may *voluntarily* adopt (or not adopt) such leave policies.

The opposition may suggest a different policy alternative, neither supported by the affirmative nor the present system. Such an alternative is called a *counterplan.*

The principle that underlies the opposition's alternative policy or stance in the debate should be expressed as a *counterposition,* a statement of underlying philosophy that contrasts and competes with the position defended by the affirmative. In the aforementioned family leave example, the opposition may construct a counterposition involving certain principles of the proper relationship between government and business: government should refrain from interference with the free market system; voluntary guidelines for business are preferable to regulation. In issuing his veto of the 1990 Family Leave Act, President Bush defended this counterposition while endorsing the desirability of family leave itself. Employers should provide such leave, he maintained, but voluntarily so.

It is generally insufficient to express what one is *against;* it is also important for the debaters of the opposition to express an alternative position that they *support*. This principle has long been conventional wisdom in political campaigns. "Negative campaigning," in which one candidate indicts the record or character of another, rarely wins elections by itself. Most people must be persuaded to vote *for* a candidate if they are to vote at all. Thus, negative campaign advertisements, for example, are generally complemented by spots that present the mud-slinger's own positions and character in a favorable light.

In this chapter, we examine the ways in which the opposition may best present its own case. In all types of debate, the opposition will find it wise to construct a counterposition that explains its alternative philosophy or stance. In policy debates, the opposition may find it desirable to articulate and defend an explicit policy alternative to that offered by the affirmative, whether in the form of a compelling defense of the present system or a counterplan.

## COUNTERPOSITIONS

Before presenting its own position in the debate, the opposition may find it advisable to offer (or at least *possess*) a clear conceptualization of the affirmative's position. The value of the counterposition rests in its ability to provide a superior answer to the crucial issues involved in a given debate. For the counterposition to be effective, then, the central issues and the other side's approach to them must be identified.

During the American Civil War, President Lincoln personally plotted military strategies for the Union army and often challenged the battle plans of his commanding officers. In 1862, Lincoln held a strong difference of opinion with Major General McClellan, the Commander of the Union forces, regarding the deployment of the Army of the Potomac. Their debate on the matter raged through a series of dispatches between the two men. In conducting the dispute, Lincoln took care to make clear his understanding of McClellan's position and of the central issues that should be used to determine whose approach was superior.

LETTER FROM PRESIDENT
LINCOLN TO MAJOR GENERAL MCCLELLAN
Executive Mansion, Washington, February 3, 1862.

Major-General McClellan.
   *My dear Sir:* – You and I have distinct and different plans for a movement of the Army of the Potomac – yours to be down the Chesapeake, up the Rappahannock to Urbana, and across land to the terminus of the railroad on the York River; mine to move directly to a point on the railroad southwest of Manassas.

If you will give me satisfactory answers to the following questions, I shall gladly yield my plan to yours.

*First.* Does not your plan involve a greatly larger expenditure of time and money than mine?

*Second.* Wherein is a victory more certain by your plan than mine?

*Third.* Wherein is a victory more valuable by your plan than mine?

*Fourth.* In fact, would it not be less valuable in this, that it would break no great line of the enemy's communications, while mine would?

*Fifth.* In case of disaster, would not a retreat be more difficult by your plan than mine?

Yours truly,
   ABRAHAM LINCOLN

(Baker & Huntington, 1905, p. 54)

Thus, Lincoln summarized in the opening paragraph his understanding of McClellan's position. He then identified what he believed to be the most important issues in the dispute: comparative expense, likelihood of victory, the ability to break the enemy's lines of communications, and the viability of retreat, if necessary. Lincoln clearly established the terms of the dispute and prepared the ground for a comparison of his own position with that of McClellan.

An effective counterposition must always be responsive to the key issues in the dispute. If not, it is unlikely to prove decisive itself. On the other hand, a well-wrought counterposition can reshape the dispute to some extent, drawing certain issues into focus while eclipsing others. In the Family Leave Act example discussed in the introduction of this chapter, President Bush's counterposition (family leave should be provided voluntarily by employers, not through government regulation), he draws one set of issues into focus (voluntary vs. mandatory provision of leave) while attempting to render other issues moot (by embracing the claimed value of family leave itself).

A similar technique may be observed in the opening paragraph of Supreme Court Justice Harry Blackmun's opinion in *University of Pennsylvania vs. E.E.O.C.* (1990), wherein he identified the two central issues in the appeal.

As it had done before the commission, the District Court and the Court of Appeals, the university raises here essentially two claims. First, it urges us to recognize a qualified common-law privilege against disclosure of confidential peer review materials. Second, it asserts a First Amendment right of "academic freedom" against wholesale disclosure of the contested documents. With response to each of the two claims, the remedy petitioner seeks is the same: a requirement of a judicial finding of particularized necessity of access, beyond a showing of mere relevance, before peer review materials are disclosed to the commission. (p. 136)

Justice Blackmun clearly identified the two central claims and the proposed remedy of the petitioner in order that he might better rebut them. Blackmun wrote to reflect the unanimous opinion of the Court that the claims of the University were unfounded and that the proposed remedy was undesirable. The Court's decision to compel the opening of previously confidential personnel files is thereby couched in the clear preliminary understanding of the central issues in the dispute.

Conceptualization of one's adversary's position is a vital prerequisite to the establishment of one's own position. It enables clear contrast of the two sides in the dispute – showing how they differ and why. By identifying the central issues that divide the two sides, the opposition also provides a yardstick with which to compare them.

## Dismissal of False Preconceptions

As the advocate or opponent on a given proposition, it will often be as important to explain what one's position will *not* entail as to describe the position itself. Indeed, unless prevailing misconceptions have been set aside, the presentation of one's actual position and arguments may be misunderstood or wrongfully evaluated.

Audiences may have strong preconceptions of one's position. These preconceptions may, of course, be *wrong* and interfere with their comprehension or approval of your actual arguments. Before you begin to speak, the audience may have a mistaken idea of what your position will be and how you are likely to support it. Such misconceptions may result from the audience's prior knowledge of the issues and how others have discussed them, from the audience's own preliminary thoughts on the topic, or from false characterizations of one's position by an opponent who has spoken previously. These misconceptions should be cleared up as soon as possible. As Foster (1908/1932) advised, "It is well to show clearly in the introduction what you are *not* obliged to do in order to establish your case, and what you do not purpose to do, whenever your audience may expect you to do more than is necessary" (p. 36). These two suggestions warrant separate consideration.

1. The demonstration of what one need not prove in order to support one's position is a way of dismissing irrelevant concerns and arguments, thus enabling one to concentrate on what *is* important. Edmund Burke

(1729–1797) employed this method to focus the discussion in a debate over marriage between minors:

> The question is not now, whether the law ought to acknowledge and protect such a state of life as minority, nor whether the continuance, which is fixed for that state, be not improperly prolonged in the law of England. Neither of these in general is questioned. The only question is, whether matrimony is to be taken out of the general rule, and whether the minors of both sexes, without the consent of their parents, ought to have a capacity of contracting the matrimonial, whilst they have not the capacity of contracting any other engagement. (cited in Foster, 1908/1932, p. 37)

Burke thereby narrowed his burden of proof, excluding irrelevant considerations in order to direct his (and his audience's) attention to the issues in genuine dispute.

The exclusion of irrelevant matters from consideration is extremely important in legal argument as well. The court rules as to whether evidence and lines of questioning are admissible, partly on the basis of their potential relevance (probative value). Even so, not all admitted evidence and the arguments to which it pertains will ultimately prove relevant to the charges as framed by the disputants.

In 1780, Lord George Gordon, a young Scottish member of the House of Commons, was tried for high treason. As the president of the Protestant Association, he had sought the repeal of a bill favoring Catholics. He requested that members of the association meet him at St. George's Fields and march to Parliament, where they would present a petition for repeal. Forty thousand unarmed supporters did so, and their petition was peaceably presented by Lord George in the House of Commons. When the House refused to consider the petition, a riot ensued in which Catholic chapels were destroyed, prisons were opened and set afire, and the city of London fell to mob rule for several days.

Lord George was charged with high treason, on the grounds that he assembled the crowd in order to intimidate the legislature and to "enforce his purposes by numbers and violence." In his defense, Lord Erskine sought to separate the genuine issues of the case from those that had captured the public's attention.

> I trust that I need not remind you (members of the jury) that the purposes of that multitude, as *originally* assembled on that day, and the purposes and acts of him who assembled them, are the sole object of investigation. All the dismal consequences which followed, and which naturally link themselves with this subject in the firmest minds, must be altogether cut off and abstracted from your attention further than the evidence warrants their admission. (Baker & Huntington, 1905, p. 44)

The skillful advocate attempts to exclude irrelevant concerns, narrow his or her burden of proof, and direct attention to the heart of the matter.

2. It is sometimes also important for the advocate to explain what s/he does not advocate. When U.S. Representative Patricia Schroeder argued in 1987 at a Harvard Law School forum in favor of reducing the number of American troops stationed abroad, she took care to explain what this position did *not* entail:

> I do not advocate that the United States cut and run from its commitments. Rather, I think there are strong arguments that now is the time to begin reducing the number of troops we have stationed abroad. And this argument does not come from any recurrence of isolationism or a Fortress America mentality. (in Johannesen et al., 1988, p. 246)

After distinguishing her position from these damaging associations at the outset of her speech, Schroeder proceeded to support the claim that troop reduction would not affect the viability of American security commitments or active engagement in world affairs.

A second example of this technique may be found in the contemporary abortion debate. Many proponents of legal abortion (especially politicians confronted with vehement constituents on both sides of the issue) have sought to distinguish their support for abortion *rights* from the support of abortion itself. This distinction has often been made in the form of a qualifier such as "Although I would never seek an abortion *myself*. . . ." Advocates have thus sought to narrow the focus of discussion to the question of who should make the abortion decision.

In the trial of Lord George Gordon discussed earlier, Lord Erskine's defense also included a careful distinction between his actual claim regarding the defendant and the case that the jury or prosecutor might have expected him to make.

> Though I am perfectly convinced of the purity of my noble friend's intentions, yet I am not bound to defend his prudence, nor to set it up as a pattern for imitation: since you are not trying him for imprudence, for indiscreet zeal, or for want of foresight and precaution, but for a deliberate and malicious predetermination to overpower the laws and government of his country by hostile, rebelious force. (Baker & Huntington, 1905, p. 45)

Lord Erskine differentiated the case he will (and must) make from the arguments that might otherwise be expected of him. He simultaneously lessened his own burden of proof (not needing to show Lord George to be prudent) while increasing the burden of the prosecutor (to show that Lord

George *planned* the riots that ensued). Having cast aside the false conception of his position, he had set the stage for an elaboration of his actual case.

## Presentation of the Counterposition

Having explained, when necessary, what one's counterposition is *not*, it is then appropriate to explain what one's counterposition *is*. The counterposition should be clearly and succinctly described; it is normally a brief statement of principle that you hold in contrast to that of your adversaries. In the example of the Family Leave Act controversy discussed earlier, President Bush's description of his counterposition consisted of two components: support for the *concept* of family leave and support of a different way in which employers should provide it (voluntarily).

Explanation, support, and use of the counterposition may be accomplished through the following three steps.

*Contrast the Counterposition With the Position Advocated by Your Adversary.* A counterposition, by definition, exists in opposition with some other, competing system. The counterposition is most effective when this competition can be succinctly framed, creating a duality from which the arbiter must choose. In the Family Leave Act dispute, President Bush framed the dispute as one between *voluntary* and *compelled* provision of leave by employers. This framing not only provided a basic point of contrast between the two sides in the debate, but framed the dispute in powerfully connotative terms. According to this formulation, Bush was for voluntarism, his opponents for compulsion; Bush was for free enterprise, his opponents for government regulation. In this duality, he had painted his adversaries in a highly pejorative light.

Another effective use of the contrastive counterposition may be found in the long-standing dispute over a proposed amendment to the U.S. Constitution that would limit the presidency to a single, 6-year term. Proponents, such as former U.S. Attorney General Griffin Bell and other members of the Committee for a single 6-year presidential term, argue that the single 6-year term would free the president from reelection pressures that "lie at the heart of our inability to manage complex, long-term national problems" (Barnet & Bedau, 1987, p. 102) Bell and others argue that presidents are unwilling to face up to tough decisions before reelection, postponing important matters. It has been suggested, for example, that President Reagan failed to tackle the federal budget deficit in his first term for fear that to do so would damage his chances for reelection in 1984; and that President Kennedy failed to pull out of what he believed to be a doomed intervention in Vietnam for fear that this would be perceived as weakness in a reelection bid. By limiting the presidency to a single 6-year term, proponents argue, presidents would be more likely to do what they believe is right and necessary, rather than worrying so much about how it will affect their chances for reelection.

In response, historian Arthur Schlesinger, Jr., (1986) offered a compelling contrast between the competing principles of his counterposition and the position of his adversaries who support the proposal.

> The proposal of a single six-year Presidential term has been around for a long time. High-minded men have urged it from the beginning of the Republic. The Constitutional Convention turned it down in 1787, and recurrent efforts to put it in the Constitution have regularly failed in the two centuries since. Quite right: It is a terrible idea for a number of reasons, among them that it is at war with the philosophy of democracy.
>
> The basic argument for the one-term, six-year Presidency is that the quest for reelection is at the heart of our problems with self-government. The desire for reelection, it is claimed, drives Presidents to do things they would not otherwise do. It leads them to make easy promises and to postpone hard decisions. A single six-year term would liberate Presidents from the pressures and temptations of politics. Instead of worrying about reelection, they would be free to do only what was best for the country.
>
> The argument is superficially attractive. But when you think about it, it is profoundly anti-democratic in its implications. It assumes Presidents know better than anyone else what is best for the country and that the people are so wrongheaded and ignorant that Presidents should be encouraged to disregard their wishes. It assumes that the less responsive a President is to popular desires and needs, the better President he will be. It assumes that the democratic process is the obstacle to wise decisions.
>
> The theory of American democracy is quite the opposite. It is that the give-and-take of the democratic process is the best source of wise decisions. It is that the President's duty is not to ignore and override popular concerns but to acknowledge and heed them. It is that the President's accountability to the popular will is the best guarantee that he will do a good job.
>
> The one-term limitation, as Gouverneur Morris, final draftsman of the Constitution, persuaded the convention, would "destroy the great motive to good behavior," which is the hope of reelection. A President, said Oliver Ellsworth, another Founding Father, "should be reelected if his conduct prove worthy of it. And he will be more likely to render himself worthy of it if he be rewardable with it."
>
> Few things have a more tonic effect on a President's sensitivity to public needs and hopes than the desire for reelection. "A President immunized from political considerations," Clark Clifford told the Senate Judiciary Committee when it was considering the proposal some years ago, "is a President who need not listen to the people, respond to majority sentiment or pay attention to views that may be diverse, intense and perhaps at variance with his

own. . . . Concern for one's own political future can be a powerful stimulus to responsible and responsive performance in office."

We all saw the tempering effect of the desire for reelection on Ronald Reagan in 1984. He dropped his earlier talk about the "evil empire," announced a concealed passion for arms control, slowed down the movement toward intervention in Central America, affirmed his loyalty to Social Security and the "safety net" and in other ways moderated his hard ideological positions. A single six-year term would have given Reaganite ideology full, uninhibited sway . . . "By seeking to determine by fixed constitutional provision what the people are perfectly competent to determine by themselves," (Woodrow) Wilson said in 1913, "we cast a doubt upon the whole theory of popular government."

A single six-year term would release Presidents from the test of submitting their records to the voters. It would enshrine the "President-knows-best" myth, which has already got us into sufficient trouble as a nation. It would be a mighty blow against Presidential accountability. It would be a mighty reinforcement of the imperial Presidency. It would be an impeachment of the democratic process itself. The Founding Fathers were everlastingly right when they turned down this well-intentioned but ill-considered proposal 200 years ago. (Schlesinger, 1986, p. 104–105)

In the opening paragraph, Schlesinger offered a brief glimpse of the principle at stake that he would support in his counterposition: "the philosophy of democracy," with which he believed the proposal for a single-term 6-year presidency to be "at war." In the second paragraph, he offered a clear conceptualization of the proponents' position, stating their case from their perspective. He acknowledged that the promises of their case are "superficially attractive."

Beginning in the third paragraph, Schlesinger constructed his counterposition, exemplified through a series of dualities in which he contrasted his position with that of his adversaries. In its simplest form, he portrayed the conflict as between those who are "anti-democratic" (the proponents of the Amendment) and those who believe in democracy (himself). This basic contrast is elaborated through a series of further dualities. Schlesinger framed the positions of the two sides as follows:

### The Two Sides According to Schlesinger

| BELL'S POSITION | SCHLESINGER'S POSITION |
|---|---|
| Presidents know best. | People know best. |
| Disdain for American people. | Belief in American people. |
| (Assumes they are "wrongheaded and ignorant.") | (Assumes they are "the best source of wise decisions.") |
| Imperial Presidency. | Democratic accountability. |

Thus, Schlesinger constructed a counterposition based not simply on the negation of the proponent's position but on the *affirmation* of another, competing principle (democratic accountability). His framing of the dispute highlighted what he believed to be the central issue and cast his opposition in an unflattering light: as elitist enemies of democracy. Because this debate was a public one, carried out in the popular press, Schlesinger's framing of the dispute was especially damaging to the proponents of the Amendment. According to Schlesinger, the readers were being asked by the proponents to discredit themselves and to limit their own ability to check unwanted actions of their president.

Precisely because the framing of the two sides can be so powerful, it is important to remember that it is subject to debate. The proponents of the single 6-year presidential term would be unlikely to accept the framing of the dispute provided by Schlesinger. To accept Schlesinger's portrait of what they stand for and what he stands for would be to accept likely defeat. Debates often feature considerable dispute over how the two sides should be portrayed and contrasted, as each side attempts to draw the lines in a way most favorable to its own cause.

When potential United States sanctions were considered against China following the repression of demonstrators in Tienanmen Square and elsewhere, each side in the dispute tried to frame the debate in a particular way. Those who favored severe sanctions against China framed the dispute as one of: hypocrisy versus principled action.

Proponents of sanctions accused the Bush administration of hypocrisy in not supporting strict sanctions, arguing that the administration's actions were inconsistent with its (and the nation's) professed ideals (commitments to human rights).

But the opponents of stricter sanctions offered their own framing of the dispute. Instead of accepting the proponents' portrayal of themselves as hypocrites who had betrayed their principles, opponents depicted themselves as *upholding an alternate principle*. In the opponents' reformulation of the debate, the dispute amounted to a conflict between: coercion versus diplomacy, or isolation versus communication.

Opponents of sanctions argued that those who proposed them were turning their backs on diplomacy when it was most needed. Maintaining trade and diplomatic relations, opponents insisted, was essential in order to encourage reform. Instead of cutting off relations, we should *use* our relations with the Chinese, they argued.

The debate in the U.S. Congress over what course of action should be followed centered around these very different views of the dispute. The construction by one side of a particular duality to frame the debate need not be accepted by the other. The other side may seek to dispel the unflattering way in which it has been portrayed by constructing an alternative view of what each side stands for.

*Explain the Reasons* or Philosophy Behind Your Position.   It is not enough to explain what your position is and how it differs from that of your opponent. You must also explain the reasons that have led you to support the position: the principles that undergird the position and reasons why these principles deserve support.

Just as it is important to distinguish one's actual position from false preconceptions of it, it is often necessary to distinguish one's actual reasons for supporting a position from false preconceptions of them. People may support the same judgment or policy for very different reasons. Debaters should distinguish their actual reasons from others that might be imagined, especially when there exist other supporters of the policy *with whose reasons you disagree.*

An example of this technique of differentiation may be seen in the anti-pornography campaign of Susan Brownmiller and other feminists. In opposing pornography, feminists have found themselves strangely allied with religious fundamentalists and political conservatives. Because these associations may prove damaging in Brownmiller's efforts to enlist the support of other feminists for her position, she took care to explain in a 1979 manifesto, "Let's Put Pornography Back in the Closet," that her *reasons* for opposing pornography were quite different:

> The feminist objection to pornography is not based on prurience, which the dictionary defines as painful, itching desire. We are not opposed to sex and desire, with or without the itch, and we certainly believe that explicit sexual material has its place in literature, art, science and education. Here we part company with old-line conservatives who don't want sex education in the high schools, for example.
>
> No, the feminist objection to pornography is based on our belief that pornography represents hatred of women, that pornography's intent is to humiliate, degrade and dehumanize the female body for the purpose of erotic stimulation and pleasure. We are unalterably opposed to the presentation of the female body being stripped, bound, raped, tortured, mutilated and murdered in the name of commercial entertainment and free speech. (Barnet & Bedau, 1987, p. 259)

Brownmiller thus contrasted *her* reasons for support of antipornography measures from those of other supporters with whom she preferred not to be identified. Having distinguished the two, she then elaborated on her own reasons in more detail.

*Explain Why Your Position Should Win the Debate.*   It is not enough to express a position different from that of one's adversary; reasons must be given as to why these differences should prove decisive. The counter-position (as opposed to a counterplan in which some alternate course of action is advocated) is normally a statement of the opposition's philosophy. If, as in the example of the debate over the 6-year presidency, the counterposition consists of an alternate value or principle (e.g., "democracy vs. imperial presidency"), a hierarchical relationship must be established between these principles demonstrating the superiority of the value upheld by the opposition. Do not assume that the superiority of the value upheld in the counterposition is self-evident. Despite the fact that most of his intended audience would have assumed "democracy" to be a desirable state, Schlesinger took care to:

1. Demonstrate that this value was at risk in the dispute; that the proposal for a single 6-year term jeopardized democratic accountability for the most important elected office; and
2. Demonstrate why, in the specific issues covered in the dispute, the countervalue was superior. Schlesinger offered a series of historical examples in which the reelection-based popular check on Presidential action produced wise policy.

The counterposition should offer a clear synthesis of the opposition's philosophy in the debate and a basis from which individual arguments proceed. It should offer the audience or judge something to vote *for* in the opposition's position, elevating their arguments from mere denial of the proponents' claims. In presenting its counterposition, the opposition should seize the opportunity to dismiss damaging preconceptions of its position that may result from false portrayal by the other side or from potential misunderstandings on the part of the audience itself. Finally, the counterposition should offer a clear, succinct explanation of the differences between the two sides and why these differences should govern the outcome of the dispute.

## COUNTERPLANS

Every moment of decision is a nexus of possibilities, a fork in the road through the future. In deciding which path to walk, we try to judge what lies ahead: where each path will lead us and what we are likely to encounter along the way. In his poem "The Road Not Taken," Robert Frost (1915/1971) wrote of his confrontation with such a choice:

Two roads diverged in a yellow wood,
And sorry I could not travel both
And be one traveler, long I stood
And looked down one as far as I could
To where it bent in the undergrowth. (p. 270)

Just as Frost's protagonist peers ahead through the yellow wood, all decision makers must struggle to see what the future will hold if they decide to walk one road instead of another. Policy debate is always a dispute between different predicted outcomes of a given decision. Each side defends a particular vision of the future. At a minimum, each side must imagine what the world would be like if the proposed policy existed and what it would be like if it did not. Would the policy yield significant benefits? Produce terrible costs? Encounter significant obstacles? Because these questions about the proposed policy require one to speculate about events that have not yet happened (the policy has not yet been adopted), the answers to them are always uncertain and debatable.

The central fact of decision making is that the proposed policy is not the only road through the future. As economic cost analyst R.E. Bickner (1971) has observed:

The costs and benefits of a decision lie in the differences between two alternative worlds. Even in retrospect, even after a certain decision has been made and implemented, we cannot fully determine its costs and benefits without estimating the different state of the world that would otherwise have ensued. (p. 44)

What would the world be like if we chose not to adopt the proposed policy? One way to answer this question is to predict what would happen were we to continue our current course, retaining the "present system." If the affirmative proposes that economic sanctions against South Africa should be eliminated, it would be necessary to compare the potential outcomes of dropping sanctions with the likely consequences of retaining them. Both judgments require predictions of the future. If the opposition were to defend the "present" system against a proposed change, it would really be defending the future performance of that system. The opposition would argue that the future outcomes of the present system are superior to the predicted outcomes of the affirmative plan. Evidence about the success or failure of the sanctions in the past or present would be relevant to the decision only insofar as they provide a basis for predicting the future performance of the sanctions policy.

All policy decisions, whether in the legislature, corporate board meeting, or mundane world of personal affairs, place the decision maker at a fork in the road through the future, requiring that he or she peer ahead and compare the probable outcomes of possible choices. In Charles Dickens' *A Christmas Carol*, it is Scrooge's terrifying vision of "Christmas yet to come" that induces him to mend his miserly ways. He adopts a new attitude when shown what will happen if he retains his present one, a future in which he is despised even in death, his accumulated wealth is dispersed, and in which Tiny Tim, the sickly but angelic son of his underpaid clerk, has died for lack of the money necessary for proper medical care. Scrooge is left at the fork in his personal road: If he continues his current course, the awful events he has just witnessed will come to pass; If he takes the advice of his ghostly guides and truly embraces the spirit of Christmas "all year 'round," they tell him, these undesirable outcomes may yet be avoided. Scrooge changes the course of his life by taking the latter road.

We each make hundreds of decisions, big and small, every day; each of which places us at a fork in the road through the future. Like Scrooge, we too face moral and ethical decisions; we are surrounded by temptations to wrongful deeds and by possibilities for good ones. We also face more mundane decisions that have the same basic properties. When we decide what clothes to don in the morning, for example, we are faced with a range of choices whose outcomes must be predicted. Choosing among the available options, we may peer ahead through the day to come, predicting what the weather will be like and what functions we will attend. We may then determine what clothing will be most comfortable and appropriate to the day we have projected.

At all moments of decision making, we face a fork in the road through the future. In order to decide which path to take, we peer ahead through the yellow wood to see what outcomes each choice may hold. When we finally decide to walk one path, we are also deciding not to walk another. As policy analyst Aaron Wildavsky (1979) has noted:

> In choosing to do any one thing, whether we realize it or not, we are rejecting alternate activities, at least at the same time, usually making at least implicit decisions on how we personally value things by actually giving up some for others. (p. 161)

In Frost's poem, the narrator chooses one road over the other and, in the poem's famous final lines, expresses confidence that he has made the right choice:

> I shall be telling this with a sigh
> Somewhere ages and ages hence:
> Two roads diverged in a wood, and I—

I took the one less traveled by,
And that has made all the difference. (p. 271)


Yet despite the confidence expressed in its final lines, the title of Frost's poem draws attention to the *other* road, the "road not taken." It seems at odds with the self-assuredness of the final lines and draws attention to the unresolved question of the poem: What lay down that other road?

The job of the opposition in any policy debate is to identify and defend what lies down that other road, the "road not taken" if the proposed policy is adopted. In order to win the debate, the opposition must demonstrate that what lies down that other road is more valuable and/or less risky than what lies down the road proffered by the affirmative. The counterplan is the clearest way in which the opposition may articulate what lies down the road not taken. The counterplan is simply an alternative course of action, the benefits of which are foregone if the affirmative's policy is adopted. In the field of economics and formal policy analysis, the counterplan is referred to as an "opportunity cost."


## Opportunity Costs


The concept of opportunity cost is a simple one, as E.S. Quade (1982) explained:

> It is in the alternatives, that is, in the foregone opportunities, that the real meaning of cost must always be found. An estimate of the cost of any decision is then an estimate of the benefits that could otherwise have been obtained if some other decision had been made. (p. 118)


Sometimes referred to as "economic costs" or "alternative costs," opportunity costs force attention to the roads not taken if a given policy is adopted. We usually think of costs as the "price tags" attached to an action; if we buy a new car, we think of it as costing *x* amount of money. But the true cost of that car consists not of a certain amount of money, but rather of *the lost benefits we might have obtained by buying something else with that money.* Instead of "outlay costs," the direct price tags attached to an action, opportunity costs measure the potential benefits lost by taking that action instead of another.

Every decision entails opportunity costs. By deciding to do one thing, we lose our opportunity to do others. The true cost of our decision to do one thing consists of the benefits we have foregone by not taking the best alternative course of action.

The true cost of a college education at University Q consists not of the tuition and fees paid to that university, but rather of the benefits lost by not devoting those resources (money and time) to something else, such as attending a different university, investment, or going directly into the job market.

The true cost of a city's decision to build a public swimming pool consists not of the amount of money it will take to build it, but rather of the value attached to the best alternative use of the resources (money, land, planning) that will be devoted to it.

The true cost of a business firm's decision to allocate more of its budget to television advertising consist of the value assigned to the best alternative use of that budget line (e.g., advertising in another medium, plant expansion, salary bonuses).

Whether we realize it or not, we often compute opportunity costs in making personal decisions. The aphorism, "You can't have your cake and eat it, too" is a statement of opportunity cost (Wildavsky, 1979, p. 161). Choice is forced between competing alternatives; the value of one is the true cost of the other. In deciding to read this chapter at this time, you have foregone many alternatives. Instead of reading it now, for example, you could be watching a television program now being broadcast, exercising, or doing charitable work. The true cost of reading this chapter consists of the value placed on the best of these foregone activities.

Economist Paul Samuelson (1976) illustrated the concept of opportunity cost by reconstructing Robinson Crusoe's decision as to how he should spend his time after he is marooned on a tropical island. In deciding whether to pick strawberries, Crusoe must imagine how else he might spend that time.

Some of the most important costs attributable to doing one thing rather than another stem from the foregone opportunities that have to be sacrificed in doing this one thing. Thus, Robinson Crusoe pays no money to anyone, but realizes that the cost of picking strawberries can be thought of as the sacrificed amount of raspberries he might otherwise have picked with the same time and effort or the sacrificed amount of foregone-leisure. (Samuelson, 1976, p. 475)

Thus, all decisions, whether personal, corporate, or legislative, present opportunity costs. By choosing to do one thing, we forego the benefits of having done another. In a policy debate, the opposition may attempt to identify an alternative course of action and its foresaken benefits through the presentation of a counterplan.

## Counterplans as Opportunity Costs

The presentation of a counterplan amounts to an argument by the opposition that **the true cost of the affirmative's policy lies in the foregone benefits of an available alternative.** By adopting the affirmative plan, they argue, we will sacrifice the benefits that could be achieved by adopting another, superior course of action.

In the 1990 Congressional debate over a proposal that the United States should suspend China's trading status as a "Most Favored Nation" (M.F.N.; which entitles it to lower tariffs and other trade benefits) following that government's crackdown against political dissidents, a counterplan was advocated by some opponents. By rescinding China's M.F.N. status, they argued, we would sacrifice the ability to use that status as a lever with which to encourage reforms. These opponents proposed an alternative: We should extend China's M.F.N. status for 1 year, on the condition that the Chinese government undertake specified political reforms (such as the release of political prisoners). If these conditions had not been met by the end of the year's extension, *then* China's M.F.N. status would be rescinded. The true cost of a decision to rescind M.F.N. status *now*, opponents argued, consists of whatever political reforms might be achieved by extending it on these conditions.

In order to calculate the opportunity costs entailed by a particular decision, it is necessary to identify the best (most beneficial) foregone alternative. As Wildavsky (1979) insisted, it is "only by the value of the best alternative that must be foregone to take such action" that an opportunity cost can be assigned (p. 156). In presenting a counterplan, the opposition declares it to be the best available alternative to the policy being debated, "best" because it would provide the most significant benefits that would be sacrificed if the affirmative plan were to be adopted.

In presenting a counterplan, the opposition should:

1. Provide a clear explanation of what the counterplan *is* and how it would work. Just as the affirmative speakers must describe the policy they advocate in sufficient detail for its operation and outcomes to be assessed, so too must the opposition in presenting an alternative course of action;

2. Identify the benefits that the alternative policy would yield. These benefits may be of three sorts:

A. Benefits gained by *both* plan and counterplan, demonstrating that the counterplan achieves some or all of the benefits that the affirmative speakers have claimed for their own proposal;

B. Benefits *unique* to the counterplan, that the affirmative plan will not yield; and/or

C. Avoidance of *dis*advantages unique to the affirmative plan. Any disadvantage uniquely attributable to one policy is a comparative advantage to a competing policy. If, in the process of buying a car, you learn that the exhaust system of one model you are considering is prone to failure, the *lack* of such problems would be considered an advantage of a competing model;

Ultimately, the counterplan must be shown to be comparatively advantageous.

3. Demonstrate that the counterplan advantages will be *sacrificed* if the affirmative plan is adopted. The opposition must do more than demonstrate that their proposal will yield benefits; they must show that these benefits are a *cost* of adopting the affirmative proposal. In order to establish that one is a cost of the other, the two must be shown to *compete*.

Competition between plan and counterplan is usually the central issue in a counterplan debate. In order for the counterplan to constitute a reason for rejecting the affirmative plan, the two proposals must be shown to be competitive. Some reason must be demonstrated that the two proposals *could not* or *should not* both be adopted. Stated in terms of opportunity costs, the opposition must demonstrate that by adopting the affirmative plan, potential benefits available through the counterplan would be sacrificed. The key question thus becomes: In what sense does the counterplan represent a *cost* of the proposal?; or, more pointedly, Why and to what extent are the benefits of the counterplan sacrificed by adopting the affirmative proposal?

Let us imagine that you are invited to a party this evening. In deciding whether or not to attend, you weigh the option of the party against another alternative: staying home to watch a favorite program on television. Is the value you attach to watching the television program an opportunity cost of attending the party? Must you sacrifice the values of watching the program if you decide to attend? Not necessarily. If, for example, you own a videocassette recorder, you might set it to record the television program *while* you are attending the party, then watch it after you return. In this way, the benefits of watching the television program would not be sacrificed by choosing to attend the party. It is then not an opportunity cost and does not constitute a reason not to attend the party.

Similarly, if one were to oppose a policy to send food supplies to Iranian earthquake victims on the grounds that medical assistance would be more valuable, one must confront the simple question: Why not do *both?* By sending food assistance, do we sacrifice our ability to send medical supplies? Are the medical supplies an opportunity cost of sending food? There may be some argument that they are in the short run, because of limited transportation and distribution systems. Only so much material can be distributed in the first 48 hours following the disaster, and we must choose what these shipments will and will not contain. Beyond that period of time, however, there may be no reason to sacrifice one form of relief in order to provide another—more airplanes, pilots, and relief workers can be dedicated to the task of distribution in order to dispense both medical supplies *and* needed food.

The question "Why not do both?" is the primary basis for determining whether a plan and counterplan are in competition. This question, in turn, is best answered through the application of the "net benefits" standard: **In presenting a counterplan, the opposition must demonstrate that the benefits of adopting the counterplan *alone* outweigh the benefits of adopting *both* plan and counterplan.**

This requirement may be expressed in the following formula: CP > P + CP. It must be shown that some potential benefits of the counterplan are sacrificed if the affirmative plan is adopted. Unless this is demonstrated, the counterplan does not constitute a true opportunity cost of the affirmative plan.

Let us imagine that on the last evening of your vacation in a foreign land, you must decide where to dine among several restaurants that you find appealing. If you choose restaurant $Q$, must you sacrifice the pleasures of consuming the famous nine-course meal served at restaurant $R$? It may be physically possible for one to pursue both these dining options in a single evening. Yet in doing so, your enjoyment of the dining experience as a whole will be markedly diminished.

Even when it is physically possible to pursue both of two suggested options, it is not always best to do so. A city faced with difficulty in choosing between two public works projects in a given fiscal year (e.g., repairing streets and bridges and building a new elementary school) may decide to pursue both, only to discover that the tax increases necessary to fund the two projects instead of one has produced great personal hardship for many people.

Another instance in which adoption of the counterplan alone may prove preferable to adoption of both plan and counterplan is when co-existence with the plan substantially reduces the benefits produced by the counterplan. In the widespread public debate over how to handle the problem of illegal drug use, some prominent politicians have argued in favor of legalizing drugs (which, by lowering prices, may reduce property crime and other undesirable consequences of drug use). Some opponents have argued for increased efforts in drug education and counseling, decreasing use through prevention and treatment. These seem on the surface to be compatible; there is no physical reason to regard legalization and education as mutually exclusive. Yet education efforts might be *undermined* by legalization. Drug education and counseling attempt to convince people to avoid or cease taking drugs because they are harmful. Legalization, regardless of its actual purposes, would send a powerful implicit message that the government regards drugs as safe and acceptable. If drug education were rendered less effective by legalization, it would constitute an opportunity cost of the decision to legalize.

When the benefits of adopting the counterplan alone exceed those of adopting both plan and counterplan, plan and counterplan are competitive. One *should not* adopt both, even if it is possible to do so (Lichtman & Rohrer, 1975, pp. 75–78).

All counterplan debates, then, require that the alternative be clearly specified, comparatively advantageous, and competitive with the affirmative proposal. In "The Road Not Taken," Frost's narrator uses precisely these factors to decide between the two paths he confronts. One path, he decides, presents intangible but significant benefits that will be sacrificed if he chooses to walk the other. He begins by assessing the virtues of each path. After looking down one as far as he could, he

Then took the other, as just as fair,
And having perhaps the better claim,
Because it was grassy and wanted wear.

The narrator admits that this difference in wear is not a very large one: "Though as for that the passing there/ Had worn them really about the same." But even minor differences may produce significant advantages. In the poem's final stanza, the narrator declares the advantage that this slightly less-worn path presents over the other. He imagines his future self looking back at this moment of decision. Taking the road "less traveled by," he pronounces, "has made all the difference."

But is this unconventional benefit truly an opportunity cost of the other road? If the narrator had chosen to walk "the road not taken," would he necessarily have sacrificed the benefits to be obtained by walking the other? Frost's narrator answers this question in part by establishing that the unconventional benefits are *unique* to the road that he has chosen. But *must* he choose between the roads? He must, of course, choose only one to walk *now* ("I could not travel both and be one traveler"). He could, however, return later to walk the other. Frost's narrator at first reassures himself with this idea ("Oh, I kept the first for another day!"), then realizes that this is self-delusion: "Yet knowing how way leads on to way,/ I doubted if I should ever come back." There is no escaping the need to choose between the roads before him; by deciding to walk one, he abandons the other.

Frost's narrator weighs plan and counterplan. He decides that they are *competitive* (he must choose between them; by adopting one he foregoes some benefits of the other). He examines the potential benefits of each, and ultimately adopts one rather than the other because of a perceived advantage: It is "less traveled by." In all counterplan debates, the decision maker must peer ahead through the yellow wood of prospective outcomes and determine what lies down "the road not taken" as well as down the path advocated by the affirmative. The process of decision making followed by Frost's narrator involves the same basic considerations and issues as more conventional policy disputes involving a counterplan.

## Case Study in Counterplan Advocacy: An Alternative to the Bombing of Hiroshima

In June 1945, U.S. President Harry Truman and his advisers decided to use the atomic bomb against Japan as soon as possible and without notice. The Potsdam Declaration issued on July 26 reiterated the American demand for unconditional surrender, a demand to which the Japanese responded with indignant silence. On August 6, the United States dropped an atomic bomb on Hiroshima and another 3 days later on Nagasaki. Japan surrendered soon after the Nagasaki bombing.

But this course of action was not the only one available. During the deliberations over the plan to drop the bomb, various alternatives had been considered. One of the most interesting was outlined in a top secret memorandum delivered on June 28 to George L. Harrison in the War Department by Under Secretary of the Navy Ralph Bard:

Memorandum on the Use of S-1 Bomb
Ever since I have been in touch with this program I have had a feeling that before the bomb is actually used against Japan that Japan should have some preliminary warning for say two or three days in advance of use. The position of the United States as a great humanitarian nation and the fair play attitude of our people generally is responsible in the main for this feeling.

During recent weeks I have also had the feeling very definitely that the Japanese government may be searching for some opportunity which they could use as a medium of surrender. Following the three-power conference emissaries from this country could contact representatives from Japan somewhere on the China Coast and make representations with regard to Russia's position and at the same time give them some information regarding the proposed use of atomic power, together with whatever assurances the President might care to make with regard to the Emperor of Japan and the treatment of the Japanese nation following unconditional surrender. It seems quite possible to me that this presents the opportunity which the Japanese are looking for.

I don't see that we have anything in particular to lose in following such a program. The stakes are so tremendous that it is my opinion very real consideration should be given to some plan of this kind. I do not believe

under present circumstances existing that there is anyone in this country
whose evaluation of the chances of the success of such a program is worth a
great deal. The only way to find out is to try it out.
(signed) Ralph A. Bard
27 June 1945
(Sherwin, 1987, pp. 307–308)

Bard's counterplan proposed that instead of dropping the bomb without
warning or diplomatic contact, that the U.S. should:

1. Make clear to the Japanese what would happen to them if they
   were to surrender. The Japanese, as the U.S. knew at the time,
   were especially concerned with whether they would be allowed to
   retain the Emperor and whether he would be tried for war crimes;
2. Offer warning that we were about to introduce a new and devastating weapon; and
3. Notify the Japanese that the Soviets were about to declare war on
   them.

Bard's proposal and Truman's policy to attack without warning or
diplomatic contact are mutually exclusive, hence competitive. The unique
benefits of each constitute a cost of choosing the other.

Bard suggested two comparative advantages borne by his counterplan:

1. An improved chance of surrender with fewer casualties (particularly if surrender could be achieved without use of the bomb); and
2. More humane action (Bard implied that the U.S. bore a moral
   obligation to try to avoid the use of the bomb, relying on its
   destructiveness only as a last resort).

The prospects for the success of Bard's counterplan in inducing Japanese surrender is supported by American intelligence of the time. According to U.S. intelligence reports, the Emperor had decided to surrender as early as June 20, 1945. In July, the Japanese tried to arrange
surrender terms by using the Soviets as intermediaries through which to
approach the United States. U.S. forces had broken the Japanese codes
prior to the war, and were able to intercept and read the transmissions
between the Japanese government and its envoys in the Soviet Union.
Truman's diaries, first published in 1979, show that he regarded the
willingness of the Emperor to surrender as genuine. He knew from the
July 13 cable of Japanese Foreign Minister Togo that "Unconditional
surrender is the only obstacle to peace" (because they regarded the terms
as too dishonorable), yet was unwilling to clarify to the Japanese what such

surrender would mean for them. (Sherwin, 1987, p. 235) Bard proposed that those conditions be clarified in advance (that the Japanese Emperor would be retained and not prosecuted), which we were ultimately to accept anyway. By doing so, he argued, an earlier surrender might have been achieved without the atomic bombing of Hiroshima and Nagasaki.

Bard's proposal that the United States notify the Japanese of the imminent Soviet entrance into the Pacific war was also aimed at securing earlier and less costly surrender. It should be remembered that the Japanese believed that the Soviets would assist them in initiating peace negotiations with the U.S. When the Soviets suddenly declared war on Japan and invaded Manchuria on August 9, it stunned the Japanese and was, according to a U.S. Army Intelligence Report issued in April, 1946, the decisive factor in convincing them to surrender:

> While the Japanese were awaiting an answer from Russia, there occurred the disastrous event which the Japanese leaders regarded as utter catastrophe and which they had energetically sought to prevent at any cost— Russia declared war on Japan and began moving her forces into Manchuria. Events had moved too swiftly for the Japanese, and Premier Suzuki, at about 0700, 9 August, presented the Emperor with two alternatives: to declare war on the Russians and continue the war, or to accept the Potsdam Declaration. The latter course was decided upon and the machinery was put into operation to implement this decision. (Ennis, 1946, pp. 4–5)

Based on interrogations of the Japanese cabinet members, the U.S. intelligence report concluded that "there was little mention of the use of the atomic bomb by the United States in the discussions leading up to the 9 August decision" to surrender. Instead, it was the Soviet entry into the war that convinced the most ardent militarists that it was impossible to continue "without all of Japan being destroyed and her people exterminated." The Soviet entry into the war, the report concludes, "would almost certainly have furnished this pretext" for surrender in itself, without the necessity of atomic bombing. Truman's own diary entries during the Potsdam conference seem to support this hypothesis. After Stalin agreed to invade Japan, Truman himself wrote "Fini Japs [*sic*] when that happens" and, in a letter to his wife: "We'll end the war a year sooner now, and think of the kids who won't be killed" (Alperovitz, 1989, A23). Nevertheless, Truman kept the Soviet entry into the war secret until after the bombing of Hiroshima.

Thus, it may be argued that Bard's counterplan presented a reasonable chance of gaining the Japanese surrender without having to drop the atomic bomb, by clarifying surrender terms and by notifying them of the Soviets' plan to enter the war. The advantages of doing so include the avoidance of massive casualties associated with the atomic bombings and the satisfaction of a moral requirement to exhaust reasonable alternatives before resorting to mass destruction. These advantages constituted opportunity costs of Truman's decision to drop the bomb without warning or prior diplomatic contact.

### Countering the Counterplan

The counterplan, although a potentially powerful form of argument, is certainly susceptible to refutation on a number of grounds. Successful refutation of a counterplan normally relies on the following arguments.

*Deny That the Counterplan Is Competitive.* Unless the counterplan competes with the affirmative plan, we are not forced to choose between them. No reason has been provided to vote against the plan.

The mere demonstration that the counterplan presents more significant advantages does not establish that they are competitive. If a bill were introduced in the U.S. Congress to prosecute those who burned the American flag, a counterproposal to send additional food aid to sub-Saharan Africa might be more significant, but would not be competitive with the original proposal. It would not constitute a reason for rejecting the original proposal.

In refuting a counterplan, advocates of the original proposal should always ask themselves: Why can't we do both? It may be demonstrated that the two proposals themselves are compatible. In the preceding example, both pieces of legislation could be adopted without diminishing the benefits of either. In other cases, it may be shown that the *benefits* of the counterplan can be gained even if the plan is adopted, and that they therefore do not constitute true opportunity costs of the affirmative's proposal.

*Diminish the Significance of the Counterplan Advantages.* The advantages of the counterplan are opportunity costs of the affirmative plan, benefits that are foregone if the plan is adopted. The opportunity costs attributed to the affirmative's plan must be shown to be more significant than the unique advantages of the plan. Thus, proponents of the original plan may seek to diminish the significance of the advantages claimed for the counterplan. In the example of the Bard alternative to the atomic bombing of Japan, a proponent of the bombing might well argue that the prospects for gaining surrender through Bard's mechanisms were miniscule – that it was the destructiveness and shock of the bomb that provided the pretext for honorable surrender. This argument suggests that the counterplan will be less likely to *gain* the advantage (less costly surrender) claimed for it.

The significance of the counterplan advantages may also be reduced by disputing their *value*. Even if gained, it may be argued, they are less valuable than claimed. In the Hiroshima example, the moral advantage claimed by Bard might be refuted by arguing that the United States was under no moral obligation to provide surrender terms or initiate negotiations; that this is properly the role of the nation that wishes to surrender. If so, there may be no moral advantage to be gained from U.S. initiation of the process.

By diminishing the claimed advantages of the counterplan, proponents of the plan lessen the costs of foregoing these benefits.

*Identify Significant and Unique Disadvantages of the Counterplan.* The counterplan may produce problems as well as benefits. If these disadvantages are shown to outweigh the unique advantages available through adoption of the counterplan, it should be avoided.

In response to Bard's counterplan, it might be argued that if the Soviet entrance into the Pacific war, rather than the dropping of the American atomic bomb, were acknowledged as the clear cause of the Japanese surrender, this would have given the Soviets a basis for increased post-war territorial demands. The Soviets might well have insisted, for example, on joint occupation of Japan as it did in Germany. Soviet occupation would have lessened the chances of post-war democratization in Japan and may have greatly increased Soviet influence in Asia. It might have consigned the Japanese to the same sort of oppressive subjugation endured by Eastern European nations. Those refuting Bard's counterplan might argue that these disadvantages outweigh the potential benefits.

*Identify Unique Advantages of the Original Proposal.* A unique advantage of the original proposal is one that cannot be obtained under the counterplan. Just as the counterplan functions as an opportunity cost of the plan, so does the original plan function as an opportunity cost of the counterplan. If we choose to adopt the counterplan, we may sacrifice certain benefits available only through the plan. In the aforementioned Hiroshima example, it may be argued that it was the American insistence on unconditional surrender that gave the United States extraordinary latitude in reforming the Japanese political system after the war. This enabled the American occupation forces to dismantle the Japanese military state, write a new constitution (that banned offensive military spending, for example), and establish a democratic government. By opening up terms for negotiation before surrender, as proposed in the counterplan, it might be argued that these American powers would have been vitiated and political reforms reduced.

When confronted with a counterplan, proponents of the original plan should always scrutinize their own advantages to determine which might be obtained under the counterplan and which are unique, thus functioning as opportunity costs of the counterplan.

<u>Countering the Counterplan</u>
1. Deny that the counterplan is competitive;
2. Diminish the significance of the counterplan advantages;
3. Identify significant and unique disadvantages of the counterplan;
4. Identify unique advantages of the original proposal.

## CONCLUSION

The counterplan is not unique to academic debate, but rather a type of argument common to all forms and forums of policy decision making. At all moments of decision, we confront a fork in the road through the future. By choosing to walk one road, we choose not to walk another. The counterplan represents an attempt to show what lies down the "road not taken" if a proposed policy were to be adopted. Counterplan advocates show what will be missed if we walk one road instead of the other. These foregone benefits are opportunity costs of the proposed policy.

The true cost of any proposed action lies in the foregone benefits associated with the best available alternative. "Opportunity costs," Miller and Starr (1967) explained, "are penalties suffered for not having done the best possible thing" (p. 35), and are therefore at the center of most policy disputes, whether in the legislature or our personal lives.

# STRATEGIES FOR MORAL ARGUMENT

Most debates involve moral argument. The values at issue may be explicitly stated in the proposition ("Resolved: that capital punishment is immoral") or may be revealed in the course of computing the costs and benefits of proposed courses of action. In order to *evaluate* a potential course of action, one must not only predict its outcomes, but assess and compare these outcomes. As discussed in chapter 2, all policy debates therefore involve moral argument.

Moral disputes in debate usually take one or both of the following forms:

- Evaluation of a given act, principle, or condition – Is it right or wrong, just or unjust, good or evil?
- Comparison of competing values – When two values are in conflict (such as one person's right to free speech and another's right to privacy), which should prevail?

Such disputes are best conducted through special strategies of argumentation, designed to make values more tangible, to test their practical implications, and to provide some sort of scale through which different values may be contrasted. The most important of these is the analogy.

## ANALOGY

Arguments from analogy draw a conclusion about one thing based on its similarity to another. The *primary subject* is that about which the conclusion is drawn; the *analogue* is that with which it is compared.

When President Lincoln ran for reelection in 1864, he employed an analogy to answer those critics who urged his replacement as commander in chief, saying "it is not best to swap horses while crossing the river" (*Reply to National Union League*, June 9, 1864). Lincoln used the analogy to highlight the risks associated with such a change, concluding that "I am not so poor a horse that they might not make a botch of it in trying to swap."

Normally, the analogy features a comparison among four terms in the following relationship:

A is to B as C is to D.

In the case of Lincoln's analogy, swapping horses in mid-river is compared to swapping presidents in the middle of the Civil War. The easily visualized risk of the former is used to make clear the less apparent risks of the latter. Thus, the risks (A) of swapping horses in mid-river (B) are like the risks (C) of changing presidents in mid-war (D).

Analogies are used to construct a pattern of inference by which what is known about one case may inform us about another similar case. For this reason, the analogy has sometimes been referred to as a means of arguing about the unknown (or lesser-known) on the basis of the known. According to the four terms just listed, a given fact (A), known to be true of B, may be more likely to be true of D if D and B share certain essential properties. As Foster (1908/1932) observed, "we base an argument from analogy on a preponderring resemblance between two individuals or classes, which is sufficient, we believe, to warrant us in inferring that the resemblance in known particulars extends to unknown particulars" (p. 111).

The advocate who employs an analogy must demonstrate that the two instances are alike in those respects *essential* to the issue at hand. When such a parallel is constructed, the analogy may be a very powerful form of argument possessing great strategic value.

## The Strategic Value of Analogies

Analogy plays an important role in many debates, particularly those concerned with moral disputes and those that revolve around prediction of future consequences of contemplated actions. Some analogies have achieved enormous political power and framed the basic discussion of public policy. Much of the public debate in the early months of allied intervention in the Persian Gulf, for example, centered on the dispute as to which historical analogy for the conflict was more appropriate: World War II (the "Good War"), or Vietnam (a prolonged and costly failure, by most accounts).

Well-wrought arguments from analogy possess certain strategic values that enhance their popularity.

*Analogies May Clarify Muddled Disputes and Simplify Complex Issues.*  Arguments based on analogies take an issue under dispute (the primary subject) and compare it to one that is not (the analogue). A properly selected analogue is one about which some normative judgment already exists and may be drawn on to resolve the issue being contested. It does no good to compare one confused situation with another. In order to be effective, the analogue must be a case in which our judgment is clear.

The strategic value of analogy in clarifying muddled disputes makes it especially valuable in the conduct of moral argument. Moral disputes may rage over abstract principles (i.e., "Is the right to individual privacy more important than the public's right to know?"), but are generally conducted with reference to specific examples. Analogies may be used to clarify the tangled debate over one example by reference to another in which a clear normative judgment exists. Thus, analogies may be used to support the transferral of a normative judgment from the analogue to the primary subject, as in Lincoln's analogy of changing horses in mid-stream. We should regard the prospect of changing presidents as we do that of changing horses, according to Lincoln.

Analogies may also be used in moral argument to *test* the principles defended by one's opponent. Usually, a moral principle is derived from the analogue that may be applied to the primary subject. But it is also sometimes useful to construct an analogue to which the moral principle used by the opponent in arguing about the primary subject may be applied and found unsatisfactory. In this use of analogy, the argument runs as follows:

1. If the two cases are parallel and
2. The opponent's moral principle is unsatisfactory in the case of the analogue; then
3. The principle should also be rejected as unsatisfactory in the case of the primary subject.

During the years in which the South African government remained openly committed to the maintenance of *apartheid*, many American investors were compelled to deliberate as to whether their continued investment in South Africa was immoral. The advocates for divestiture normally argued as follows:

— *Apartheid* is evil (providing a social structure based on racial injustice).

– Investment from abroad supports *apartheid* (by propping up the economy and by providing items such as computers needed to administer the *apartheid* system).

– Therefore, investment is immoral.

Two principal arguments were used to counter these claims: (a) By maintaining investments, we maintain leverage and the ability to encourage a shift away from *apartheid* (a policy termed "constructive engagement" by the Reagan administration); and (b) If we divest, others will simply take our place (thus our actions would be an empty and costly gesture). Both arguments from opponents of divestiture are vulnerable to certain analogies that might be drawn by proponents of divestiture.

The construction of effective analogies should begin with the distillation of the moral principles that underlie the arguments. From the perspective of the proponents of divestiture, the underlying principles in the two arguments might be stated as follows: (a) In order to reform evil forces, we should first join them; and (b) It is moral to do harm if that harm will occur anyway.

The distillation of the moral principle behind an opponent's argument is an important first step for discovering analogies. The moral principle is the essential parallel; a usable analogue must be based on it. Having identified the principle, the advocate of divestiture would attempt to construct an analogous situation in which following the principle would be clearly unacceptable, contrary to normative standards.

In the case of the first principle, such an analogy might be as follows: We should join the Mafia in order to convince them to renounce their lives of crime (or, more generally, "We may best reform criminals by joining them in their criminal enterprises"); or We should make financial contributions to the Ku Klux Klan so that we might change their racial beliefs and actions.

These arguments, although arguably analogous to those about South Africa, are more clearly absurd. In both instances, the moral principle of the opponent's argument against divestiture is likely to be found unacceptable. Moreover, the selection of these particular analogues emphasizes other parallels to the primary subject: The criminality of the Mafia and KKK suggests a moral characterization of those who administer *apartheid;* the unlikelihood of changing the minds of those in the Mafia or KKK suggests the dim prospects for success in the "constructive engagement" of South Africa; and the "financial contribution" to the KKK highlights the investor's direct complicity in the actions of the South African government.

In the case of the second principle ("It is moral to do harm if that harm will occur anyway"), the following analogies might be constructed to expose the principle as false: It is morally acceptable to join a lynch mob because if your hand isn't on the rope, someone else's will be; or It is morally acceptable for Virginia farmers to buy slaves because if they had not, someone else would have.

Again, both arguments are analogous to those offered by opponents of divestiture—they operate from the same moral principle. Yet these two arguments more clearly expose the deficiencies of the principle.

In presenting such analogies to an audience, an organizational pattern should be followed identical to the steps outlined earlier for their discovery:

1. Summarize the opponent's argument;
2. State the general moral principle beneath it;
3. Construct an analogous situation in which the principle is clearly unacceptable;
4. Explain why the principle is similarly unacceptable when applied to the primary subject.

By following these procedures, the first strategic value of the analogy may be seen, as its use may clarify muddled disputes and simplify complex issues.

*Analogies May Lend Credence to Predictions.* When we confront a problematic situation, we may well ask—how have others handled similar situations in the past, and with what results? Analogies are often drawn in debate between some past event and a situation currently faced. Because the outcome of the past situation is known, it may be argued that the present situation will, unless changes are made, produce similar results. Such uses of history are quite ancient. Thucydides voiced the hope that his history of the Peloponnesian wars might prevent future leaders from duplicating past mistakes, urging clear understanding of "the events which happened in the past and which (human nature being what it is) will at some time or other and in much the same ways be repeated in the future" (cited in Neustadt and May, 1986, p. 232).

Great disasters of the past are often used to construct analogies with present situations. The fall of the Roman Empire, the Munich "appeasement" of 1938 (thought to embolden Hitler and precipitate World War II), the 1929 stock market crash and ensuing Great Depression, and the American debacle in Vietnam, among others, are commonly used as warnings against arguably similar tendencies in the present.

The forms of these arguments should be familiar:

— Iraq's invasion of Kuwait is similar to Hitler's annexation of Czechoslovakia.

- When Western leaders failed to stand up to Hitler's move, he invaded other nations.

- Unless the U.S. stands up to Iraq, Hussein will invade other nations.

Or,

- If the U.S. decides to invade Nicaragua, it will face much popular resistance, protracted guerrilla warfare in difficult terrain, substantial opposition from within the U.S., and the likelihood that any government installed by the U.S. will be unstable.

- These conditions spelled disaster for the U.S. intervention in Vietnam.

- Nicaragua could become "another Vietnam."

In these sample arguments from historical analogy, parallels are drawn between the past and the present. Each of the historical events just cited has been used literally hundreds of times to warn of the potential consequences of later policies or situations. This fact alone may encourage skepticism. The fall of Rome has been attributed by various observers over the centuries to hundreds of different causes and employed to warn against policies ranging from pacifism to water fluoridation. Such claims are obviously vulnerable to challenges of their causal reasoning. The advocate in these cases, moreover, bears the additional burden of demonstrating essential parallels between the historical situation and the present one.

Nevertheless, some historical analogies, particularly the Munich and Vietnam analogies, have exerted immense influence in shaping public policy debate on major issues. Since 1975, whenever the United States or Soviet Union has contemplated or engaged in military intervention, the question has been asked in public debate over the proposed action: "Will this be another Vietnam?" Do shared characteristics of the contemplated intervention (as in Iraq, Nicaragua, or Afghanistan) and the war in Vietnam (such as popular resistance, difficult terrain, absence of a strong government to support, and the lack of public support inside the intervening country) foreshadow similar results (protracted and futile struggle)? Even where important differences between the target country and Vietnam exist, consideration of the analogy may alert decision makers to important issues and potential risks.

The frequent use of poorly constructed analogies should by no means serve to invalidate the use of historical analogies in decision making. In their book, *Thinking in Time: The Uses of History for Decision-Makers*, Richard Neustadt and Richard May (1986) identified some crucial decisions in which the construction and careful analysis of analogies contributed to the success of the process. In the Cuban Missile Crisis of 1962, for example, the analogy of the Japanese surprise attack on Pearl Harbor (and the understanding of that attack as barbarous) helped dissuade the Kennedy administration from an air strike against Cuba. The historical analogy was used in this instance partly to predict the likely world reaction to an American attack on Cuba, but mainly to draw into clearer focus the moral principle at stake for the decision makers.

On the other hand, Neustadt and May pointed to the failure of the Johnson administration to consider the analogy between their intervention in Vietnam and the failed campaign of the French a decade earlier. Relevant analogies, they argued, assist decision makers in the process of sorting out relevant from irrelevant concerns. They encourage political decision makers to determine what is known, unknown, and presumed in the case at hand, then to construct multiple historical analogies and scrutinize the likenesses and differences between them and the primary subject.

Neustadt and May also observed the extraordinary popularity and power of analogies in the public advocacy of policies. "The 'lessons of the thirties,'" they wrote, "have provided, among other things, the underlying theme for every argument supporting stern approaches toward Communist regimes abroad from Truman's time forward. As a form of advocacy, nothing is more familiar to Americans of almost any age" (Neustadt & May, 1986, p. 47). Advocates must, therefore, be prepared to employ and rebut arguments of historical analogy.

*Analogies May Draw the Opponent Onto Unfamiliar Ground.*    A successful argument from analogy moves the focus of the debate from the case at hand to the analogue. The analogue becomes the lens through which the primary subject is then viewed. If the analogy has been thoughtfully prepared, this forces the opponent to move onto ground that you have constructed and into a range of arguments and counterarguments that you have already anticipated.

In the case of the analogies to investment in South Africa described earlier, the advocate who employs them does so to draw a powerful conclusion: Investment is immoral. The opponent must therefore contest the analogy. Generally, as is discussed in more detail at the end of our discussion of arguments from analogy, this is done by disputing the facts of the analogue itself or by disputing the link between the analogue and the primary subject. In either case, the opponent is forced to enter the world of the analogue – a world presumably designed to his or her disadvantage in argument.

*Analogies May Place the Opponent in an Untenable Position.*    If the terms of the analogy hold, supporting the existence of a genuine parallel between the primary instance and the analogue, the opponent may be induced either to buck the "common wisdom" established for the analogue (a consensus that presumably includes the judge or audience) or to appear inconsistent by ignoring the wisdom of the derived principle when applied to the primary instance. In the case of a moral dispute, one might term these two unsavory options *hypocrisy* or *deviance:* The opponent may appear hypocritical if he or she accepts the normative judgment in the analogous case, but defends a different standard of judgment in the primary instance; or The opponent may appear deviant if he or she denies the normative judgment in the analogous case, thereby imperilling the credibility of his or her arguments regarding the primary instance.

In order to avoid being boxed into these two undesirable alternatives, the opponent should attempt to defeat the analogy by using one or more of the strategies described later in this chapter.

The trap posed by the analogy is based on the value accorded consistency. The claim of the analogy is warranted by the belief that similar cases should be treated similarly. In the administration of criminal justice, for example, the circumstances of one criminal act are often compared with those of another. If a convicted criminal in one case has received a particular sentence, it might be argued that another criminal should receive approximately the same sentence for a similar offense. The claim that the two cases are similar must be supported by a demonstration that they are alike in their essential particulars: the type of the crime, effect on the victim, previous record of the criminal, and so forth. If the two criminal acts are essentially alike (analogous), it may be reasoned that their perpetrators should receive similar sentences.

In such legal reasoning, the comparison of the two cases provides a basis for resolving a disputed judgment (sentencing in the new case) by reference to an agreed judgment (the sentence already passed in the prior case). The power of the analogy is rooted in a basic consensus that justice requires equity, and thus similar cases should be treated similarly.

## A Case Study in Argument From Analogy

One of the most difficult moral and policy issues facing the United States during the past two decades has been the use of "affirmative action" procedures in personnel and other decisions. The notion of affirmative action emerged from legislation passed in the mid-1960s to prohibit discrimination against women, African-Americans, and other minorities in employment, commerce, and admissions to higher education.

Although a broad consensus has emerged in America to support the abolition of discrimination, there has been little consensus about what that *means.* Does it mean that employers and admissions officers should process applications on a *color-blind* basis, for example? Or does it require that they compensate for *past* discrimination by giving *preference* to members of these groups, whether through formal quotas or general commitments to personnel diversification? These questions have proven very difficult to resolve.

One of the most skillful advocates of affirmative action is Jesse Jackson. He employs an argument from analogy to cut through the complexities of the issue and recast it in the context of a parallel case in which normative judgments are more clear.

Let me illustrate the point [this] way, using the familiar athletic example. "Runners to your mark, get set, go!" Two world-class distance runners begin the grueling human test of trying to run a sub-four-minute mile. Two minutes into the race, officials observe that one runner, falling far behind, still has running weights on his ankles. They stop the race, and hold both runners in their tracks. The weights are removed from the runner far behind, the officials refire the starting gun, and both runners continue from the points where they were when the race was stopped. Not surprisingly, the runner who ran the entire race without the ankle weights comes in with a sizable lead.

The fundamental moral question one could ask about that theoretical race must be, Would anyone call it fair? Again, not surprisingly, the answer would certainly be a simple and resounding No. If one could devise some means of compensating the second runner (for example, comparing the runners' times for the last two laps and projecting them over the entire race), a more accurate appraisal of each runner's ability and performance could be made. And if a reasonable means of compensation could be devised, no one would say that such compensation constituted "reverse discrimination" against the first runner or "preferential treatment" for the second. All would agree that compensation was fair and just.

Everyone can follow this example and see the "reasonableness" and morality of the solution because racial attitudes are not involved. Yet this is similar to the position in which blacks find themselves in the United States. We have been running the race with weights on our ankles – weights not of our own choosing. Weights of "no rights that a white must respect," weights of slavery, of past and present discrimination in jobs, in education, housing, health care, and more.

Some argue that there now are laws forbidding discrimination in education, in public accommodations and employment, in politics, and in housing. But these laws only amount to removing the weights after years of disadvantage. Too often, when analyzing the race question, the analysts start at the end rather than at the beginning. To return to the track-meet example, if one only saw the last part of the race (without knowing about the first part), the compensation might seem unreasonable, immoral, discriminatory, or a form of preferential treatment. Affirmative action programs (in light of the history and experience of black people in the United States) are an extremely reasonable, even conservative, way of compensating us for past and present discrimination. (Jackson, 1978, pp. 27–29)

Jackson employed the extended analogy of the mile race in order to recast disputed issues in the affirmative action debate. The analogue is, as Jackson noted, a "familiar" one in which "everyone can follow and see the 'reasonableness' and morality of the solution because racial attitudes are not involved." Jackson believed that his audience's judgment regarding the mile race itself would be clear: the race would be seen as unfair and compensation to the disadvantaged runner would be seen as just. By establishing the issues at stake in the analogue as identical in essential ways to those in the primary subject (affirmative action), Jackson hoped to transfer the moral judgments his audience had made in the former instance to the latter.

Jackson constructed his analogy in such a way as to draw certain parallels between details of the mile race and details of the primary subject.

| ANALOGUE | PRIMARY SUBJECT |
| --- | --- |
| runners | blacks and whites |
| mile race | competition for jobs |
| ankle weights | "weights of 'no rights that a white must respect' . . . slavery, of past and present discrimination in jobs, in education, housing, health care, and more." |
| removal of weights at mid-point of race | recent laws forbidding discrimination |
| unfairness to weighted runner | unfairness to blacks in job market |
| compensation of runner | affirmative action |

These parallels mark the most important points of the affirmative action dispute. Once the parallels had been established and the two situations may be seen as analogous, Jackson believed that his opponents' arguments would be exposed as untenable. He spoke for the audience when he answered the "fundamental moral question" about the race ("Would anyone call it fair?") with "a simple and resounding No." He then imagined that some way of compensating the weighted runner might be devised and posed arguments against that compensation that have been used against affirmative action. These arguments, as he realized, would clearly seem ill-founded in discussing the mile race: "Noone would say that such compensation constituted 'reverse discrimination' against the first runner or 'preferential treatment' for the second. All would agree that compensation was fair and just." The point of Jackson's analogy is now clear: If the two cases are indeed parallel, then what is just in one instance should be just in the other. Jackson called for consistency in the application of moral standards to the two situations.

Jackson accounted for the arguments of his adversaries on the affirmative action issue by returning to the analogy. Those who saw affirmative action as unfair were looking only at recent history in which discriminatory barriers had been reduced, not at the long history of oppression and disadvantage that came before. "If one saw only the last part of the race (without knowing about the first part), the compensation might seem unreasonable, immoral, discriminatory, or a form of preferential treatment," he said. Jackson's analogy was designed to broaden and alter the vision of those who might be sympathetic to such charges.

As should be apparent in this example, a well-wrought analogy can be a powerful instrument in reshaping the terms of a debate. Jackson had been careful to establish clear parallel details, to choose an example in which the audience's judgment should be relatively clear, to delineate the moral principles that govern the situations, and to move arguments from the primary subject into the analogue and vice versa. An opponent facing Jackson's argument would have been forced not only to generate arguments against affirmative action (such as the claim that it constitutes "reverse discrimination"), but either to deny the applicability of the analogue or attempt to defend the principle of his or her argument in the case of the analogue as well.

## Tests and Counterstrategies for Analogies

Because of the potential persuasiveness of the analogy, opponents must have a clear understanding of how such arguments may be tested and countered. Although logically sound and relevant analogies may be constructed, many (if not most) analogies used in public debate are specious.

If a principal virtue of the analogy is its ability to simplify complex issues, a chief liability lies in its tendency to *over*-simplification. Analogies may be used to substitute for the careful scrutiny and complicated analysis the primary subject deserves. If a strength of the analogy is its ability to bring already achieved consensus on some past issue to bear on a present one under dispute, a weakness lies in failure to scrutinize that past judgment. "Common knowledge" is often, in fact, disputable.

Furthermore, the use of a powerful analogy, such as an apt historical parallel, may blind decision makers to the existence of other useful parallels, the "lessons" of which may deviate from or even contradict that of the first.

In order to test and refute analogies, opponents should consider one or more of the following strategies.

*Argue That the Cases Are Not Sufficiently Similar.*    If the logical basis of the analogy may be found in the principle that "similar cases should be treated similarly," one obvious line of refutation is the argument that the two cases at hand are *not* in fact similar (and hence need not be treated similarly). The most direct way in which this line of refutation may be supported is by denial of the claimed similarities themselves.

Assuming, however, that there *are* some genuine similarities between the analogue and primary subject, two additional (and more demanding) questions should be raised.

1. **Are the details of comparison and contrast *essential* to the issue at hand?** The usefulness of an analogy is not demonstrated by showing simple similarities between it and the primary subject. The two cases must be demonstrably alike in those qualities *essential* to the dispute under consideration. What is essential in the comparison of two cases will therefore vary according to the dispute.

As Foster (1908/1932) explained,

> What would be an essential difference between two tariff policies with reference to one question might be safely neglected as irrelevant on another question. Two financial panics are essentially *similar* when their differences may be ignored for the purposes of drawing conclusions as to a monetary policy. Two child-labor laws are essentially *different* when their likenesses may be ignored for the purpose of drawing conclusions as to enforcing such laws. (p. 113)

In order to test an analogy, one must first determine the most important *issues* in the dispute over the primary subject. Having done so, the opponent should ascertain whether the parallels drawn between the primary subject and the analogue actually engage these issues, or merely others non-essential to the dispute at hand.

2. **Do the essential points of similarity between the two cases outweigh the differences?** In the comparisons drawn between analogues and primary subjects, there will obviously be differences as well as similarities between any two cases that are compared. The opponent should determine whether these differences are sufficiently important to render the analogy useless.

Among the most influential analogies of the past half-century has been that of the 1938 Munich "appeasement," in which the leaders of France and

Britain sought to avoid a war with Germany by ratifying Hitler's claims to portions of Czechoslovakia. Upon his return to England, Prime Minister Neville Chamberlain waved the treaty papers before a cheering crowd and proclaimed that a lasting peace was at hand. The following year, a presumably emboldened Germany invaded Poland and began its conquest of Western Europe.

The Munich analogy has since been used to oppose diplomatic negotiations or concessions designed to end or avert conflict. It influenced President Truman's policies during the Korean war, was frequently cited by President Reagan in downplaying diplomatic solutions to the arms race with the Soviets and the conflicts in Central America, and was an important rhetorical touchstone of President Johnson's public defense of the war in Vietnam. The form of the analogy is roughly the same in each case: "Just as the Munich appeasement emboldened Hitler (convincing him of our weakness) in the initiation of World War II, agreeing to terms with $x$ will encourage this enemy to further aggression."

In refuting the analogy of Munich to Vietnam, Howard Zinn, a critic of American involvement in Vietnam, identified several essential differences between the two cases:

> 1. The Munich accord ratified a seizure of land from one nation by another. Vietnam, however, was a civil war, with much opposition to the government from rebels in South Vietnam itself;
> 2. The Czech government was democratically elected, stable, and effective. The South Vietnamese government was unpopular, undemocratic, corrupt, and unstable; and
> 3. Where Hitler sought Czechoslovakia as a base for the conquest of Poland and others, the North Vietnamese sought unification of Vietnam as an end in itself. (cited in Sproule, 1980, p. 150)

On the basis of these differences between the primary subject (Vietnam) and the analogue (Munich), Zinn dismissed the analogy drawn between them.

The discovery of differences between the primary subject and analogue does not necessarily warrant rejection of the parallel. One must establish whether or not the similarities on the essential issues outweigh the differences to such an extent that the parallel is a useful one.

*Deny Your Opponent's Analysis of the Analogue.*    It should be remembered that the effectiveness of an analogy depends on the existence of a clear and shared judgment regarding the analogue. If an opponent can cast doubt on the "lesson" of the analogue, the power of its application to the primary subject will be greatly diminished.

It might be argued from analogy, for example, that the United States should deregulate the postal service because of its success in deregulating the airlines. But not all (or many, in fact) would agree that the government's deregulation of the airlines has been a success. Proof of the failure of airline deregulation not only evaporates the original "lesson" of the analogy (the prediction that postal deregulation will be successful), but actually turns the analogy to the use of the opponent (just as airline deregulation failed, so too might postal deregulation).

In the public debate over policies designed to decrease drug use in the United States, legal penalties for drug distribution and use have been compared by some opponents to the American prohibition against alcohol earlier in this century. Those who construct this analogy are drawing on an assumed "common knowledge" that Prohibition was a failure, widely circumvented by bootleggers, smugglers, and speakeasies. But this common knowledge has been challenged by some recent historians who claim that per capita alcohol consumption did actually *decline* during the Prohibition era, in spite of the fact that many broke the law.

By denying the opponent's analysis of the analogue, its "lesson" for the primary subject may be discredited. Indeed, it may be turned against those who originally introduced the analogy.

*Deny the Virtue of Consistency.*   As discussed earlier, the logic of the analogy suggests that similar cases should be treated similarly. Advocates who employ analogies claim that the way we judge the analogue should govern our judgment of the primary case. One common abuse of the analogy involves, as Trudy Govier (1985) put it, the attempt "to defend one thing that is allegedly wrong by pointing out that another thing that really is wrong has been done, or has been accepted. In doing this, he is arguing that since we have allowed some wrong, we should (in consistency) permit more" (p. 247).

In the debate that has raged for decades over whether or not the atomic bombing of Hiroshima was justified, defenders of the atomic bombing have often compared it to the devastation already wrought upon Tokyo and other cities by incendiary weapons. In a single incendiary bombing raid on Tokyo in March 1945, for example, an estimated 125,000 people were killed, more than died (initially, at least) in the atomic bombing of Hiroshima. This comparison has been used by some scientists and government leaders associated with the atomic bombing (such as Arthur Holly Compton) to claim that it was morally justified.

A simple and effective response to such reasoning is: "Two wrongs do not make a right." The fact that the incendiary raids occurred and were, to a great extent, morally acceptable to most Americans at the time does not render them morally justified. Those who oppose the atomic bombing of Hiroshima might reasonably oppose the incendiary raids on Tokyo as well.

*Use the Opponents' Analogy Against Them.*   It is often possible for the same analogue to be used by opposing debaters. As in the deregulation and Prohibition examples discussed earlier, opponents may draw different parallels between the analogue and primary subject and must derive a different "lesson" from the analogue. Doing so may neutralize the analogy for the advocate who originally presented it: The clear consensus regarding our judgment of the analogue will have been dispelled. Indeed, if fully turned to the advantage of the opponent, the analogy may become a considerable liability to the original presenter rather than an asset.

Abraham Lincoln's analogy of changing horses in mid-river might have been countered by an opponent who attempted to answer two questions: Under what circumstances *might* it be less risky to change horses in mid-river than to continue with one's current mount?; and, Do such circumstances exist in the current presidential election?

It might, in fact, be *wise* to change horses while crossing a river:

– If one's horse had stopped in the middle;

– If one's horse were drowning in a raging current; or

– If one's horse were heading in the wrong direction.

An opponent might then have sought to identify a parallel for one or more of these circumstances in Lincoln's presidential performance during his first term, charging, for example, that Lincoln's poor performance as commander in chief had failed to bring the Civil War to an expeditious conclusion.

In this strategy, the opponent seeks to enter the fictional world constructed in the analogy and draw a different lesson from it. An alternative strategy uses the advocate's analogy in an indirect fashion. Instead of accepting the notion of the advocate that the analogue and primary subject are related only *in principle,* the opponent takes the terms of the analogy *literally* and applies them to the primary subject.

In early 1990, Judge Leonard Sand of New York ruled that solicitations by panhandlers in subway stations deserved protection under the First Amendment to the U.S. Constitution. Begging, the judge argued, is a form of political expression in which more affluent commuters are asked to confront "how the other half lives" and to consider their own responsibility toward those less fortunate than they. Syndicated columnist George Will objected to this ruling, and supported his objection with an argument from analogy:

James Q. Wilson of UCLA says that if a broken window goes unrepaired, the remaining windows will be broken, because an unrepaired window sends a message that no one cares. Disorder and crime are linked in a developmental sequence. Disorder atomizes communities . . . Beggars, many of them deranged by alcohol or other drugs or mental illness, and dangerous in fact or appearance – are human "broken windows." (Will, 1990, p. 4)

But an opponent of Will's position might well have used the "broken window" analogy against him, noting perhaps that for the homeless men and women begging to survive in the subways, even a house with broken windows might seem a palace, or that if the city had paid more attention to fixing the real broken windows and averting the destruction of low-cost housing, far fewer would be forced to beg in the subways.

One effective strategy, then, for dealing with an opponent's analogy is to embrace it, take it farther, and turn it against the advocate who originally employed it.

*Construct a Counteranalogy.* Any primary subject may always be paralleled with more than one analogue. Interestingly, different analogues may yield quite different – even opposite – "lessons" for application to the primary subject. Thus, Neustadt and May (1986), among others, urged decision makers to construct and analyze alternate historical analogies in their search for useful precedents: "Reach for possibly relevant analogues, the more the better, spelling out *likenesses* and *differences*. That helps guard against illusions" (p. 89).

In the public debate over abortion rights, much use has been made of analogies. Dr. Jack Willke, President of the National Right-to-Life Committee, is one of many opponents of abortion rights who argue that an embryo is a human being from the moment of conception (and therefore should receive full legal protection). "Contained within the single cell who I once was," he argued, "was the totality of everything I am today" (cited in Gardner, 1989, p. 557).

The analogy of the *blueprint* is often used to support such claims: Just as blueprints contain all details of what a house will be like, it is argued that the DNA of the embryo contains all determinants of the adult human life, from physical appearance to talents and interests.

Charles Gardner, a member of the Ann Arbor Committee to Defend Abortion Rights, attempted to counter the blueprint analogy in several ways. First, he argued that the essential differences between analogue and primary subject outweigh the similarities:

But an analogy between a blueprint and the DNA is misleading. If a human being were a house, then the DNA would specify doorknobs, hinges, lumber and nails, window panes, wires, switches, fuses and a thousand other individual parts. But it would not tell how to put all those parts together in the right order and the right time. . . . The fertilized egg is clearly not a prepackaged human being. There is no body plan, no blueprint, no tiny being pre-formed and waiting to unfold. It is not "complete" or the "totality" of a person. The fertilized egg may follow many different paths; the route will be penned in only as the paths are taken; the particular person that it might become is not yet there. (Gardner, 1989, pp. 557–558)

Gardner then attempted to make these claims of difference more tangible by constructing a counteranalogy: "The fertilized egg cell does not contain its fate, just as a grape seed does not contain wine" (p. 559).

By presenting alternative analogues, the opponent hopes to at least diminish the credibility of the original analogy. If the alternate analogy is at least as sound as the original one, the "lesson" to be drawn with respect to the primary subject will be rendered equivocal. If the counteranalogy is in fact shown to be *superior* to the original one (drawing closer parallels on essential issues), then the counteranalogy may in fact take precedence and replace the original analogy in the audience's resolution of the dispute.


## SUMMARY: COUNTERSTRATEGIES

1. Argue that the cases are not sufficiently similar;
2. Deny your opponents' analysis of the analogy;
3. Deny the virtue of consistency;
4. Use the opponents' analogy against them;
5. Construct a counteranalogy.

### Case Study in the Refutation of Analogy: "Shouting 'Fire!' in a Crowded Theater"

In 1917, U.S. Supreme Court Justice Oliver Wendell Holmes employed an analogy in his argument that a defendant was rightly convicted of protests against the First World War. He likened the defendant's actions to "falsely shouting fire in a theater," and claimed that they were no more deserving of constitutional protection. Holmes' analogy has been widely used ever since in disputes over the proper limits of free speech. Yet Harvard Law Professor Alan Dershowitz (1989) maintained that Holmes' analogy was wrong-headed in the first place and wrongly applied ever since.

In spite of its hallowed position in both the jurisprudence of the First Amendment and the arsenal of political discourse, it is and was an inapt analogy, even in the context in which it was originally offered. It has lately become – despite, perhaps even because of, the frequency and promiscuousness of its invocation – little more than a caricature of logical argumentation.

The case that gave rise to the "Fire!"-in-a-crowded-theater analogy – *Schenck* v. *United States* – involved the prosecution of Charles Schenck, who was the general secretary of the Socialist Party in Philadelphia, and Elizabeth Baer, who was its recording secretary. In 1917 a jury found Schenck and Baer guilty of attempting to cause insubordination among soldiers who had been drafted to fight in the First World War. They and other party members had circulated leaflets urging draftees not to "submit to intimidation" by fighting in a war being conducted on behalf of "Wall Street's chosen few." Schenck admitted, and the Court found, that the intent of the pamphlets' "impassioned language" was to "influence" draftees to resist the draft. Interestingly, however, Justice Holmes noted that nothing in the pamphlet suggested that the draftees should use unlawful or violent means to oppose conscription: "In form at least [the pamphlet] confined itself to peaceful measures, such as a petition for the repeal of the act" and an exhortation to exercise "your right to assert your opposition to the draft." Many of its most impassioned words were quoted directly from the Constitution.

Justice Holmes acknowledged that "in many places and in ordinary times the defendants, in saying all that was said in the circular, would have been within their constitutional rights." "But," he added, "the character of every act depends upon the circumstances in which it is done." And to illustrate that truism he went on to say,

> The most stringent protection of free speech would not protect a man in falsely shouting fire in a theater, and causing a panic. It does not even protect a man from an injunction against uttering words that may have all the effect of force.

Justice Holmes then upheld the convictions in the context of a wartime draft, holding that the pamphlet created "a clear and present danger" of hindering the war effort while our soldiers were fighting for their lives and our liberty.

The example of shouting "Fire!" obviously bore little relationship to the facts of the Schenck case. The Schenck pamphlet contained a substantive political message. It urged its draftee readers to *think* about the message and then – if they so chose – to act on it in a lawful and nonviolent way. The man who shouts "Fire!" in a crowded theater is neither sending a political message nor inviting his listener to think about what he has said and decide what to do in a rational, calculated manner. On the contrary, the message is designed to force action *without* contemplation. The message "Fire!" is directed not to the mind and the conscience of the listener but, rather, to his adrenaline and his feet. It is a stimulus to immediate *action*, not thoughtful reflection. It is – as Justice Holmes recognized in his follow-up sentence – the functional equivalent of "uttering words that may have all the effect of force."

Indeed, in that respect the shout of "Fire!" is not even speech, in any meaningful sense of that term. It is a *clang* sound – the equivalent of setting off a nonverbal alarm. Had Justice Holmes been more honest about his example, he would have said that freedom of speech does not protect a kid who pulls a fire alarm in the absence of a fire. But that obviously would have been irrelevant to the case at hand. The proposition that pulling an alarm is not protected speech certainly leads to the conclusion that shouting the word *fire* is also not protected. But the core analogy is the nonverbal alarm, and the derivative example is the verbal shout. By cleverly substituting the derivative shout for the core alarm, Holmes made it possible to analogize one set of words to another – as he could not have done if he had begun with the self-evident proposition that setting off an alarm bell is not free speech.

The analogy is thus not only inapt but also insulting. Most Americans do not respond to political rhetoric with the same kind of automatic acceptance expected of schoolchildren responding to a fire drill. Not a single recipient of the Schenck pamphlet is known to have changed his mind after reading it. Indeed, one draftee, who appeared as a prosecution witness, was asked whether reading a pamphlet asserting that the draft law was unjust would make him "immediately decide that you must erase that law." Not surprisingly, he replied, "I do my own thinking." A theatergoer would probably not respond similarly if asked how he would react to a shout of "Fire!"

Another important reason why the analogy is inapt is that Holmes emphasizes the factual falsity of the shout "Fire!" The Schenck pamphlet, however, was not factually false. It contained political opinions and ideas about the causes of the war and about appropriate and lawful responses to the draft. As the Supreme Court recently reaffirmed (in *Falwell* v. *Hustler*), "The First Amendment recognizes no such thing as a 'false' idea." Nor does it recognize false opinions about the causes of or cures for war.

A closer analogy to the facts of the Schenck case might have been provided by a person's standing outside a theater, offering the patrons a leaflet advising them that in his opinion the theater was structurally unsafe, and urging them not to enter but to complain to the building inspectors. That analogy, however, would not have served Holmes's argument for punishing Schenck. Holmes needed an analogy that would appear relevant to Schenck's political speech but that would invite the conclusion that censorship was appropriate.

Unsurprisingly, a war-weary nation – in the throes of a know-nothing hysteria over immigrant anarchists and socialists – welcomed the comparison between what was regarded as a seditious political pamphlet and a malicious shout of "Fire!" Ironically, the "Fire!" analogy is nearly all that survives from the Schenck case; the ruling itself is already most certainly not good law. Pamphlets of the kind that resulted in Schenck's imprisonment have been circulated with impunity during subsequent wars.

Dershowitz relied on two of the counter-strategies discussed earlier in his refutation of Holmes' analogy. He argued that the two cases are not sufficiently similar (or, in his words, the analogy is "inapt") because:

1. Unlike shouting "Fire!," Schenck's pamphlet contained a "substantive political message" (paragraph 5);

2. Unlike one who shouts "Fire!" in the hope of a reflexive response, Schenck encouraged his audience to thoughtfully reflect upon his message (paragraph 5);
3. People don't respond to political rhetoric as schoolchildren do to a fire drill – they engage in critical analysis (paragraph 7); and
4. Schenck's pamphlet was not factually false as in the false shout of "Fire!," it simply contained different political ideas (paragraph 8).

Dershowitz also constructed an effective counteranalogy to that posed by Holmes. A closer analogy to Schenck's act, Dershowitz argued, would be that of a person standing outside a theater, handing people a pamphlet as they enter saying that in his opinion the building is unsafe and urging them to complain to public authorities. Dershowitz argued that this analogue is far more similar to the primary subject than that offered by Holmes. It further served Dershowitz's purpose, because few would believe that the safety-minded pamphleteer outside the theater deserves to be punished. If it is analogous to the Schenck case, then presumably Schenck should also have been exonerated.

### Presentation of Analogies

In light of the available counterstrategies, those who employ arguments from analogy must be careful in constructing them. A poorly constructed analogy can easily backfire, hurting one's case rather than helping it. A well-prepared analogy, on the other hand, can be an extremely persuasive figure of thought that reshapes the basic terms of the dispute.

*Anticipation.*   Those who intend to employ analogies should use the aforementioned list of counterstrategies as a checklist for argument preparation. What differences between analogue and primary subject might an opponent raise? What counter-analogies might be constructed? How might opponents turn the analogy to their own use? By attempting to answer these questions, the advocate may prepare responses, redesign the terms of the analogy to avert potential objections, or avoid presenting an unsatisfactory or dangerous analogy.

*Use of "Understated" Analogies.*   Because the most common challenges to analogies center on the computation of essential differences and similarities between the analogue and primary subject, an effort should be made when possible in presenting analogies to explain why the conclusion drawn from the analogue *is even more true* of the primary subject. This strategy may be seen at work in the *New Testament*, when it is argued that: "Wherefore, if God so clothe the grass of the field, which today is, and tomorrow is cast into the oven, shall he not much more clothe you, O ye of little faith?" (Matthew 6:30).

In arguing for greater representation of the American colonies in Parliament, Edmund Burke compared their representation with that accorded the territories of Ireland, Wales, Chester, and Durham. After arguing that the American colonies are similar to the others in essential respects, he decried the difference in the way they are represented:

> But your legislative authority is perfect with regard to America. Was it less perfect in Wales, Chester, and Durham? But America is virtually represented. What! does the electric force of virtual representation more easily pass over the Atlantic than pervade Wales, which lies in your neighborhood – or than Chester and Durham, surrounded by abundance of representation that is actual and palpable? But, Sir, your ancestors thought this sort of virtual representation, however ample, to be totally insufficient for the freedom of the inhabitants of territories that are so near, and comparatively so inconsiderable. How then can I think it sufficient for those which are infinitely greater, and infinitely more remote? (cited in Foster, 1908/1932, p. 114)

Burke reasoned from accepted premises regarding the territories close at hand. The reasons behind these provisions, he argued, apply in even *greater* force to the American colonies.

The use of this "even more so" strategy may also be observed in the extended analogy presented by Jesse Jackson on affirmative action. When Jackson compared the ankle weights worn by the runner with the weights borne by African-Americans ("Weights of 'no rights a white must respect,' weights of slavery, of past and present discrimination in jobs, in education, housing, and health care, and more"), he was careful to note that *unlike* those worn by the runner, these are "weights not of our own choosing." This makes his argument even more compelling.

There will always be differences between the analogue and primary subject. By using this presentational strategy, the advocate argues that certain differences actually *strengthen* the point of the analogy, rather than weakening it.

*Cross-Examination.*    Debate formats that feature the cross-examination of speakers by their opponents provide an ideal opportunity for the construction of analogies. Cross-examination enables the questioner to place the respondent directly in the situation of the analogue and to compel him or her to reason through it. Let us imagine, for example, that in the debate over investment in South Africa described earlier, the opponent of divestiture, who has argued that "withdrawing our investments is pointless because someone else will step in and invest anyway," is asked the following question: If you were walking down the street in a bad section of town, came upon an unlocked car with a portable stereo on the front seat, and you were convinced that if you didn't steal it, somebody else would– would it be morally acceptable for you to take it?

After an answer is gained, nothing more should be said until the following speech. The analogy should not be explained during cross-examination, either before or after it is presented. As a general rule: *The questioner should never move from the analogue to the primary subject during cross-examination.* As questioner, do not allow the respondent to speculate about or refute the link between analogue and primary subject during the cross-examination period; insist that the respondent answer the question as posed.

Posed in cross-examination, the analogy forces the respondent to enter its world and confront a dilemma: If the respondent offers the "common sense" answer ("No" to the aforementioned question), s/he has provided a damaging moral standard by which the primary subject may then be addressed. If the respondent senses the trap and tries to be difficult by violating the common sense answer (answering "Yes" or "Maybe" to the question), then the respondent has violated common moral standards in ways that may discredit his or her arguments regarding the primary subject.

Arguments from analogy are common and persuasive features of public argument and private deliberation. When faced with one problem, we often try to envision it in terms of another we have already faced and resolved.

The construction of potential analogies should be part of the preparation for debates on most topics, particularly for those to be waged in the public forum. Properly used, analogies can both clarify and make vivid the terms of a discussion. Advocates for either side of any given dispute would be well-advised to prepare analogies for their own use and to prepare to refute the analogies that their opponents may employ.

## OTHER STRATEGIES OF MORAL ARGUMENT

The argument from analogy involves not only a comparison between the characteristics of two similar situations, but a claim that the *principle* governing our judgment of one instance should be transferred to the other. In the axiom, "Similar cases should be treated similarly," the question of how a case should be treated is the matter of principle.

"A principle," wrote noted conservative speaker William Rusher (1981), "is an argument that is derived from the general experience of the race and has been enshrined in some permanent form: Honesty is the best policy. Thou shalt not kill. Never drink until the sun is over the yardarm. In theory, a principle governs any situation to which it is applicable" (p. 66).

All debate cases embody core principles. Every piece of social legislation embodies (perhaps unstated) principles of the responsibility of the state for the maintenance of its citizens' welfare. Every foreign policy initiative is constructed from assumptions about the proper role of the nation in worldly affairs. A decision by the United States to intervene militarily in another country, for example, is founded on principles regarding the limits of the other nation's sovereignty. Every criminal prosecution rests on principles of what constitutes wrongful behavior and what constitutes just punishment.

These principles, although of fundamental importance to the case, may remain implicit and unstated. Discover the unstated principle(s) behind your opponent's case. Having discovered one, decide whether it is possible to convincingly refute it.

As explained in the preceding section, the analogy may be used to test the principle that undergirds an opponent's arguments. It is not, however, the only strategy by which to challenge such principles.

*Discover Anomalies and Exceptions to the Opponent's Principle.*  A principle is a form of generalization. As such, it may be refuted to the extent that it is less generally true than is required to support the case. During the American Civil War, Henry Ward Beecher traveled to England in an effort to convince the British not to support the Confederacy. He determined that one of the most important principles on which British sympathy for the Confederacy rested was a sense that the Southerners were "underdogs," a weaker minority bravely battling against a superior foe. In his speech to an audience in Liverpool, Beecher identified exceptions to this principle that "Underdogs deserve sympathy and support":

> But who ever sympathized with a weak thief, because three constables had got hold of him? [Hear, hear!] And yet the one thief in three policemen's hands is the weaker party. I suppose you would sympathize with him. [Hear, hear! laughter, and applause.] Why, when that infamous king of Naples, Bomba, was driven into Gaeta by Garibaldi with his immortal band of patriots, and Cavour sent against him the army of Northern Italy, who was the weaker party then? The tyrant and his minions; and the majority was with the noble Italian patriots, struggling for liberty. I never heard that Old England sent deputations to King Bomba, and yet his troops resisted bravely there. [Laughter.] (cited in Baker & Huntington, 1905, pp. 187–188)

Beecher disproved the principle by identifying exceptions to it. We do not *always* side with the underdog. By proving that the principle does not always hold true, Beecher thus directed his audience to the questions where he believed the debate should properly rest: Under what circumstances *do* we support the underdog? and Does the Confederate *cause* deserve support?

The identification of anomalies and exceptions to case principles is enormously important in legal argument. Legal principles are used to guide judgment. Cases establish precedents for principle and acceptable exceptions that may influence the outcome of later cases. In early 1990, the U.S. Supreme Court considered the case of the *University of Pennsylvania vs. the Equal Employment Opportunity Commission,* regarding the right of the University to withhold confidential personnel files from scrutiny, even when a charge of employment discrimination had been lodged against it. The University rested its case on the claim that confidential peer review is an essential part of the University's decision as to who will teach and, hence, of the University's freedom of expression under the First Amendment.

Justice Harry Blackmun wrote the unanimous opinion of the Court in rejecting the University's claim. Blackmun (1990) identified the principle behind the University's case: That anything which negatively affects the University's ability to hire whomever it chooses to teach is an infringment on its First Amendment rights. He then refuted this claim by identifying widely accepted exceptions to it:

> Indeed, if the universities attenuated claim were accepted, many other generally applicable laws might also be said to violate the First Amendment. In effect, petitioner says no more than the disclosure of peer review materials makes it more difficult to acquire information regarding the "academic grounds" on which petitioner wishes to base its tenure decisions. But many laws make the exercise of the First Amendment more difficult. For example, a university cannot claim a First Amendment violation simply because it may be subject to taxation or other government regulation, even though such regulation might deprive the university of revenue it needs to bid for professors who are contemplating working for other academic institutions or in industry. We doubt that the peer review process is any more essential in effectuating the right to determine "who may teach" than is the availability of money. . . . (1990, p. 86)

It is important to remember that in presenting an anomaly or exception to a principle one is only proving that the principle is not *always* true, not that it is *never* true. One may uphold the proposition that "It is better to die on one's feet than to live on one's knees" as generally true, even if there are some instances (if, e.g., by prostrating oneself, others could be saved) in which it is not true. If one's opponent has been foolish enough to argue such a principle as an absolute truth ("It is *always* better to die on one's feet than to live on one's knees"), then a single exception might suffice to win the point, but such instances are rare.

Generally, the strategic value of identifying anomalies and exceptions lies in the ability to dismiss the principle as an absolute truth, thereby directing attention to the question: Under what circumstances is it true or not true? In short, it is a strategy by which one redirects the debate toward the specific issue at hand.

*Enforce the Consequences of the Opponent's Principle.* Principles may be defended in the abstract, may be invoked to lend guidance to a particular instance, or may be derived from a particular instance or set of instances. A second important counterstrategy for the refutation of an opponent's principle is to see where it will *lead;* looking beyond the case at hand to other instances in which this case might be applied. A principle used to govern one judgment may presumably be applied to others. An even stronger claim is that the case at hand may serve as a *precedent* for the application of the principle to other instances.

In the case of *Cohen v. State of California* discussed in chapter 5 (in which the defendant was arrested for wearing a jacket emblazoned with a scurrilous epithet opposing the draft during the Vietnam War), Justice John Marshall Harlan bolstered his opinion on behalf of the majority to overturn the conviction based on the precedent it would set.

> We cannot indulge the facile assumption that one can forbid particular words without also running a substantial risk of suppressing ideas in the process. Indeed, governments, might soon seize upon the censorship of particular words as a convenient guise for banning the expression of unpopular views. We have been able, as noted above, to discern little social benefit that might result from running the risk of opening the door to such grave results. (Barnet & Bedau, 1987, p. 256)

If the principle (that the State has the right to excise certain words from the public discourse) is affirmed in this case, Harlan argued, it may then be applied to others. In order to be effective, the precedent argument moves the principle from the relatively innocuous case at hand (suppression of the scurrilous epithet) to a case of greater value (suppression of more thoughtful political speech).

Using this strategy, the speaker seeks to enforce the consequences of the opponent's position, showing where it will or could predictably lead.

*Reduce the Opponent's Principle to Absurdity.* Like the strategy of enforcing the consequences, the strategy of *reductio ad absurdum* applies the opponent's principle to instances unforeseen by the opponent. In this case, however, there is no claim that these instances *will* be covered by the principle, no claim of precedent or "slippery slope." In *reductio ad absurdum*, it is argued that:

1. If we accept the opponent's general principle, we would do $X$ in situation $O$.
2. Doing $X$ in situation $O$ is absurd.
3. We should not accept the opponent's principle as true.

Such an argument may employ an analogy between the case at issue in the debate (the case to which the opponent has applied the principle) and some similar but unforeseen instance. British essayist Macaulay often employed such arguments, as in the following:

> Many politicians of our time are in the habit of laying it down as a self-evident proposition, that no people ought to be free until they are fit to use their freedom. The maxim is worthy of the fool in the old story, who resolved not to go into the water until he had learned to swim. If men are to wait for liberty until they become wise and good in slavery, they may indeed wait forever. (cited in Foster, 1908/1932, p. 178)

The principle that Macaulay attacked was, as he noted, a popular belief in his time (and, for that matter, in more recent times). By removing it from its intended context and applying it to an instance it which it seems preposterous, Macaulay at least succeeded in making the principle seem less "self-evident."

In *Cohen v. State of California*, Supreme Court Justice Harlan applied the strategy of *reductio ad absurdum* to the principle advanced by the attorneys for the State. The State's attorneys claimed that it had the power to prohibit the wearing of a jacket bearing an obscene four-letter epithet against the draft for the Vietnam war. Harlan distilled the principle here—the State has the right to excise objectionable language from the public discourse—and reduces it to absurdity:

> The principle contended for by the State seems inherently boundless. How is one to distinguish this from any other offensive word? Surely the State has no right to cleanse public debate to the point where it is grammatically palatable to the most squeamish among us. Yet no readily ascertainable general principle exists for stopping short of that result. For, while the particular four-letter word being litigated here is perhaps more distasteful than most others of its genre, it is nevertheless often true that one man's vulgarity is another man's lyric. Indeed, we think it is largely because governmental officials cannot make principled decisions in this area that the

Constitution leaves matters of taste and style so largely to the individual. (Barnet & Bedau, 1987, p. 256)

Harlan did not argue that if the State were allowed to ban the four-letter epithet, this would lead to the establishment of grammar police. Instead, he used the grammar example to indict the general principle that the State should be allowed to excise objectionable language from public discourse. This principle, he argued, applies equally well to the grammar offense as to that of the four-letter epithet. If we find the State's hypothetical assertion of a right to police grammar to be ridiculous, the generality of the principle has been successfully indicted. Now the defenders of the principle must *limit* the principle in such a way that to accept it does not entail the approval of grammar police. Harlan and the majority of the Supreme Court found that no such line could be drawn, and overturned Cohen's conviction.

*Extrapolate the Opponent's Principle.* If the opponent's principle gains its force by the assertion of a general axiom to govern our judgment in a given instance, one frequently successful strategy for countering the appeal to principle is to reverse this process of application: Instead of *particularizing* the principle by applying it to a specific instance, *extrapolate* or *broaden* the principle by imagining what the world would be like if it were governed by the principle.

The process of extrapolation is sometimes used to establish moral principles. In explaining to a child why s/he should not walk on the grass or pick a flower from the grounds of a landscaped estate, we might ask the child to imagine "What would happen if *everybody* did that?"

Testing accepted principles through extrapolation is a staple technique of political fiction. This is particularly true of *dystopian* fiction, in which the author depicts an evil future world, usually extrapolated from some already existing tendency in our own. George Orwell's (1949) *1984* is perhaps the best known dystopian novel. In it, he extrapolated from his experience of government information control during and shortly after the Second World War. Most of Orwell's contemporaries might have accepted the value of government information control during the war, even when it meant exaggerating victories and downplaying losses, as necessary to the maintenance of morale. Orwell's *1984*, however, shows us a world in which the government tells its citizens they are *always* at war and such information control has become its central operation. Orwell did not intend to write a predictive novel about what the future would be like in the actual year 1984. Indeed, the original title of the novel was *1948*, the year it was completed. Orwell's novel was designed to extrapolate or hyperbolize a principle of governance in his own time so that its pernicious nature might be more clearly revealed.

Kurt Vonnegut's short story, "Harrison Bergeron," makes use of a similar technique in order to indict the principle that "Government should strive to promote absolute equality." Vonnegut (1970) imagined a world in which this principle has been fully accepted:

> The year was 2081, and everybody was finally equal. They weren't only equal before God and the law. They were equal every which way. Nobody was smarter than anybody else. Nobody was better looking than anybody else. Nobody was stronger or quicker than anybody else. All this equality was due to the 211th, 212th, and 213th Amendments to the Constitution, and to the unceasing vigilance of agents of the United States Handicapper General. (p. 7)

The Handicapper General makes sure that everybody is equal by establishing handicaps for people with some advantage: Attractive people must wear ugly masks, strong people must carry weights, smart people must wear earphones that disrupt their thoughts. Vonnegut's extrapolated vision of a perfectly egalitarian society was not meant as a prediction of things to come, but rather as a test of a principle that has influenced contemporary social reform efforts.

The strategy of extrapolation is often equally useful in actual debate. When confronted with a statement of principle by one's opponent, ask yourself: "What would the world be like if we *lived* by this principle?"

Let us consider the controversy over prohibition of flag-burning in the United States. One argument launched in favor of criminal penalties has been that they *enhance* the effectiveness of the act as political dissent by increasing the publicity and audience. This argument may seem clever at first glance; it attempts to coopt the position of the other side (as opponents of criminal penalties will undoubtedly support the value of flag-burning as political expression) into a reason to vote *for* penalties. But the true absurdity of the claim can be revealed by (a) exposing the underlying principle (people should be jailed for political expression because it increases their audience) and (b) extrapolating it into a more general system of law and speech. Imagine what the world be like if governed by the principle that any just action should be punished in order to produce sympathetic publicity.

*Appeal to a Higher* Principle.    One way to challenge a principle is to subordinate it to another. This strategy is especially useful when the opponent's principle seems beyond dispute in itself. Many of those who agreed, for example, with Senator Joseph McCarthy's principle ("We should be wary of Communist infiltration") disapproved of his methods for executing it. Senator Margaret Chase Smith, among other critics of McCarthyism, invoked a higher principle of proper governmental action with which to censure his activities.

To subordinate one principle to another is to construct a *hierarchy* of values. How may we say that one value is more "valuable" than another? One way is to demonstrate that one value is a *prerequisite* for the other. When the U.S. government tried to suppress the publication of the "Pentagon Papers," classified government documents that contained embarassing information about American operations in Vietnam, the issue at one level required a comparison of the value of press freedom versus that of national security. Proponents of publication argued that the freedom of the press to investigate and expose government fraud, mismanagement, and wrongful action is a safeguard of national security, hence, the higher value.

Psychologist Abraham Maslow's (1954) "hierarchy of needs" constructs a graduated list of basic human needs in order of their perceived importance – from more basic needs of physical security and sustanance to more advanced psychological needs of self-fulfillment. Each level of human requirement is portrayed as a prerequisite for the next.

All such hierarchies are subject to dispute. Moreover, the notion that the status of one value as a prerequisite for another establishes it as a *greater* value is itself easily disputed. We may just as easily value the needs (such as self-fulfillment) at the top of Maslow's hierarchy as of greater value because they subsume and expand on those below them.

One useful way of comparing competing values is to construct a situation in which they conflict. Doing so may produce interesting results and potent arguments. Although, for example, we may regard the maintenance of life as a prerequisite for the enjoyment of liberty, we know that when given a choice, widely admired people often make the opposite choice (as in Patrick Henry's famous pronouncement: "Give me liberty or give me death!").

The appeal to principle is a powerful force in debate, investing arguments about a particular case with the moral authority of common wisdom and experience. Yet, as William Rusher (1981) has observed, "As a practical proposition in debating, you will rarely if ever come across a principle that wholly forecloses argument" (p. 77). Principles may be disputed as false or pernicious, limited in their scope, challenged as to their applicability in the case at hand, or subordinated to higher principles. Through a variety of available strategies, an opponent's appeal to principle may be effectively countered.

## SUMMARY: TESTS OF PRINCIPLES

1. Discover anomalies and exceptions to the opponent's principle.
2. Enforce the consequences.
3. *Reductio ad absurdum.*
4. Extrapolate the opponent's principle.
5. Appeal to a higher principle.

# THE FORM AND TECHNIQUES OF DEBATE

Success in debating requires not only a mastery of the subject debated and of strategies for argument, but also a thorough understanding of how a debate *works:* the format for the debate; the responsibilities of individual speakers; how notes should be taken to record the flow of arguments; and of techniques for the clear and effective delivery of arguments.

## DEBATE FORMATS

Debate may be conducted in formats as diverse as a series of letters-to-the-editor or a panel discussion among experts on a television news show. An early debate textbook, *The Young Debater* (Anonymous, 1856), offered "a model for juvenile debating clubs" and "for classes in public and private schools" consisting of a fully scripted debate on the character of Julius Caesar, divided into 32 speeches. Even today at the university level, there are many different forms of organized debate. Indeed, new ones are frequently invented to suit the specific needs of a given class or occasion.

Nevertheless, it is helpful to know the formats most commonly employed in organized debate, and the conventional responsibilities assigned to the individual speaker positions in each format. Most debate formats share at least the following characteristics:

1. **The affirmative (supporting the proposition) begins and ends the debate.** Because propositions normally call for some change in action or

belief, the affirmative must begin by constructing a case for such a change and conclude the debate by demonstrating that, after all objections have been accounted for, the case is still sufficiently intact to support change.

2. **Speeches alternate between representatives of the two sides in the debate.** After the first affirmative speaker has finished, a member of the opposition should follow, and *vice versa*. This heightens clash between the two sides. If the affirmative is both to begin and end the debate and both sides are to have an equal number of speeches, however, there must at some point in the format be an *exception* to the strict alternation of sides. Two speakers for the opposition must speak consecutively, usually by having the first opposition rebuttalist follow the last opposition constructive speaker.

3. **Different speeches are designated as *constructives* or *rebuttals*.** Constructives are speeches in which the debaters construct their cases and argumentative positions and, accordingly, come first in the debate. Rebuttals are speeches in which no *new* argumentative positions are constructed, but instead the debaters must synthesize and extend previously introduced positions, as well as refuting the extended arguments of the other side. The rebuttals will normally be assigned a shorter speaking time than the constructives, reflecting the need to winnow and coalesce the most important arguments.

4. **The time period in which the debate occurs is limited.** Unlike the "pure talk" debates of medieval China, most formal debates end when the allotted time has expired, not at the end of all controversy. Speaking time is evenly divided between representatives of the two sides.

Beyond these shared characteristics, however, debate formats and procedures vary considerably. The most important factor influencing these variations is the *audience*. Who is the decision maker to whom the debaters appeal? Are the debaters to appear before a *public* audience or an *expert* one? Does the audience look to the debate as a way in which to decide some issue, as a source of entertainment, as a training exercise for the participants, or some combination of these? The different possible answers to these questions have produced very different formats for debates.

**Parliamentary Debate**

Modified parliamentary debate is the form of intra- and intermural debate most commonly practiced by students around the world. University teams from over 30 nations have participated in the World (Parliamentary) Debate Championships in recent years. Because of its flexibility, simplicity, and audience appeal, it is also ideally suited to the classroom.

Modified parliamentary debate is loosely derived from the model of the British legislature and the intramural debates of the Oxford Union. As John Rodden (1985) has written:

> Founded in the 1820s, the Oxford and Cambridge unions were conceived as miniature parliaments, designed to improve speaking skills, to facilitate professional contacts, and to enlarge political opportunities. The unions were the oral counterpart to the student university newspapers, charting from week to week those events of local and national concern to the university community. (p. 308)

There are many variations in the parliamentary format, but the two most commonly used are these:

| | |
|---|---|
| Prime Minister | 8 minutes |
| Leader of the Opposition | 8 minutes |
| Member of the Government | 8 minutes |
| Member of the Opposition | 8 minutes |
| Leader of the Opposition | 4 minutes (rebuttal) |
| Prime Minister | 4 minutes (rebuttal) |

*OR*

| | |
|---|---|
| Prime Minister | 8 minutes |
| Member of the Opposition | 8 minutes |
| Member of the Government | 8 minutes |
| Leader of the Opposition | 12 minutes (the last 4 of which are restricted to rebuttal arguments) |
| Prime Minister | 4 minutes (rebuttal) |

No preparation time is permitted between speeches.

The Prime Minister and Member of the Government (sometimes referred to as the "Minister of the Crown") are obliged to affirm the proposition for the debate, the Leader and Member of the Opposition to negate it. The number of participants in a parliamentary debate is flexible. Teams usually include two, three, or four debaters per side. With more than two participants, the individual debaters may "specialize" by presenting only a constructive or a rebuttal speech, rather than both.

Parliamentary debates may feature "set topics," agreed on in advance, or "extemporaneous" topics, which the debaters first learn only a few minutes before the debate. Extemporaneous debates emphasize inventiveness and the ability to organize one's thoughts and responses in a spontaneous fashion; placing a premium on the ability to "think on one's feet." The 1990 World Debate Championships held in Glasgow, Scotland, included the following topics, each announced 15 minutes prior to the start of a round of debate: "Be it Resolved that . . .":

"The Second Amendment to the U.S. Constitution should be repealed";

"No community has the right to force another to be civilized";

"The art of being a good lover is knowing when to leave"; and

"We have reached the end of history."

The topics employed in extemporaneous debate are often abstract or indefinite, permitting many possible interpretations by those who would affirm them. Advocates are obliged to interpret the topic in such a way as to *enable meaningful debate*. The case presented on behalf of the proposition in an extemporaneous debate must not rely on special knowledge unlikely to be shared by opponents or audience and must not foreclose debate by being truistic, or one-sided.

Parliamentary debates may also feature "set topics," agreed on in advance to enable more thorough research and preparation of arguments. The Oxford and Cambridge debate unions, like many others, publish schedules of upcoming debates to be held on-campus during each academic term. A sampling of topics published in advance of the 1981 Spring term at Cambridge University illustrates the range of issues discussed:

"Britain should control imports, leave the European Economic Community, and expand public expenditure to restore full employment";

"This House believes that the Arts today are in decline";

"Private lives of public figures should be solely their own concern";

"Soviet foreign policy poses no threat to the West";

"This House would support a realignment in British politics."

Public parliamentary debates may be held on an intramural basis as an exhibition for the university community. On-campus debates may also involve teams from other universities, sometimes arranged as "home and home" contests in which debaters from each university agree to appear on the campus of the other. Parliamentary tournaments, involving teams from a variety of schools, are also held.

Unlike the more specialized debate formats generally employed in the United States, public parliamentary debates are geared toward direct involvement of the audience. Members of the *audience* may actively participate in public parliamentary debates in four ways: by presenting "floor speeches"; by rising to a point of order or information; by heckling; and, in many cases, by voting on the outcome of the debate.

*Floor speeches* are formal remarks delivered by a member of the audience. These speeches may be offered in support of either team or, if delivered as "cross-bench" remarks, may reject the arguments of *both* teams. Floor speeches are usually presented during a designated period between the constructives and rebuttals. The moderator of the debate should announce procedures for the delivery of a floor speech (e.g., alternation of sides and time limits), then recognize speakers from the floor at the appropriate time. The opportunity to deliver a floor speech may be left open to any member of the audience or restricted to a group of speakers approved in advance.

Floor speeches add enormously to the excitement of a public debate. They provide an opportunity for many participants to speak and generate direct audience involvement in the dispute. A prize is sometimes awarded to the best floor speaker in a public debate.

Floor speeches are also excellent training exercises for new debaters. Because they encourage the speaker to identify and address a single important issue in the debate (whether raised or neglected by the formal debaters in their constructive speeches), they help develop argumentative *perspective* and decision-making skills. Because floor speeches are normally limited to a short period (1 to 2 minutes), they are also less intimidating for beginning debaters.

Members of the audience may also speak in some parliamentary debates by raising *points of order* (objections to some violation of procedural rules by one of the debaters – such as making insulting references to "the Queen and members of the Royal Family," prohibited by the rules of the Glasgow Union) or *points of information*. Points of information are delivered when a speaker cedes the floor to a debater from the other side or a member of the audience so that a brief (usually hostile) statement or question can be made.

*Heckling* is a long-standing tradition in parliamentary debate (and still avidly practiced in the British Parliament itself). Proper heckles are short, witty, pointed remarks shouted from the floor during a debater's speech. Heckles usually point out some flaw in the speaker's argument, raise a challenge or counterexample, or jokingly insult the speaker. It is improper to heckle in such a way as to prevent the speaker from being heard. When A. Craig Baird coached the first American college team (Bates) to visit Oxford in 1921, he observed that proper heckling serves to enhance the performance of accomplished debaters. "The constant heckling," he noted, "may inspire him to unexpected power in argument" (Baird, 1923, p. 215).

Through these opportunities for direct audience participation, public parliamentary debates are often quite lively events, exciting and challenging for both debaters and audiences.

A decision may or may not be announced at the end of public debates. Proponents of no-decision debating claim that it "allows for the fairest possible analysis of the proposition under discussion," by purging elements of competition (Grether, 1929, p. 14). When public debates *do* feature decisions, they may be arrived at by vote of assigned judges, the general audience, or both. The basis of the decision also varies. Decision makers may be encouraged to vote on the basis of their actual opinions regarding the proposition, on the basis of the issues as debated in the round (apart from their own opinions on the matter), or on the basis of the speaking and analytical skills exhibited by the debaters.

Audience votes may be taken by ballot, show of hands, or some form of house division, such as route of egress. In this last method, audience members choose a door through which to exit the chamber—one designated for the affirmative, one for the opposition, or one for those who remain undecided. Some institutions have attempted to gauge shifts in audience opinion by asking for ballots on the question both as the audience enters the chamber and as it exits. These shifts in opinion are sometimes made evident during the debate when members of the audience are invited to shift their seats from one side of the chamber to another according to changes in their allegiance.

Public debate, whether in parliamentary or other formats, is designed to generate public interest and understanding of issues and to enhance public participation in discussions about them. The success of a public debate may be gauged by the degree to which it has motivated the audience to speak and provided them with a coherent framework for the dispute in which their opinions may be brought to bear.

## Speaker Responsibilities in American Policy Debate

The American policy debate format (also practiced in Japan) is a set of conventions that have derived mainly from intermural tournament competition. In the National Debate Tournament (N.D.T.) circuit of competition, a single broad resolution (such as "Resolved: that the United States should significantly increase its exploration of outer space") is employed by all tournaments during an academic year. These debates are judged by trained specialists, place a premium on the use of evidentiary quotations to support arguments, and feature technical vocabulary and conventions of argumentation that may render them inaccessible to general audiences. Debates are judged according to the balance of a proposed policy's costs and benefits as constructed by the debaters during the round.

The format of American policy debate is adaptable to other purposes and audiences, however, and is frequently used for classroom and even public debates. The speaking order and two most popular speaking-time limits are as follows:

| Speech | 60-minute | 72-minute |
|---|---|---|
| First affirmative constructive | 8 | 10 |
| Cross-examination of first aff. | 3 | 3 |
| First negative constructive | 8 | 10 |
| Cross-examination of first neg. | 3 | 3 |
| Second affirmative constructive | 8 | 10 |
| Cross-examination of second aff. | 3 | 3 |
| Second negative constructive | 8 | 10 |
| Cross-examination of second neg. | 3 | 3 |
| First negative rebuttal | 4 | 5 |
| First affirmative rebuttal | 4 | 5 |
| Second negative rebuttal | 4 | 5 |
| Second affirmative rebuttal | 4 | 5 |

There are other variations on these time limits, notably formats which lengthen rebuttal speech times relative to those of constructives (allowing, for example, a 9-minute constructive and 6-minute rebuttal). These variations place greater emphasis on argument extension and make it easier for less experienced debaters to cover all significant issues in the rebuttal period.

There are conventional responsibilities assigned to each of these speaker positions. In some cases, these conventions reflect the logical requirements for meaningful discussion (such as the requirement that the first affirmative speaker present a case on behalf of the resolution). In other instances, the conventional responsibilities merely reflect the stylistic habits of past debaters and are subject to change.

The first affirmative constructive, as described in chapter 2, must present a *prima facie* case on behalf of the proposition, complete on its "first making" and obliging the opposition to respond.

The first negative constructive should both refute the arguments offered by the first affirmative speaker (as described in chapter 2) and launch the negative's own position and arguments in the debate. As discussed in chapter 6, these arguments should include a coherent explanation of the negative's counterposition in the debate: a description of what they *support* as well as of what they oppose.

The second affirmative constructive speaker should rebuild the case after the first negative's attack on it. He or she should: (a) Refute arguments made by the negative speaker; (b) make note of elements of the first affirmative speech that were *not* attacked by the negative (and explain their significance), and (c) augment important original arguments of the case with additional evidence, emphasis, or development (regardless of whether the point has been refuted by the negative). The second affirmative speaker should make sure that the basic structure of the original case (its organization and labeling of issues) is revived.

The second negative constructive may extend arguments initiated by the first negative speaker, answer arguments extended by the second affirmative constructive, and/or initiate new arguments on new issues. Traditionally, the first negative constructive speech was devoted primarily to refutation of the affirmative *case* and the second negative speech was devoted to the refutation of the affirmative *plan* (presenting plan-meet-advantage arguments and disadvantages). In recent years, however, this strict division of responsibilities has largely been abandoned. The first negative constructive may initiate a disadvantage, for example, that will be extended by the second negative speaker. This strategy permits greater depth in extension than could be provided in the first negative rebuttal. On the other hand, not *all* issues from the first negative constructive can be handled in this way, lest the first negative rebuttalist be left with nothing to say. Also, because the second negative constructive is the last opportunity for the negative to construct *new* issues, it may be wise to do so.

The first negative rebuttal follows the second negative constructive, with no intervening speech from the other side. As a result, one may look at the primary responsibility of the first negative rebuttalist as extending whatever important arguments from the first negative constructive that have *not* been covered by the previous speaker. But the first negative rebuttalist has other important responsibilities as well; he or she must begin the process of winnowing the negative's best arguments from less telling ones. The best arguments – those that have been poorly handled by the affirmative and/or have the greatest potential impact on the case – should receive further development and evidence, the less important ones should probably be abandoned at this point in the debate.

The first affirmative rebuttal, and the two rebuttals that follow, should cover all important (i.e., consequential to the decision) issues in the debate. This is no small task for the first affirmative rebuttalist, who must respond to the arguments of *two* consecutive previous speakers for the opposition. The first affirmative rebuttalist should begin by addressing any *new* issues raised in the second negative constructive, because no affirmative responses to these arguments have yet been issued in the debate. The first affirmative rebuttalist must then provide responses to all remaining issues of importance. The responses must be sufficiently detailed to enable extension by the second affirmative rebuttalist and, because of time constraints, should be restricted to the strongest available arguments on the point.

The two final rebuttalists each have the responsibility of drawing the vital issues together and explaining why, on the basis of these issues, their side should win the debate. The second affirmative and negative rebuttal-ists should each attempt to look at the debate as the judge might – What issues are important? Which side is winning them? How do the costs and benefits of the proposal balance out? Issues that are not likely to have much of an impact on this equation should be abandoned. "The last speaker," admonished Foster (1908/1932), "has no time for minor matters. He must subordinate the insignificant odds and ends, which are more or less confused in the minds of the hearers, to the main issues. His task is to muster the whole forces of his side for an orderly, unified, final attack" (p. 306).

The two final rebuttalists should be able to narrow the decision of the debate to a definable, measurable contrast between the positions of the two sides. This "debate about the debate" is among the most difficult and rewarding aspects of competition. "Rebuttal," wrote Professor George Pierce Baker (Baker & Huntington, 1905) of Harvard, "may be said to be the life of debate, for it links part with part, brings the immediate and unexpected into relation with the prearranged, keeps a discussion from going off on secondary issues, and places emphasis correctly" (p. 410). A successful rebuttalist is one who assembles an incisive portrait – the "big picture" – of the debate, persuading the audience to step back from the debate and view its issues from a holistic perspective favorable to the debater's own position.

Most of the speaker responsibilities just described (with the exception of those assigned to the opening and closing speakers) are the products of convention rather than necessity. Whether or not you decide to abide by the conventional division of speaker responsibilities as described here, you should arrive at some sort of agreement with your teammates prior to the debate (or during it when necessary) about how responsibilities for the introduction or coverage of various arguments will be divided. In this way, you will minimize repetition and maximize the range and depth of arguments you present.

## Non-Policy Debate

American debate reformers have created several alternate formats and leagues for debate in recent decades. The two most popular of these are "Lincoln–Douglas (L–D) debate" and Cross-Examination Debate Association (CEDA) debate. Both have attempted to employ non-policy proposi-tions, usually in the form of value propositions. Competitive tournaments are widely held in both formats.

Lincoln–Douglas debate features only one debater per side. The format was inspired by the 1858 Illinois Senate campaign debates between Abraham Lincoln and Stephen A. Douglas – a contest of verbal single-combat between two great orators that centered on one of the greatest value-conflicts in American history: slavery. The modern Lincoln–Douglas debate format was introduced by the U.S. National Forensic League in 1980 and has since become the most popular form of debate among American high school students.

The order of speeches in a Lincoln–Douglas debate is as follows:

| | |
|---|---|
| Affirmative constructive | 6 minutes |
| Cross-examination by negative | 3 minutes |
| Negative constructive | 7 minutes |
| Cross-examination by affirmative | 3 minutes |
| Affirmative rebuttal | 4 minutes |
| Negative rebuttal | 6 minutes |
| Affirmative rebuttal | 3 minutes |

The Lincoln–Douglas format balances the amount of speaking time for the two sides (13 minutes each), but allows the affirmative three speeches and the negative two. In this way, the format enables the affirmative to both open and close the debate while maintaining the alternation of sides throughout the round.

Lincoln–Douglas debate differs from traditional policy debate in more than its format or team size, however. It was designed to encourage different stylistic practices from those employed in tournament policy debate. In introducing the Lincoln–Douglas format in 1980, the National Forensic League *Rostrum* outlined its principal differences from policy debate:

1. The emphasis is on abstract reasoning, and stock issues may not apply at all.
2. Evidence is of less importance and handled as information would be handled in oratory or extemporaneous speaking.
3. Only general or major propositions are signposted.
4. Value propositions call for decisions based on a system of values.

The topics for Lincoln–Douglas debate change on a monthly basis and are worded differently than N.D.T. propositions, as in the following examples:

"Resolved: The emphasis on sports in America's high schools is unjustifiable."

"Resolved: Civil disobedience is morally unjust."

"Resolved: Technological advancement is of greater value than ecological preservation."

"Resolved: The unilateral nuclear freeze is beneficial for mankind."

"Resolved: The government is best that governs least."

The propositions of value employed in Lincoln–Douglas debate are of three general types: those that evaluate a given institution or action (as in the "government" and "civil disobedience" topics just mentioned); those that require the comparison and hierarchical arrangement of different values (such as the aforementioned "technological advancement"/"ecological preservation" topic); and those that logically require a defense of policies (as in the "high school sports" and "nuclear freeze" topics just mentioned), although they are couched in evaluative terms. This last category of topics should make clear the difficulty of distinguishing between propositions of policy and value. All propositions of policy require the support and contrast of value propositions; the concepts of significance, cost, and benefit are only meaningful when placed on scales of value. At the same time, propositions of value often prescribe and are tested by exemplary actions.

The choice of a format (whether one of those just described or one you have devised) should be made according to the number of desired participants (dictating more or fewer speakers per side), the audience for the event (e.g., public or specialized), the subject to be debated, and the experience level of the participants.

Most of the analytical skills and strategic perspectives on argument developed in earlier chapters are applicable to any of the available formats.

## CROSS-EXAMINATION

Cross-examination is a popular feature of many competitive debate formats, and is common in other formal disputes as well. Questioning of advocates and opponents is an important part of legal disputes, legislative hearings, and other exchanges. Whereas much of the speaking in a debate takes the form of a series of monologues (one person speaks to the audience for a set period of time, then is followed by another), cross-examination brings advocates for opposing sides together in dialogue. Because it is the one time in most debates that the audience will see a direct and immediate exchange between the two sides, cross-examination can be exciting and yield insights to the issues unobtainable in other ways.

Cross-examination is best directed toward the achievement of one or more of the following objectives:

1. **Information.** Cross-examination may be used to gain details needed in order to refute the answerer's position. Such questions may center on the methods used in an important study cited by the opponent, or on the intended meanings of vague terms (e.g., "democracy") important to the opponent's case. The clearer your understanding of the opponent's argument, the more relevant and damaging may be your refutation of it.

2. **Focus.** The cross-examination period is an opportunity to narrow the audience's attention to what you believe to be the most vulnerable aspects of an opponent's position: those areas in which the opponent's evidence is lacking or weak, for example.

3. **Consensus.** The most important strategic function of cross-examination is its ability to generate agreement between the two sides, in the form of admissions or other statements elicited from the respondent that may then be used to the questioner's benefit. Remember: the strongest evidence in any debate is that statement, principle, or data used by your opponent, which you have been able to convert to your own purposes. Cross-examination offers the best opportunity to gain such evidence.

## Techniques of Questioning

Proper questions should be clear, simple, and brief. Do not set them up by providing background information – the respondent will soon look at you and ask, "What's the question??" The question period should be used to gain information from your opponent, not to make statements yourself. A question that is too long and complicated confuses audience and respondent alike as to what is expected in answer. More than once, a lengthy and complex question has been defused by the simple response: "Would you please repeat that?", usually followed by laughter from the audience.

Except in asking informational questions (Purpose 1 listed earlier), the questioner should either know the answers to the questions in advance or have prepared for a variety of possible answers. When the questioner knows the answer to a question, its purpose may be to gain some public statement of the answer from the respondent, which may then be used by the questioner in subsequent speeches. The questioner may also choose to press for an answer that is obvious not only to the respondent but to the audience, which encourages the audience to follow the line of question and see its point as if it were their own challenge to the respondent. In the early 1980s, at the height of renewed Cold War tensions between the United States and the Soviet Union, the Olympic Games were twice boycotted (in 1980 and 1984) by one of the two superpowers. Some observers proposed the establishment of Athens as a permanent home for the Olympics, claiming that to do so would lessen boycotts and, as a result, reduce tensions between the superpowers. In one debate over the proposal, its advocate was asked the following questions regarding this claim:

Is there tension between the United States and U.S.S.R. over nuclear arms in Europe?

Is there tension between the United States and U.S.S.R. over Central American policy?

Is there tension between the United States and U.S.S.R. over Jewish emigration?

Is there tension between the United States and U.S.S.R. over Star Wars?

Is there tension between the United States and U.S.S.R. because of President Reagan's characterization of the Soviets as an "Evil Empire?"

And so on. The answer to each question was obvious to audience and respondent alike, as was the purpose of the questions. The audience was led to view the claim that a permanent home for the Olympics in Athens would lessen superpower tensions within the context of all the other tensions between them. After completing this list of questions, the questioner simply asked: "How much of the tension between the United States and U.S.S.R. would a permanent home for the Olympics eliminate?" This question is unanswerable, of course, which is precisely its point.

Cross-examination should generally be used to *set up* arguments to be made in a subsequent speech. When used for such purposes, questions should elicit needed information without telegraphing your forthcoming argument to your opponent. Never give the opponent an opportunity to anticipate and answer a forthcoming argument in cross-examination. As discussed in chapter 7, this is especially important when using analogies. Cross-examination can be used to put the respondent in an analogous situation but should not be used to draw a parallel between the analogue and the primary subject or offer the respondent an opportunity to dispute the analogy between them during the cross-examination period.

All useful points made or information gained in cross-examination must be introduced in a subsequent speech in order to have an impact on the outcome of the debate. It is not enough to lay out an analogy or gain some damaging admission in cross-examination; the implications of the analogy or admission must be spelled out in a speech that follows, converting *information* gained in cross-examination into an *argument*. The questioner should take notes about what he or she has gained in cross-examination and use them to prepare arguments.

The questioner should remain courteous but in control of the cross-examination period. Do not allow the respondent to make speeches. Phrase your questions so that they require precise answers and avoid terms in your question (such as "why" and "how") that signal open-endedness. When respondents go astray, pull them back to the question; when they ramble on, politely cut them off. It is the questioner who decides when to move from one line of questioning to the next, abandoning lines of questioning that have proven fruitless or been exhausted.

When responding to questions, one should be gracious, open, and honest. Answer questions directly, rather than engaging in evasive tactics likely to be transparent to the audience. One should, however, be aware of the questioning strategies just described: Try to see ahead to where a line of questioning is leading, to what implications it might have for the debate. This may influence your answer or afford you the opportunity (especially against a less-skilled questioner) to dispute or preempt the implication before it is fully drawn.

Cross-examination is perhaps the most difficult aspect of debate to master, because its success depends on the mastery of so many other difficult skills—such as anticipation, analogy, strategic agreement, and perspective. Even when it is less than expertly managed, however, it adds the excitement of dialogue and direct confrontation to debate.

## THE FLOWSHEET

Even the most narrowly drawn disputes may involve many separate issues and arguments. Because debates, by definition, feature the extension of disputed issues through an ongoing exchange, keeping track of all the important points that have been raised is no easy matter. The flowsheet is a system of notation specially designed to record the issues in a debate and to facilitate clear discussion of them. Each participant in a debate should make a flowsheet.

A properly designed flowsheet assists the speaker in several ways:

1. The flowsheet enables comprehensive coverage of the issues. All important arguments should be recorded, lessening the chance that the speaker will fail to address a crucial point;

2. The flowsheet permits better refutation of specific details and supportive reasoning. It is often not sufficient for the respondent to address only the broad outline of an opponent's argument. It is in the details of supportive evidence, examples, and reasoning (best recalled by use of the flowsheet) that the debate usually rests;

3. The flowsheet enhances the organization of a speaker's presentation, by outlining the major and subordinate arguments in the cases of both sides and by tracking the discussion of any given issue from speech to speech;

4. The flowsheet enhances strategic decision making in rebuttals, by allowing the debater to identify the most important issues in the debate and everything that has (or has not) been said about them; and

5. After the debate, the flowsheet enables the debater to reassess the debate and learn from mistakes (particularly after receiving a judge's comments regarding the debate). If filed, the flowsheet becomes a resource for future competition, providing a record of the arguments a particular team has used against you in the past.

The flowsheet provides a graphic representation of the true debate round. It shows the development and organization of positions, the points of clash between the two sides, the extension and refinement of arguments throughout the course of the debate, and enables an overall perspective on the issues.

The flowsheet organizes the record of the debate in two ways: by speaker and by issue. The division of the debate by speaker is designated by the vertical columns of the flowsheet, which may be drawn on blank pages prior to the debate (see Fig. 8.1–8.3). Each speech in the debate is recorded in a different vertical column, moving left-to-right from first speech to last speech. The speeches of each side may be recorded in different color ink (e.g., blue for the affirmative and red for the negative) for clear differentiation at a glance.

The case presented by the first affirmative (or government) speaker should be outlined from top to bottom in the far-left column of the flowsheet. Additional pages (using the same format) may be used to record a longer speech. All arguments by both sides in the debate pertaining to the initial case structure offered by the affirmative should be recorded on these sheets.

| 1AC | 1NC | 2AC | 2NC/1NR | 1AR | 2NR | 2AR |
|-----|-----|-----|---------|-----|-----|-----|
|     |     |     |         |     |     |     |

**FIGURE 8.1.**  Case flowsheet format for policy debate.

| AC | NC | 1AR | NR | 2AR |
|----|----|-----|----|-----|
|    |    |     |    |     |

**FIGURE 8.2.** Case flowsheet format for Lincoln–Douglas debate.

| PM | LO | MG | MO | LOR | PMR |
|----|----|----|----|-----|-----|
|    |    |    |    |     |     |

**FIGURE 8.3.** Case flowsheet format for parliamentary debate.

## Dividing the Debate by Issue

The flowsheet also divides the debate according to issue. Whereas the vertical columns of the flowsheet separate the debate by speaker, the horizontal planes of the flowsheet divide the discussion of one issue from that of another. The principle is a simple one: With a properly designed flowsheet, one should be able to point at a given argument made in the first affirmative speech and, by moving one's finger straight across the page from left to right, trace all discussion of that issue throughout the debate. Arrows are normally drawn from left to right between the arguments on an issue by one speaker and the arguments on that same issue by the next speaker.

In order to achieve the horizontal division of the flowsheet by issue, certain guidelines must be observed.

*Arguments Presented by Different Speakers Regarding the Same Issue Should Be Flowed Next to Each Other.*   When recording the first speech in which an issue is raised, the notetaker sets the location for that issue on the page. Whenever that issue is addressed in later speeches (whether in refutation or further support), the new argument should be flowed in the same horizontal plane as the original one.

This principle must be followed regardless of the order in which the issues are covered in the later speech. Let us assume, for example, that the first speaker in support of a proposition raises three arguments: A, B, and C. The next speaker, opposing the proposition, begins his/her speech by discussing Argument C, then covers Arguments A and B. If recorded in the order of presentation, the flowsheet of this exchange would resemble the following:

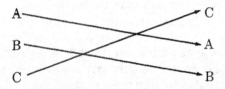

In this instance, the horizontal principle of the flowsheet has been violated: Arguments on the same issue have not been flowed next to each other. As a consequence, it will be far more difficult to follow the development of any given issue, particularly as the debate continues.

A proper flowsheet of the preceding exchange would be as follows:

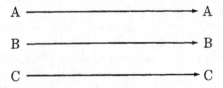

Regardless of the order in which they are presented by subsequent speakers, arguments on a given issue should be flowed in the same horizontal plane as their original presentation.

*Adequate Vertical Space on the Flowsheet Must Be Provided for Each New Issue.*   There will often be more arguments about a given issue in later speeches than were offered in the original presentation. A single original argument may provoke several counter-arguments, each of which may in turn be answered with several arguments from the supporters of the original argument. Although the original argument may have taken only two lines of the flowsheet to record, the discussion of that issue in the fifth speech of the debate, for example, may take 10 or 12 lines.

If in recording the original presentation, the notetaker failed to leave adequate space for the later expansion of that issue, the horizontal principle for *other* issues would be violated. The space next to them would wrongly be filled with arguments regarding the first issue.

By leaving adequate space below each issue recorded, the notetaker will be able to record expanded discussion of that issue in subsequent speeches without violating the horizontal principle for other issues. The provision of adequate space between different issues also makes it easier to distinguish them and trace their development at a glance.

*Every Important Issue Should Be Flowed Across the Page, Even if It Has Been Dropped by One Side.*   One important function of the flowsheet is its ability to highlight the failure of one's opponent to respond to an important issue. Normally this is done by drawing an arrow from the prior speaker's discussion of the issue to where the next speaker's response to that issue *should* have appeared, and by then drawing an "X" in that spot.

By noting important arguments that have been dropped by one's opponent, you will be less likely to drop them yourself.

*When an Argument in a Later Speech Raises a New Issue* That Does *Not* Respond to an Argument Raised in Prior Speeches, It Should Be Flowed on a Separate Page or Notepad.   The first speaker in support of a proposition will normally provide the structure of the affirmative case. As noted earlier, all arguments pertaining to that case structure (rebutting or supporting the arguments made within it) should be recorded on the same page(s). Some arguments may be presented, however, that do *not* pertain to the affirmative's case structure. The opposition, for example, may present an overview of its competing philosophy in the debate, a counterplan, or arguments against the affirmative plan (such as disadvantages) that do not directly address points raised in the affirmative's case structure. Such arguments, and all discussion of them in subsequent speeches, should be recorded on separate pages, ideally on a separate flowpad.

The first speech in which these issues are presented (e.g., the presentation of several disadvantages in the second constructive speech of the opposition) should be flowed in the left-hand column of the additional page. All responses and extensions of these arguments should also be flowed on these new pages. In order to keep the different pages of the flowsheet distinct and to be able to find the right one while speaking, a bold marker should be used to label the contents (i.e., "CASE" or "DISADS") of each page.

## Comprehensiveness

The proper flowsheet should provide a comprehensive record of the important arguments in the debate. It should contain all elements of case and argument structure for both sides. If the affirmative structures its case with three contentions, the numbers and some description of each should be recorded. If each of the three contentions is supported by several arguments, these too should be numbered and described. An outlined organization should be provided for each speaker's arguments, even if the speaker has failed to do so. The flowsheet should sort out and structure different strands of argument, identifying main and subordinate points, independent and dependent arguments.

The flowsheet should also record the substance and support for arguments made in the debate. It is not enough to record the mere label or claim of an argument. The debate will generally center on the support for these claims, the evidence and reasoning provided for them. The flowsheet record of an argument should note the jist and key components, such as statistics or examples, for any evidence used. The flowsheet should also note the source of any authoritative testimony employed in the debate. By recording the source, it is easier to refer to a specific piece of evidence in a later speech or to challenge the source in the manner described in chapter 3.

The ideal flowsheet, a comprehensive and organized record of argument structure and substance, is difficult to execute and necessitates patient practice. Early efforts at flowing are likely to be rather sparse, missing many arguments and failing to record the details of those that are recorded. One of the main reasons for these early difficulties is the tendency of most people to listen, analyze, *then write*, rather than performing these tasks simultaneously. The debater who pauses to hear and think about an argument, writing it on the flowsheet only as the speaker concludes it, is likely to miss the speaker's *next* argument. There is no necessary conflict, however, between listening to an argument and simultaneously analyzing and recording it. With practice, flowing sharpens critical listening skills by forcing one to find the key parts and phrases of an argument. Debaters should be writing at all times during a debate when they are not speaking – either recording the arguments of another or drafting their own arguments for an upcoming speech.

Even if one is constantly writing during a debate, it is neither possible nor desirable to transcribe every word that is spoken in it. While striving for comprehensiveness in the recording of arguments, it is vital to remain selective in choosing the words and symbols with which to represent those arguments. Descriptions of arguments should be brief and clear, stripped of the rhetorical flourishes that may have accompanied their oral presentation. Thus, a speaker's argument that "the government's proposal for greater use of coal will promote global warming and ecological catastrophe," may be labeled simply "global warming" or "climate" on the flowsheet and still provide clear reference. The supportive reasoning and evidence for the claim must be flowed with similar selectivity.

A second technique for increasing the comprehensiveness of one's flowsheet is the extensive use of symbols and abbreviations. Terms commonly used in debate become sufficiently familiar that one may abbreviate or symbolize them. Instead of writing the term "disadvantage," for example, one might write "DA." The abbreviation in this case takes only one-sixth the time to write that the full word does; if extended, this would mean that one might be able to record six times as much in the same amount of time, thus producing a far more comprehensive flowsheet.

Figure 8.4 lists some examples of commonly used symbols and abbreviations for various recurring features of debate argumentation.

Other symbols and abbreviations should be developed for specific cases and issues that you debate. If one is debating fetal tissue research policies, the phrases "fetal tissue" and "fetal tissue research" will be uttered many times. The acronyms "FT" and "FTR" might be substituted on the flowsheet.

The great danger in the use of symbols and abbreviations is that, as a speaker, one may not be able to recognize and translate them when glancing at the flowsheet. This danger can be minimized in two ways. First, one may begin by using less radical abbreviations for unfamiliar terms. Although "R," used in the preceding example, might stand for many things, "rsrch" is clear at a glance and still saves one-third of the time it takes to write the full word. Second, use only those symbols and abbreviations that are completely clear and immediately recognizable to you. Symbols and abbreviations are idiosyncratic—each debater may have slightly different ways of symbolizing or abbreviating certain terms. There is no one "right" way to symbolize an argumentative contradiction. Find a symbol or abbreviation with which you are comfortable, whether from Fig. 8.4 or from your own imagination.

### Flowing to Make Arguments

The flowsheet is more than a record of the arguments made by others; it is also an invaluable device for the preparation of one's *own* arguments. Before you rise to speak, it is imperative that you have outlined on your flowsheet the arguments you are about to present, and that if you are going to address issues previously introduced in the debate, the connec-

| Debate Terms | | Common Periodicals | |
|---|---|---|---|
| T | topicality | WSJ | Wall Street Journal |
| Inh | inherency | NYT | New York Times |
| DA | disadvantage | CR | Congressional Record |
| PMA | plan-meet-advantage | CQWR | Congressional Quarterly |
| PMN | plan-meet-need | | Weekly Report |
| Circ | circumvention | WP | Washington Post |
| PS | present system | BW | Business Week |
| SQ | status quo | CSM | Christian Science Monitor |
| TA | turnaround | USN | U.S. News & World Report |
| CP | counterplan | | |
| Sig | significance | **Common Source Abbreviations** | |
| OBS | observation | | |
| OVW | overview | J | Journal |
| UVW | underview | Rvw | Review |
| U | unique | LR | law review |
| NU | non-unique | Comm | committee |
| thr | threshold | Hrgs | hearings |
| OTB | on the brink | | |
| $ | dollars, money, finance, revenue, funding | **Relationships** | |
| )( | contradiction | > | greater than |
| MR | minor repair | < | less than |
| EXT | extratopicality | ↑ | increase |
| Lin | linearity | ↓ | decrease |
| NC | non-competitive | → | causes |
| I | Impact | ─//→ | does not cause |
| | | = | equals, is |
| | | ≠ | does not equal, is not |
| **Flowing Notes** | | w/ | with |
| | | w/o | without |
| x | dropped argument | w/in | within |
| NE | no evidence used | ∴ | therefore |
| ?? | (used before an argument or card to show you're not sure you flowed it correctly) | b/c | because |
| | | avg | average |
| CX: | statement from cross-ex. | **Source Qualifications** | |
| --√-- | argument has been repeated without extension | atty | attorney |
| E ≠ A | evidence does not match argument or label given | prof | professor |
| | | Sen | Senator |
| | | Rep | Representative |
| | | Dir | director |
| | | Fields of Study: Ec, Soc, PS, (Political Science), Psy, etc. | |

**FIGURE 8.4.** Flowsheet symbols and abbreviations (from Branham, 1987, p. 10).

tions between your arguments and those of previous speakers be clearly traced on the flowsheet.

When debating, perhaps the most difficult task in taking a flowsheet is that of preparing and outlining one's own forthcoming speech while recording the arguments of the previous speaker. This problem can be addressed in several ways:

1. Anticipate and brief against your opponent's arguments. If you have been able to anticipate your opponent's arguments before the debate

begins, you will already be familiar with them to some extent. The more familiar you are with the arguments and evidence you are flowing, the more succinctly they can be flowed and the more time you can spend organizing your own responses. Indeed, it should also take far less time to organize your responses because you have anticipated their need and prepared them in advance of the debate. If you have fully briefed responses to the opponent's argument, record the points of your brief on the flowsheet next to the argument being delivered and try to generate new arguments that had not previously occurred to you.

2. Employ critical flowing notes when recording an opponent's arguments. One should listen *aggressively* to an opponent's arguments. Instead of passively recording them, try to determine how you can *use* them for your own purposes or what's *wrong* with them if you choose to refute them. The way in which you flow the argument should reflect this critical process. In listening to a piece of evidence, for example, one should always determine whether the evidence fully supports the debater's claim. If it does not, this should be noted with the appropriate flowing symbol (E A) along with a brief description of the discrepancy.

3. Flow the portion of an opponent's argument or evidence that you wish to use or indict. If you plan to object to some specific part of a piece of evidence (such as the conflict of interest indicated by the source's credentials or the appearance of a serious qualifier, e.g., "one cause of this problem is . . ."), make these portions of the evidence or argument the substance of your record. Similarly, if you intend to use an opponent's argument or evidence against him or her, highlight those words of the opponent that are consonant with this aim. You are thus bridging the two tasks of recording the opponent's arguments and preparing your own.

Whenever possible, you should record the exact wording of the opponent's phrase that you plan to use or indict. The phrase should be flowed in quotation marks to indicate that these are the exact words of the opponent, and this fact should be communicated to the judge or audience.

### Flowsheet Practice

Practice in using the flowsheet is easy but vital to obtain. Listening to practice debate rounds provides a good opportunity to concentrate on one's flowing skills. If possible, compare your flowsheet of the debate to that of a more experienced debater who has seen the same round. You may also find it useful to tape record rounds of debate for flowsheet practice. Flowing a taped debate enables you to stop and reassess the flowsheet between speeches. Taped debates may also be listened to more than once, enabling you to see the improvement in your flowing skills.

Mastering flowsheet techniques will dramatically improve one's performance as a debater. It allows the debater to address arguments in detail and to make wise strategic decisions based on an understanding of how different arguments have developed through the course of the debate. The flowsheet also enables the debater to communicate arguments with greater organization and clarity. Flowsheet techniques require many hours of practice, but such efforts will be greatly rewarded.

## STYLE AND DELIVERY IN DEBATE

The style and delivery with which arguments are conveyed may best be thought of as ways in which debaters enhance the ability of their audiences to see to the heart of the matter and appreciate what they find. Mill (1859/1947) observed in his essay *On Liberty:*

> Since there are few mental attributes more rare than that judicial faculty which can sit in intelligent judgment between two sides of a question, of which only one is represented by an advocate before it, truth has no chance but in proportion as every side of it, every opinion which embodies any fraction of the truth, not only finds advocates, but *is so advocated as to be listened to.* (p. 52)

The flowsheet offers much to the study of proper delivery and style in debate. The good speech, like the good flowsheet, depends at a fundamental level on clarity, emphasis, and organization. In order for one's ideas to ring true, they must first ring in such a way as to be understood. The arguments most easily incorporated into a flowsheet are those that have been clearly labeled (as discussed in chapter 5), allowing the audience to understand what the argument *is;* those marked by clear transitions, which mark the movement from one argument to the next; and those that make explicit organizational reference to arguments that have already appeared in the debate (tying the current discussion of an issue to previous discussions of that same issue).

Debaters may wish to begin by providing an organizational overview of what arguments they will cover and in what order. This overview (sometimes called a roadmap) orients the audience toward your position and makes your speech easier to follow. After such a roadmap has been provided, the debater should use signposts during the speech to note which part of the previewed structure is being covered.

Many aspects of appropriate delivery and style in a debate are dependent on the specific forum and audience for the debate. In legal advocacy, appeals dictate different (more technical) language and arguments than do jury trials. For public debates, the advocates should assume no familiarity with the language, theories, or strategies of formal argument. Where such concepts are useful, they should be presented and explained as if newly discovered.

Particularly among inexperienced debaters, there is a temptation to "script" one's debate speech, burying one's anxieties about speaking behind a prepared manuscript, mountains of quotations, or extensive notes. In some forums (particularly technical or otherwise specialized ones), such notes may be essential due to the intricacy of the arguments, the length of the presentations, or the demands for voluminous evidence. But in most cases, such props interfere with the ability of the debater to adapt to the arguments of his or her opponents or to present one's own arguments with effectiveness. The distinctive character and value of oral debate lies in the fact that it is *not* scripted, that each new speech extends the arguments in ways that cannot be fully anticipated.

Debaters must learn to state their positions with *economy*. Without sacrificing necessary development, explanation, or evidence, arguments should be presented in a succinct fashion. This necessity is usually enforced by time limits for speaking. Operating under time limits, the debater must ensure that s/he has covered the most important arguments in the time allotted. Arguments may be prioritized for coverage, with the most important ones covered first, or the debater may choose to monitor the remaining time in the speech, regulate the amount of time spent on individual arguments, and skip ahead if necessary. In his closing speech during the 1984 presidential debates, Ronald Reagan lost track of the time, running out when he was in the middle of a lengthy anecdote about driving down the California coast highway. He never finished the story, and lost the opportunity to wrap up his candidacy.

In a timed debate, debaters should constantly monitor the time remaining, making ongoing decisions about how much time to spend on a given argument and when it is necessary to move on. Even when there are no formal time limits imposed, a long-winded speaker risks losing the audience. When Governor Bill Clinton of Arkansas offered a well-reasoned but overly long address at the 1988 Democratic Convention, the audience grew restless, then openly hostile. When Clinton uttered the words, "in conclusion . . . ," the crowd cheered. His thoughtful message had been lost.

Among the most important aspects of delivery in debate is **emphasis.** If strategy in debate stems from an awareness of the "big picture"—what issues are most important, what it takes to win, how to compare and evaluate the two sides' positions—it is through emphasis in delivery that the big picture is painted for the audience. A debate speech without proper use of emphasis is an undifferentiated mass of arguments, monotonously delivered. Emphasis signals to the audience what is important, rather than leaving that decision entirely to the audience's judgment. The audience may ultimately decide that what you have emphasized is *not* the most important set of issues in the debate, but in doing so they will at least have had to consider your strategic perspective.

Emphasis can be conveyed in several ways. Orally, we convey emphasis by *varying* our delivery: setting certain words apart by changing our volume (speaking more loudly or more softly), our *rate* of delivery (generally by speaking the emphasized words more slowly), our *pitch* (highness or lowness of voice), and/or the rhythm of our speech (primarily by setting off a phrase through brief *pauses* on either side of it).

We also convey emphasis—the sense that a point is important—by our *demeanor*. It is one thing to *say* that we are outraged by some injustice or moved by some tragedy; it is another to *show* that these are our feelings. Debaters need not act out their passions by banging on tables and shouting; conviction can be demonstrated as well through quiet and thoughtful intensity.

Because debate is a competition both between ideas and between advocates of those ideas, there is sometimes an understandable but unfortunate tendency for debaters to direct personal animosity, discourtesy, invective, or ridicule toward their opponents. There are occasions in which such *ad hominem* is an entertaining part of the event—such as the British House of Commons where squelches and put-downs are hallowed arts. But for the most part, *ad hominem* attacks make debates less enjoyable for participants and audience alike. In some recent political campaigns dominated by "negative" personal charges, voters have indicated that they are left with no confidence in *either* candidate.

Most personal attacks in debate can be replaced with more effective and pleasant arguments. Instead of calling an opponent's argument "foolish," *show* it to be so and let the audience come to its own conclusion about the intelligence of one who would make such an argument. Credit your opponent's argument when appropriate, because it speaks better for your position if you have been able to defeat the *best* that might be said for the opposition. If an opponent is discourteous to you, be especially courteous in response—the contrast will be more dramatic and favorable.

You and your opponents are competitors in one sense, but partners in a larger sense. The most treasured experiences for any experienced debater are not those in which he or she has been overpoweringly dominant, slaughtering a hapless opponent, but rather those close, well-argued matches in which either side could have won. For such a match to occur, *both* sides must be at their best and a comradeship among competitors frequently develops from these experiences.

## CONCLUSION: THE ULTIMATE CHALLENGE OF DEBATE

This text has provided an overview of common practices and proven strategies in debate. But all its advice must be bracketed by one fundamental qualification: Debate is the only form of contest in which most "rules" and procedures are subject to negotiation and revision. Debaters are obliged to address not only individual arguments, but the larger issues of how these arguments should be weighed, compared, and used in the process of making a decision about the proposition.

Which issues are the most important? What *constitutes* a "better policy"? How should conflicting values be weighed? What is fallacious and what is valid reasoning? These and other matters that govern the evaluation of debates should be a part of the substantive argument in the exchange, disputed by the contending participants.

Because debates encourage *resolution* of the disputes they join, there must always be a debate *about* the debate. As we have seen, even the "facts" used to support arguments in a debate are often themselves subject to dispute. As literary critic Stanley Fish (1989) has observed:

> While debate is certainly grounded on facts, they are facts that have themselves been established as a result of debate. Membership in the category of the indisputable is determined in the course of disputes; givens are not given but made, and once made, they can serve as the basis for unchallengeable observations, until they are themselves challenged in the name of givens that have been made by someone else. (p. 193)

The theory and practice of debate are constantly reshaped by those who participate in it. It is this process, a process of becoming more self-aware in our use of arguments and formation of opinions, that constitutes the ultimate challenge in debate.

# REFERENCES

Alden, R. (1900). *The art of debate.* New York: Henry Holt.

Alperovitz, G. (1989, August 3). Did we have to drop the bomb? *The New York Times,* p. A23.

Altman, L. K. (1989, July 27). New questions on aspirin and heart. *The New York Times,* p. 8.

Amnesty International. (1989). *When the state kills . . . The death penalty v. human rights.* London: Amnesty International Publications.

Anonymous. (1856). *The young debater.* Boston: Crosby, Nichols.

Asia Watch Committee. (1990). *Punishment season: Human rights in China after martial law.* New York: Asia Watch.

Atchity, K. J. (1978). *Homer's Iliad: The shield of memory.* Carbondale, IL: Southern Illinois University Press.

Baird, A. C. (1923). Shall American universities adopt the British system of debating? *Quarterly Journal of Speech Education, 10,* 215–222.

Baker, G., & Huntington, H. B. (1905). *The principles of argumentation.* Boston: Ginn.

Barnet, S., & Bedau, H. (1987). *Current issues and enduring questions: Methods and models of argument from Plato to the present.* New York: St. Martin's Press.

Bickner, R. E. (1971). Concepts of economic cost. In G. H. Fisher (Ed.), *Cost considerations in systems analysis* (pp. 37–62). New York: Elsevier.

Blackmun, H. (1990, January 10). Excerpts from court decision requiring universities to yield tenure data. *The New York Times,* p. B6.

Boyle, F. (1989, February 9). [Op-Ed page]. *The New York Times,* p. A26.

Branham, R. (1987). *The debate flowsheet.* Kansas City, MO: National Federation of Inter-scholastic Speech and Debate Associations.

Branham, R. (1988). Debate at the crossroads in America and Japan. In *Introduction to public debate* (pp. 9–15). Tokyo: International Education Center.

Branham, R. (1989). Roads not taken: Counterplans and opportunity costs. *Argumentation and Advocacy, 25,* 246–255.

233

234    REFERENCES

Browne, S. H. (1989). Satirizing the debate society in eighteenth-century England. *Argumentation and Advocacy, 26*, pp. 1–10.

Buchanon, J. M. (1969). *Cost and choice: An inquiry in economic theory.* Chicago: Markham.

Committee for the Compilation of Materials on Damage Caused by the Atomic Bombs. (1981). *Hiroshima and Nagasaki: The physical, medical, and social effects of the atomic bombardment.* New York: Basic Books.

Cooper, M., & Soley, L. C. (1990, February/March). All the right sources. *Mother Jones,* pp. 20–48.

Dershowitz, A. (1989, January). Shouting "Fire?" *The Atlantic Monthly,* pp. 73–74.

Engler, R. (1985, April 27). Technology out of control. *The Nation,* p. 494.

Ennis, R. F. (1946). *Memorandum for chief, strategic policy section, S & P Group, OPD; Subject: Use of Atomic Bomb on Japan.* Washington, DC: National Archives.

Epstein, D. M. (1986, July). America's No. 1 song. *Harper's,* p. 14.

*Ex Parte Cavitt.* 118 p. 2d 846, 37 CA 2d 698.

Fairlie, H. (1983, August 8). Scripts for the pageant. *The New Republic, 577,* pp. 26–28.

Fawcett, T. (1980). Eighteenth-century debating societies. *British Journal of Eighteenth-Century Studies, 3,* 217–230.

Feng, G., & English, J. (1972). *Lao Tsu; Tao te Ching.* New York: Random House.

Fish, S. (1989). *Doing what comes naturally.* Durham, NC: Duke University Press.

Fisher, R., & Ury, W. (1981/1983). *Getting to yes: Negotiating agreement without giving in.* New York: Penguin Books.

Fogelman, E. (1964). *The decision to use the A-bomb.* New York: Charles Scribner's.

Foner, P. (1975). *The voice of black America* (Vol. 1). New York: Capricorn Books.

Foster, W. T. (1932). *Argumentation and debating.* Boston: Houghton-Mifflin. (Original work published 1908)

Frost, R. (1971). The road not taken. *The road not taken: An introduction to Robert Frost.* New York: Holt, Rinehart & Winston. (Original work published 1915)

Fukuzawa, Y. (1966). *The autobiography of Yukichi Fukuzawa* (E. Kiyooka, Trans.). New York: Columbia University Press.

Gardner, C. (1989, November 13). Is an embryo a person? *The Nation,* pp. 557–558.

Garrett, M. (1989, November). *"Pure talk:" Wit, games, and debate in medieval China.* Paper presented at the Speech Communication Association Convention, San Francisco, CA.

Gitlin, T. (1983). *Inside prime time.* New York: Pantheon.

Govier, T. (1985). *A practical study of argument.* Belmont, CA: Wadsworth.

Grether, E. (1929). No-decision debates. *Gavel, 11,* p. 14.

Hansen, S. (1982, September). Public policy analysis: Some recent developments. *Policy Studies Journal,* pp. 14–42.

Haskins, C. H. (1957). *The rise of the universities.* Ithaca, NY: Cornell University Press.

Hertzberg, H. (1989, July 17, 24). Flagellation. *The New Republic,* p. 4.

Hitchens, C. (1983, January 1). Give them back their marbles. *The Spectator,* p. 12.

Hitchens, C. (1987). *Imperial spoils: The curious case of the Elgin marbles.* New York: Hill & Wang.

Homer's Iliad. (1982). (D. B. Hull, Trans.). Athens, OH: Ohio University Press.

House Committee on Agriculture. (1984, September 18–19). *Improved standards for laboratory animals act hearings.* Washington, DC: U.S. Government Printing Office.

Hyde, H. (1985, June 28). Down on the farm. *The National Review,* pp. 26–28.

Jackson, J. (1978, September/October). Why reparations are justified for blacks. *Regulation,* pp. 24–29.

Jamieson, K. H. (1988). *Eloquence in an electronic age: The transformation of political speechmaking.* New York: Oxford.

Jamieson, K. H., & Birdsell, D. (1988). *Presidential debates.* New York: Oxford University Press.

Jayatilleke, K. N. (1963). *Early Buddhist theory of knowledge.* Delhi: Motilal Banarsidass.

Johannesen, R. L., Allen, R. R., & Linkugel, W. A. (1988). *Contemporary American speeches.* Dubuque, IA: Kendall/Hunt.

Kennedy, G. (1980). *Classical rhetoric and its Christian and secular tradition from ancient to modern times.* Chapel Hill, NC: University of North Carolina Press.

Krauthammer, C. (1989, November 10). Political malpractice: The research ban on fetal transplantation. *The Washington Post,* p. A27.

Lewis, J. (1987). *Before the vote was won: Arguments for and against women's suffrage 1864-1896.* New York: Routledge & Kegan Paul.

Lichtman, A. J., & Rohrer, D. (1975). A general theory of the counterplan. *Journal of the American Forensic Association, 12,* pp. 70-79.

Lippmann, W. (1982). *The essential Lippmann: A political philosophy for liberal democracy* (Rossiter & J. Lare, Eds.). Cambridge, MA: Harvard University Press.

Mallet, C. E. (1924). *A history of the University of Oxford.* London: Methuen.

Maslow, A. (1954). *Motivation and personality.* New York: Harper & Brothers.

Masters, K. (1990, April). How Art Buchwald beat Paramount. *Premiere,* pp. 41-42.

Mays, B. E. (1971). *Born to rebel.* Athens, GA: University of Georgia Press.

McDonald, D. (1980). *The language of argument.* New York: Harper & Row.

Mill, J. S. (1947). *On liberty.* Arlington Heights, IL: AHM Publishing. (Original work published 1859)

Miller, D. W., & Starr, M. K. (1967). *The structure of human decisions.* Englewood Cliffs, NJ: Prentice-Hall.

Morris, J. (Ed.). (1978). *The Oxford book of Oxford* New York: Oxford Press.

National Abortion Rights Action League. (1978). *Legal abortion: A speaker's and debater's notebook.* Washington, DC: Author.

National Abortion Rights Action League. (1990). *Who decides? A reproductive rights issue manual.* Washington, DC: Author.

National Abortion Rights Action League. (1983). *Choice, legal abortion: Arguments pro & con.* Washington, DC: NARAL.

Neustadt, R. E., & May, E. R. (1986). *Thinking in time: The uses of history for decision-makers.* New York: The Free Press.

Newman, D., & Bueno de Mesquita, B. (1989, January 26). [Op-Ed page]. *The New York Times,* p. A23.

Newman, R., & Newman D. (1969). *Evidence.* Boston: Houghton-Mifflin.

Nichols, A. (1941). *Discussion and debate.* New York: Harcourt, Brace.

Nixon, R. M. (1983). My side of the story. In H. R. Ryan (Ed.), *American rhetoric from Roosevelt to Reagan* (pp. 114-123). Prospect Heights, IL: Waveland Press.

Orwell, G. (1949). *1984.* New York: Harcourt, Brace.

Orwell, G. (1968). As I please. In S. Orwell & I. Angus (Eds.), *The collected essays, journalism and letters of George Orwell* (Vol. 3, pp. 150-152). New York: Harcourt, Brace & World, pp. 150-152. (Original work published 1944)

Paskins, B., & Dockrill, M. (1979). *The ethics of war.* Minneapolis: University of Minnesota Press.

Pellegrini, A. M. (1942). Renaissance and medieval antecedents of debate. *The Quarterly Journal of Speech, 28,* pp. 14-19.

Quade, E. S. (1982). *Analysis for public decisions.* New York: North-Holland.

Quiller-Couch, A. (1928). *A lecture on lectures.* New York: Harcourt, Brace.

Rashdall, H. (1936). *The universities of Europe in the middle ages* (Vol. I). Oxford: Clarendon Press.

Rhodes, R. (1986). *The making of the atomic bomb.* New York: Simon & Schuster.

Roberts, W. H. (1941). *The problem of choice.* Boston: Ginn.

Rodden, J. (1985). British university debating: A reappraisal. *Communication Education,*

*34*, pp. 308–317.

Rottenberg, A. (1985). *Elements of argument: A text and reader.* New York: St. Martin's Press.

Rusher, W. (1981). *How to win arguments.* Garden City, NY: Doubleday.

Ryan, H. R. (1983). *American rhetoric from Roosevelt to Reagan.* Prospect Heights, IL: Waveland Press.

Samuelson, P. (1976). *Economics* (10th ed.). New York: McGraw-Hill.

Sansom, G. B. (1978). *Japan: A short cultural history.* Stanford, CA: Stanford University Press.

Schlesinger, A., Jr. (1986, January 10). Against a one-term, six-year presidency. *The New York Times*, p. 27.

Sherwin, M. (1987). *A world destroyed: Hiroshima and the origins of the arms race.* New York: Vintage Books.

Simon, J. (1990, May 10). More immigration can cut the deficit. *New York Times*, p. A33.

Solo, P. (1988). *From protest to policy.* Cambridge, MA: Ballinger.

Sproule, J. M. (1980). *Argument: Language and its influence.* New York: McGraw-Hill.

Stark, E. (1990, July 18). The myth of black violence. *New York Times*, p. A21.

Titcomb, C. (1985, December 16). Star-spangled earache. *The New Republic*, p. 11.

Torcia, C. E. (1985). *Wharton's criminal evidence* (14th ed.). Rochester, NY: Lawyers' Cooperative Publishing.

Vagliano, B. (1981). *Brooklyn Journal of International Law*, pp. 338–351.

Vonnegut, K. (1970). Harrison Bergerson. *Welcome to the monkey house.* New York: Dell.

Walzer, M. (1977). *Just and unjust wars.* New York: Basic.

Warder, A. K. (1970). *Indian Buddhism.* Delhi: Motilal Banarsidass.

Wattenberg, B., & Zinsmeister, K. (1990, April). The case for more immigration. *Commentary*, pp. 19–25.

Webster, D. (1890). *Reply to Hayne.* Boston: Willard Small.

Wells, I. B. (1969). *On lynchings: Southern horrors, a red record, mob rule in New Orleans.* New York: Arno Press. (Original work published 1892)

Wildavsky, A. (1979). *Speaking truth to power: The art and craft of policy analysis.* Boston: Little, Brown.

Will, G. (1990, February 1). New York City judge is liberalism at its worst. *Lewiston Sun-Journal*, p. 4.

Wilson, J. Q. (1990, February). Against the legalization of drugs. *Commentary*, pp. 21–28.

*Words and Phrases.* (Vol. 11A) (1971). St. Paul, MN: West Publishing.

Wyden, P. (1985). *Day one.* New York: Warner Books.

Ye, Y. (1989, August 27). America's China policy after the June massacre: Economic sanctions as the option. *The World Journal*, p. 30.

# AUTHOR INDEX

# SUBJECT INDEX